GW01032837

MORE MONEY WITH NOEL WHITTAKER

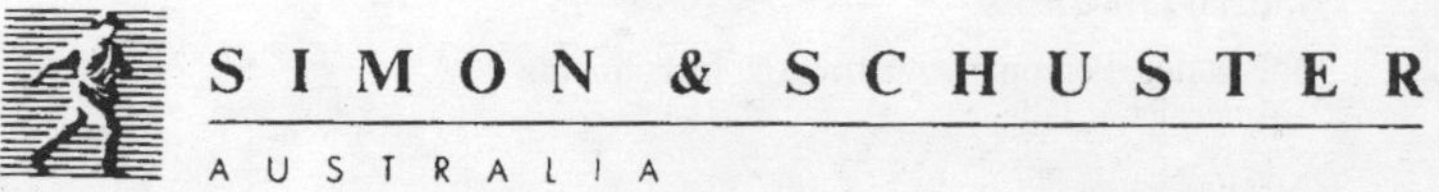

Other best-sellers by the same author:

MAKING MONEY MADE SIMPLE
GETTING IT TOGETHER
LIVING WELL IN RETIREMENT
GOLDEN RULES OF WEALTH
SUPERANNUATION MADE SIMPLE
SHARES MADE SIMPLE
CONTROLLING YOUR CREDIT CARDS
LOANS MADE SIMPLE
DRIVING SMALL BUSINESS

First Edition October 1990.
Reprinted March 1991.
Second Edition October 1992.
Third Edition July 1993.
Fourth Edition (Totally revised) March 1994.
Fifth Edition April 1995.
Sixth Edition May 1997.
Seventh Edition July 1998.
Eighth Edition February 2000.
Ninth Edition February 2002.

MORE MONEY WITH NOEL WHITTAKER

First published in Australia in 1992 by
Simon & Schuster Australia
20 Barcoo Street, East Roseville NSW 2069

A Paramount Communications Company
Sydney New York London Toronto Tokyo Singapore

Copyright © Noel Whittaker Holdings Pty Ltd

This book is copyright. Apart from any fair dealing for the purposes of private study, research, criticism or review, as permitted under the Copyright Act, no part may be reproduced by any process without written permission. Inquiries should be directed to the Publishers.

All rights reserved.

National Library of Australia
Cataloguing-in-Publication data.

Whittaker, Noel, 1940-
More Money with Noel Whittaker

Rev. ed.
Includes index.
ISBN 0-7318-0483-X.

1. Finance, Personal – Australia. 2. Investments – Australia. I. Title.

332.02400994

Cover design by Sharon Felschow.
Typeset in Australia by Ocean Graphics Pty Ltd, Bundall, Gold Coast, Queensland, 4217.
Printed by McPhersons Printing Group, Victoria.

To my wife Geraldine, and my three children Mark, James and Elizabeth, who helped me to learn about life.

The laws relating to taxation, social security benefits, and the investment and handling of money, are constantly changing and are often subject to departmental discretion. While every care has been taken to ensure the accuracy of the material contained herein at the time of publication neither the author nor the publisher will bear responsibility or liability for any action taken by any person, persons or organisation on the purported basis of information contained herein.

Without limiting the generality of the foregoing, no person, persons or organisation should invest monies or take other action on reliance of the material contained herein but instead should satisfy themselves independently (whether by expert advice or otherwise) of the appropriateness of any such action.

Acknowledgements

As you read this book and notice the detailed and technical information it contains you will appreciate the amount of work that went into its production. I am indebted to my wife Geraldine, and my business partner Cheryl Macnaught, for spending countless hours discussing with me various aspects of the contents, and providing much needed moral support.

A big "Thank you" is also due to:

Paul Resnik of Paul Resnik and Associates

Robert Maple-Brown and the staff of Maple-Brown Abbot Ltd

David Peacock and the staff of the Sydney Stock Exchange

Lyn Edgar

Ron O'Brien of O'Brien Pizzato and Co

Michael Klug and David Cominos of Clayton Utz

Jim Love of MLC Life

Alex Wickenden

Garry Connelly of Garry Connelly and Associates

Sean Leahey for the cartoons

Tony Bela for the graphics

Craig Padman, Jeff Draney and the staff of Ocean Graphics for the typesetting.

McPherson's Printing Group for production.

My research assistant Craig Higson provided his usual invaluable help in collecting data and finding all the errors I overlooked. As well, I received invaluable assistance and feedback from a team of people from all walks of life who "test drove" the original manuscript before it went to press. They include Owen Doyle, Ann Lyons, Lisa Holmes, Sandra Spurway, Kate Maloney, Linda Barry, Charles Williamson, Rosemary Kent, Jane Sharpe, Roland Lindenmayer and Rex and Val Nicholls.

Most of their many suggestions and comments have been incorporated in the text.

Contents

Introduction

In March 1987, 5 000 copies of *Making Money Made Simple* rolled off the printing presses. This may seem a timid first run when you consider that over 500 000 copies have now been sold and that local editions of the book are best-sellers in New Zealand and South Africa. However, when that first run was being planned, my publisher told me "If we can sell 5 000 copies in two years, we've got a best-seller on our hands".

Luckily, neither my readers nor I knew that few books in Australia would sell as quickly as *Making Money Made Simple,* and by Christmas 1987 sales had reached the staggering target of 100 000 copies. As I travelled around Australia to promote the book, I had the opportunity to meet many of the readers and the benefit of listening to the stories they told me about the way *Making Money Made Simple* had changed their lives. But it didn't stop there. Every day I'd receive letters from people saying "If only I'd read this 30 years ago" or "This book has changed my life" or "Why don't they teach this in schools?"

However, *Making Money Made Simple* did more than change the lives of over a million Australians; it also changed the entire Australian financial industry. The banks scoffed when *Making Money Made Simple* showed readers how they could save tens of thousands of dollars in interest by making their mortgage payments weekly or fortnightly. Now almost every bank and building society offers the service, and it is even being offered for car loans.

Unfortunately, the huge number of changes, coupled with the share boom and the subsequent crash, proved too much for most Australians and they gave the investment business away. Yet while the investment products and the laws had changed dramatically, the basic principles had not. *Making Money Made Simple* was the book that blended the principles of old with the new products of today. It gave Australians a financial manual in simple language to help them on the path to financial success. It was clear from my discussions with clients, and from the mail which still pours in, that *Making Money Made Simple* had whetted the appetites of the Australian investing public.

Now I faced a dilemma. The book is updated regularly, but if it became any bigger it would become so thick that it would frighten away the very people it is aimed at – average Australians.

The solution was to bring out a sequel – the book you hold in your hand. *More Money with Noel Whittaker* assumes you have read *Making Money Made Simple* and begins from that point.

It provides detailed techniques to get you going and to eliminate personal debt and tells the extraordinary story of the Magic Train to demonstrate the power of compound interest. It covers the stock market and the property market in a detail which was not possible in the previous book and tells you about strategies such as dollar cost averaging for creating wealth safely.

It also shows you how to speed up your wealth creation program by smart borrowing, simplifies life assurance, explains companies and trusts, and gives you an insight into the problems that can arise if your business partner dies, or becomes disabled.

The chapters on superannuation and rollovers that were in the early editions have been removed, as those subjects are now covered in much greater depth in *Living Well in Retirement*.

Now, more than ever, investors must realise their greatest enemy is lack of knowledge and experience. However, I know that many have few places to go for practical advice about business and financial matters and hope that this book, in conjunction with my other four books, will help to fill that void. Much of the material has not been published before because it is drawn from the hard school of practical experience.

You will find that some material is deliberately repeated to help you understand better certain important points. Because this book is intended to be a natural transition from *Making Money Made Simple*, the same style has been maintained. I hope you find the jump to the next level exciting and rewarding.

As a further tool, to help you with the wealth building process, I produced the Noel Whittaker Creator on CD-ROM in 1997. This contains several valuable financial calculators, a full personal budgeting program and other information to boost your knowledge. Details are at the back of the book or you can get a preview on my web-site at http://www.noelwhittaker.com.au/

Here's to health, happiness and prosperity for all of us.

Noel Whittaker

July 1998

1

Taking The First Step

As I grow older I pay less attention to what people say, I just watch what they do.

ANDREW CARNEGIE

Welcome back. By now you should have read *Making Money Made Simple* and, if you are like many of its readers who have written or spoken to me since publication, you are now inspired, much more knowledgeable, and keen to start building up your assets. There is just one problem — you are unsure of where to start. There are so many paths beckoning — budgeting, a second job, "tax free" bonds, superannuation, negative gearing, "savings plans", salary sacrifice, take a study course, pay your house off quickly — it just goes on and on. What DO you do?

This book is here to solve that problem. However, it will do more than show you where to begin — it will put you gently but surely on the road to financial independence and guide you along the way.

The aims of *Making Money Made Simple* were to give you some basic knowledge about finance and to convince you that you could have far more than you had ever dreamed possible if you made the best use of what you have now. *More Money* will take you to the next step and provide the specific techniques to enable you to do it.

It makes sense that the first step for you is to decide what goal you are trying to achieve. You may well answer "That's easy, my goal is to be wealthy."

That's a statement I hear continually, yet seldom is there a conviction that it **will** come true. It is merely a wish, like the dream of eternal youth, without a plan to back it up and without a belief that it will happen. This is not a goal, it is merely a daydream.

Let's refresh our minds about goals. A goal is an objective, or something for which you are aiming. However, an aim is not enough; unless there is a concrete plan for its achievement it will seldom happen. Therefore one of the first parts of setting goals is to determine **exactly** what you want and then formulate a plan to get there. That is probably the easiest part because it is far easier to make plans than to exhibit the discipline to carry them through.

The Strangest Secret

The force that pushes you to carry on with the plan is called "motivation". The trouble is you can't go to a shop and buy a jar of "Motivation" — it has to come from within. The feeling has to be so strong that it dominates your thinking, and keeps out all those stray thoughts that are always popping into your head and trying to lure you somewhere else. There is a recording by the American broadcaster Earl Nightingale that was released in 1953 and has been in the best seller lists every year since. Its title is *"The Strangest Secret"*. I urge you to buy a copy if you can locate one. The secret is: **we become what we think about.**

Earl Nightingale says: "The only thing strange about it, is how few people realise it. It is certainly no secret. Constant references have been made to it in the Bible and in many other writings."

Just two of the many quotations mentioned in *"The Strangest Secret"* are "A man's life is what his thoughts make of it" from the Roman Emperor Marcus Aurielus and "A man is what he thinks about all day long" from the American essayist Ralph Waldo Emerson.

According to Nightingale the main problem is that most people think only of doing what everybody else is doing — they just follow the crowd. We now know that only eight per cent attain success, so it must follow that 92% are doing the wrong thing. This is why it is both hard and easy to be successful.

The hard part is studying when almost everybody else is watching television, saving when everybody else is spending and getting out of bed when the rest of the world is sleeping. The easy part springs from the fact that 92% of people will NEVER make the sacrifices needed to be successful, so there is very little competition for anybody who is prepared to go the extra mile.

The road to achievement starts with a goal. We implant this goal in our mind, think about it all day long, take the necessary actions, and eventually reach the goal.

Here are some examples of the way motivation can be triggered. When *Making Money Made Simple* was launched in March 1987 I was told that I would be lucky to sell a total of 10 000 copies as Australians are not book buying people. Much to everybody's amazement I immediately made a goal to sell 100 000 by December 31, 1987. This target loomed so large in my brain that it dominated every other thought. I went on a lecture tour of the country, I appeared on every radio and television station that would have me and I wrote letters to our company's clients. By December 31 1987 the goal had become a reality.

In 1989 I decided to write the first edition of this book — the companion to *Making Money Made Simple*. Because I had become so busy at work, and also with my newspaper columns and my radio and television spots, I ambled along and wrote a little whenever I "could spare the time". That is no different to saving whatever money happens to be left over. You never find much.

Then in May 1990, while in Perth to give a seminar, I had a meeting with the person who was distributing my books in Western Australia. We discussed the proposed new book and he made a statement that changed the next few months for me: "You MUST have it in the shops for next Christmas which means that it will have to be released by next October at the latest; the book trade don't buy after that." I admit I had **hoped** to get the book in the shops for Christmas, but hadn't got around to planning any specific completion dates for the manuscript.

I immediately rang my publisher to break this bit of news to him. His words brought me back to reality: "If you want it released by October we shall have to have the finished manuscript by July 31st." Now I had the motivation — just a little over two months to finish it.

The dream had suddenly turned into a specific goal. No more vague generalisations like "I am working on my next book". Now it was "I have got just 78 days to have the manuscript to the publisher". Once you get as specific as that all sorts of changes take place. You develop extra energy, you suddenly become creative and you can exist on much less sleep. Anybody who has ever crammed for an examination knows what I mean. That is goal setting at its best.

Notice what gave me the motivation. It was the sudden realisation that if I did not get into action and finish it, I would still be pottering around with it until the following Christmas.

Sources Of Motivation

There are two main sources of motivation:

What will happen if you do

What will happen if you don't

Both are equally powerful. The doctor may put it either way. "If you DO give up smoking you will regain your good health within six months — If you DON'T give up smoking you will be dead in six months." They are both effective aren't they?

I have no idea what your age is but I will give some motivation triggers for all ages that may help you to start you on your journey on the road to financial independence.

The Young Person

The need at this age is to learn the value of goal setting, the value of budgeting and the value of saving. Readers of *Making Money Made Simple* tell me one of the best ways to start children on the budgeting/goal setting trail is to use the method mentioned in The Doctor's Prescription. The young person has to pass an examination based on *Making Money Made Simple*[1] and then will be given a pre-agreed sum of money from the parents. The child then has one year to increase that money by the largest amount they can. At the end of that year the parents will double whatever they have achieved.

The opportunity to get a large sum of money at the end of the twelve months is a great motivation to pursue the goal. That is not all that is needed. They also need to make a plan that works and then exhibit the discipline to carry it out. Twelve months is a good length of time for a substantial goal for a young person. They tend to get bored if it is much longer, and the last thing we want to do at that age is quell the spirit.

Once they have learned the art of making money and budgeting, the next goal may be to save for a motor car. In my book *Getting it Together* I advised young people to put a poster or photograph of the car they want on the wall, and next to it a chart recording the savings progress. It is the last thing they see at night, and as a result their subconscious mind implants the goal and helps with the achievement of it. It is particularly good if you can arrange for them to have a photo taken of themselves in the driver's seat of the car they want. This makes the goal even more personal.

---

1 Examination papers and answer sheets are obtainable free of charge from my office. The address is at the back of this book.

Stress the miracle of compound interest.

EXAMPLE: *If a person aged 15 invested $1 000 a year for 50 years at 12% they would have $3.2 million dollars at age 65. If they put off starting till they were 30 there is only 35 years for the compounding to work and the sum at the end is just $533 000. The cost of delaying the investment program is almost THREE MILLION DOLLARS.*

The Young Worker

This is the time to instil the importance of buying a house before prices go out of reach. By now the savings and budgeting habit should be implanted so you need to force into their brain a sense of the way house prices have risen. Visit a library and look up the newspapers at five yearly intervals for the last 20 years. Find large advertisements showing pictures of houses with the prices underneath, and have photo-copies made of them for the bedroom walls.

The price of the average Sydney house at $8 500 in 1960 or even $64 500 in 1980 should be enough to motivate even the most

lethargic to action. I seldom recommend buying land for reasons that are stressed elsewhere in this book.

The Married Couple

Now we should get into the habit of living on one wage, and to use the other wage to pay off the house mortgage as quickly as possible.

We have found the best way to encourage this is to have the couple draw up a budget based on the assumption that they still have the present mortgage repayments to find, but have only one wage coming in. Almost certainly they won't be able to get the figures to work out because there will be such a shortfall, and they will realise the choice is live on one wage now and pay off the mortgage, or forever give up the idea of having children. If a couple don't have their home paid off before they start a family they are **forced** into living on one income, and to struggle with the loan repayments as well. This often leads to unnecessary pressures on the relationship.

Some younger married people say they do not intend to have a family, so what is the use of paying off the house. My response is that paying off the house quickly gives them more choices in later life, whether these choices be moving to a larger home, starting an investment program or retiring early to travel. They might even decide to start a family!

Entering The Forties

Retirement is not far off and by now they should know when they wish to retire. The big question is "Can we afford to retire, and at what age".

My book *Living Well In Retirement* covers this in detail but, in any event, a good financial adviser should be able to key the data into a computer and churn out some figures.

> **EXAMPLE:** *Mr and Mrs Brown are age 40. They wish to retire at age 55 with an income of $22 000 in today's dollars. In the year after their retirement they will also spend $15 000 on a trip and $20 000 to replace the car. His present salary is $40 000 and she earns $21 000. His superannuation will pay him five times his salary at age 55 and she has just taken out a superannuation bond for $10 000. They also have $12 000 in managed funds.*

The computer print-out will show that $22 000 in present dollars will be over $43 500[2] when they turn 55. Add the trip and the car to that figure and you come up with the frightening total of $113 000 of expenditure in the year of retirement alone. By the time they are 80, the $22 000 a year living expenses in today's dollars will have become $147 000 a year. If they are to achieve their goal they will have to accumulate $685 000 at age 55. That kind of figure might frighten more than motivate.

However, their present assets are considerable and a detailed analysis will indicate that things are not as black as they look. His superannuation will be worth $396 000 at retirement, and her superannuation bond should have grown to $49 000. When you add the managed funds which should then be worth over $60 000, they are only $181 000 short of what they need. Luckily they both work so, if they can invest $5 000 a year at an average return of 12%, their retirement needs are taken care of. They should have little trouble reaching what they regard as financial independence **provided they set their target at a young enough age.**

Summing Up

A goal is the magic ingredient that makes things happen. To be effective it must be personal and specific; you cannot make an effective goal for somebody else and you cannot hit a fuzzy target.

The best approach is to break down the major goal into smaller goals. Then the overall task does not seem so overwhelming, and you enjoy the sense of accomplishment that comes when each small goal is reached.

Write your goals down; written goals are far more powerful than spoken ones.

Buy some books in goal setting and read other motivational material to keep you on track.

Stop occasionally and make sure your behaviour matches your goals. There is something basically wrong if your goal is to lose weight and you are eating a lot of chocolates or if you have a goal to retire wealthy at 55 and are spending all of each pay-packet.

---

2 Based on inflation at 5% a year.

2

Getting Rid Of Personal Debt

There can be no freedom or beauty about a home life that depends on borrowing or debt.

(HENRIK IBSEN: A Doll's House I)

Maybe you believe you will never get ahead because of the debts you have now. Take heart, for it **is** possible to be free of all that debt. Free of the monthly mortgage payments, free of the credit card statements, free of the personal loan and free of the car loan. Imagine how much money you would have to invest, or spend, if you were debt free. Naturally the best way to be debt free is not to get into that state in the first place. However this is a realistic book and I know that most of you will never get a house, or perhaps even a car, without borrowing so we'll start by assuming you are in debt now.

Becoming Wealthy By Debt Reduction

Debt is a strange thing — it has put some on the road to wealth and nearly as many on the road to ruin. Probably the reason is that borrowing enables us to buy something today for which we cannot pay cash. A wise choice such as buying a house gives us a push along the road to financial independence. The value of the house should rise as the years go by, while the debt becomes a smaller and smaller percentage of the asset value.

A bad choice may start us on the downhill track. If we borrow for items such as groceries (don't laugh — many people now put their shopping on Mastercard) we might discover that we have consumed the items we bought before we have even received the credit card statement.

You should treat this year as the one for getting debt under control so you can enjoy in the future the benefits that being free of debt brings. If you approach it systematically it is not difficult.

Start by listing all your debts. To do this you will need to phone each lender and ask the amount owing, the interest rate being charged, the penalty for early repayment and whether interest is being charged on a reducing or flat basis. Let's assume a couple have the following loans:

LOAN	DEBT	INTEREST RATE	MONTHLY PAYMENT	TIME LEFT
Housing Loan	$ 90 000	9%	$ 724	30 years
Credit Cards	$ 3 000	15%	$ 150	–
Personal Loan for car	$ 8 000	14%	$ 160	6 years
Loan on Investment House	$120 000	9%	$1 931	7 years
	$221 000		$2 965	

Notice the total monthly repayments are $2 965 a month but only the interest on the investment loan is tax deductible. This makes it the **cheapest real rate** so it should be paid off **last**.

The first step is to re-finance the investment loan on an interest only basis. This will free up that immensely valuable cash flow which is presently not being put to its best use as it is being wasted in reducing a debt for which the interest is tax deductible.

Let's assume we use finance at a fixed rate of around 9% for the next three years. Monthly repayments will drop to $900 releasing a monthly surplus of $1 031 with which to attack the other loans. This should not affect the tax deductibility much, as only the interest component may be claimed as a deduction.

The credit cards should be paid off next as they are carrying the highest interest rate. Using the $1 031 now freed up by the re-financing of the investment loan enables us to raise the monthly repayments on the credit cards to $1 181, which will have it paid off in four months.

Once there are no more payments to make on the credit cards we can use the extra $1 181 that has become available to raise the personal loan payments to $1 341. At this rate it will be paid off in just six more months making a total of nine months from when we started the debt elimination project.

At this stage we have $1 341 a month to add to our housing repayments of $724. This huge payment of $2 065 will see the housing loan liquidated in just over four years.

In five years, by the right strategy, this family has wiped out all their debts except the tax deductible one and now have **$2 065 a month free for investment**.

"One at a time"

We have spent five years of hard work, although you will notice that we did not increase the monthly payments overall. Now we can enjoy the fruits of our labours. The best part about getting out of debt is that we start to have interesting decisions to make, instead of frightening ones. There are now two options available to us. One action is to use this $2 065 to pay off the investment loan as quickly as possible. Add this $2 065 to the existing payment of $900 and total repayments jump to $2 965 a month. This will end that loan in a further four years and leave the couple with $2 965 a month to invest for the rest of their working lives. In 10 years it could grow to more than $700 000.

The alternative is to invest the $2 065 a month and leave the investment loan on an interest only basis. If they continued investing $2 065 a month for 14 years there should be well over

$970 000 at the end of the period, out of which would be deducted the $120 000 owing on the investment home.

The term of the investment plan using $2 065 a month has been shown as 14 years, as it can commence as soon as the residence is paid off. The plan using a monthly investment of $2 965 is shown as 10 years as it cannot start for four years. During those four years the $2 965 a month is used to pay off the investment house. The figures used in the illustration are based on 13% per annum. This is the actual return for the period 1 January 1980 to 31 December 1996 from a monthly investment into a share trust whose performance matched the All Ordinaries Accumulation Index would.

All calculations in this chapter have been done using my Wealth Creator on CD-ROM. Details are at the back of the book.

Becoming wealthy is not so hard is it; it's just a matter of using the right technique!

You should now understand how it is possible to get out of debt and jump into the fast lane on the road to financial independence. In the next chapter I will show you the amazing power of compound interest.

Summary

If you and your family can understand the right and wrong uses of borrowing, and use every resource available to rid yourselves of unproductive debt such as housing loans, personal loans and credit card loans, you will have almost certainly GUARANTEED yourselves a prosperous future.

The habit of going into debt at an early age is ingrained in the lower socio-economic groups and it becomes a "chicken and the egg" situation for they have to borrow because they are poor and they are poor because they have to borrow. I want YOU to break the cycle for the benefit of your future generations.

3

The Fairy Godmother And The Magic Train

Wishes, on their way to coming true, will not be rushed.

ARNOLD LOBEL

It was a warm summer's night and Margaret was propped up in a hospital bed, half asleep, musing over the events of the day. It had been the biggest day in her short life of 22 years. That morning her first child James had been born and she had that tired but contented feeling of a new mother as she rested and thought about what kind of world James would face.

Suddenly she was startled by a glow in the room and looked up in fright to see a small figure, dressed like a ballerina, coming in through the closed window. The window did not seem to impede the strange little being who seemed to have no more substance than a beam of light.

"Who are you?" whispered Margaret slowly. She had never seen anything like it before but did not feel frightened as the tiny body seemed so full of love, as well as being too small and light to harm anybody. "I am the fairy godmother of all the babies," was the reply. "I visit every new parent to tell them about my magic train and how it can carry their child on a trip to riches beyond all imagination."

Margaret was not impressed. "The idea certainly sounds fine but I don't see it happening. I wonder if I will be like most people I know; forever trying to scrape enough money together to pay for the food and the mortgage payments." She was now fully awake, her initial shock had disappeared and curiosity was slowly taking its place.

"I know," replied the fairy. "You seldom see the results of my work because I have such an uphill battle trying to convince people to come on the trip. I offer them all a ride on my train but so few bother to accept the invitation. Most of them seem content for their children and their children's children to remain poor."

Margaret was a sensible woman and by now her curiosity was thoroughly aroused. She asked if the trip was free.

"Of course the trip is not free; everything worthwhile in life has a price, but in this case the price is VERY small, IF you join the train early enough. Why don't you let me tell you how it works?" Naturally Margaret did want to hear more and what she heard was destined to change the life of her family for generations.

The fairy told her of a magical train that was given to every person, but made just one journey in their lifetime. It started on this trip when the person was born and kept going until they died. It made up to 100 stops and at every stop its tender was filled up with gold. Each time the gold filled up the tender the train grew in size so that at the next station there was a bigger tender waiting for the next load of gold to be poured in.

Margaret was intrigued by the cost of the trip for it had the strangest fare structure, just $1 000 a year or $2.73 a day; furthermore it was guaranteed never to increase provided you paid it every year.

"That's a cheap enough price," she said. "Almost everybody I know can scrape up $2.73 a day. There must be a catch."

"No, there's no catch, but there IS another rule I haven't told you about yet. It's a weird one really. The $2.73 a day only pays for the running costs of the train so you still have to pay for the train itself. However, there is a special bonus — if you get on at the terminal, but only there, the train is given to you. Remember this is a magic train, so every time the gold pours into its tender it gets bigger. We can give you one for nothing when we start the journey because the train is so tiny that it's almost worthless. If you don't board it then you have to buy the train, as well as pay the running costs. Therefore it costs more to travel as you get on at stations along the way and the bigger the train gets the more it costs."

Margaret was sceptical, but was interested enough to discuss it with her husband Jack when he came to visit next day. He was more sceptical than Margaret, but there was something about the fairy that Margaret trusted, so after about an hour of discussion Jack said "Let's give it a go. We have $1 000 saved up so we'll join the train with that".

The good fairy returned the next night and Jack and Margaret handed over their $1 000. In return they were given a tiny train — about half the size of a Matchbox toy. "This thing will be pushing to take James too far on the journey to riches," snorted Jack, but Margaret calmed him down and they settled into their new life as parents.

A year later the fairy godmother came around again with some exciting news. "Your train has just pulled into the first station and they have dumped $140 in gold into its tender. It's now 14% bigger." The train didn't look much bigger and Jack was still suspicious of the whole concept, but they had been dutifully putting their $2.73 each day away in a jar so they quietly handed over the second thousand dollars.

Another year passed quickly. James was now a big healthy two year old and the good fairy called with the latest news. "We have just got to Station Two and there is now $300 in gold pouring into your train's tender. That's more than TWICE what you got last year and your train is now worth $2 440. It's now two and a half times bigger than when I gave it to you." She was right. The train was growing nearly as fast as James.

Three more years went by and it was James' fifth birthday. They had continued putting away their $2.73 a day and the good fairy called with some incredible news. "Your train just pulled into the fifth station and they have dumped $926 of gold into it. That's almost as much as you are putting into your money box. The train is now more than seven times bigger than when you bought it. It is worth $7 537."

The once sceptical Jack was in raptures. "I have been talking to my mate Henry about this. He thought it was a stupid idea at the start but now he wants to come on the journey too. Can he have a train for his five year old daughter?"

"Of course he can," laughed the fairy. "Everybody can have their own train BUT remember the rules I told you about. The train is only free if you board at the terminal. Once it leaves there and starts the journey you have to buy the train if you intend to pay only $2.73 a day for the running costs. If Henry wants one for his daughter he will have to pay $7 537 for it, plus the $2.73 a day naturally."

Henry was stunned when he heard this, but he wasn't a fool. He had listened at first with scorn and then with ever increasing interest as Jack had told him about James' train, and now he was prepared to make the effort and scrape up the $7 537 he needed for his daughter to join the journey.

Five more years passed and the good fairy had become great friends with the two families. She called to give her yearly progress report, and to look at their children who were now bright ten year olds and watching their trains progress with interest as well as growing excitement. "You are now at Station 10. We have just tipped $2 707 of gold into your tender and your train is now worth $22 045. It has now increased in size by 22 times since I gave it to you — it is fast becoming a huge powerful locomotive. Wasn't Henry wise to get on when he did? I doubt if any of your other friends will be able to join it now; not many parents can find the $22 045 required to buy a train as big as this one has become in just 10 years."

And so the years rolled by, the train grew bigger and bigger and went faster and faster and in the year James was 21 the gold tipped into the tender was $16 195, and the train was worth $131 876. This was also the price to buy the train then for anybody who wanted to retain the cheap fare of $2.73 a day.

At James' 21st birthday a friend of James called him aside and whispered in his ear "I've heard the strangest things about this magic train of yours. Is it too late for me to join?"

"Sure you can join but the problem is buying the train. Have you got $131 876?" was James' reply.

"There's not a hope of that but I do have a good income. Would you ask the good fairy if there is anything at all she can do to help me?" James took pity on his friend and consulted the good fairy at the first opportunity. He was rocked by what she told him. "Certainly he can join the journey, but if he wants a free train we shall have to incorporate the cost of it in the fare. He will have to pay just over $20 000 a year in fares if he wants to have the same size pot of gold as you will have when you are 60."

The mathematics of that didn't make sense to James. He had paid $21 000 in the last 20 years and had just $39 000 still to pay. His friend would have to pay $20,000 a year for the next 39 years just to keep up with him. James' total fares were $60 000 while his friend's would be $780 000.

By this time the train was huge but seemed to be growing at such a pace that James could hardly believe his eyes. He had kept up the habit of giving the fairy his $2.73 a day but it now seemed so insignificant when compared to the vast shower of gold that poured into the tender each year. By the time he was 31 the train was worth over HALF A MILLION DOLLARS after over $62,000 had been added to its tender. "It is a strange train," he observed. "More gold poured into that tender in that 31st year than went in during the whole of the first 16 years. I still can't figure out the mathematics."

On his 37th birthday he had another visit from his friend the good fairy. "It's time for me to congratulate you and tell you another secret that I never told your parents. The train has just had nearly $140 000 placed in its tender and is now worth well over ONE MILLION DOLLARS. When you reach this level you can stop paying the $2.73 a day — you now have a FREE ride for the rest of your life!"

And so the journey went on and the train continued to grow. It reached SIX MILLION DOLLARS by James's 50th birthday, TWELVE MILLION DOLLARS by his 55th birthday and nearly TWENTY FOUR MILLION DOLLARS by his 60th birthday. At that stage he stopped work and lived on all the gold he had accumulated as a result of paying just $2.73 a day for the first 37 years of his life.

The good fairy still visits new parents but nothing has changed. Hardly anybody takes any notice of her. "What can you do with

$2.73 a day?" is the usual question. In reply she just smiles and thinks of James and his special train, and in her mind sees the name that has been painted on the engine — The Magic of Compound Interest.

Important Note

The world is full of sceptics and many who read this will say the figures used are unreal, that **tax** will take most of the earnings, or that the future value of the investment is made worthless by inflation.

The aim of this story is to show you the importance of starting an investment plan early, and to understand how small sums can grow. **I do NOT want it used as a tool for unscrupulous sales people to use to encourage you to sign up for long term savings plans with huge hidden charges.**

I suggest you put the $1 000 a year away in managed funds such as unit trusts run by leading fund managers — probably growth units in split trusts with all earnings re-invested will achieve the best return. You will learn more about these in the chapters on managed funds. Make sure you keep in touch with your financial adviser as the plan may work better if the money is invested in the name of a low or non income earning spouse in the early stages.

When I wrote this chapter for the original edition of *More Money* in 1990 I used a return on investment of 14% and an inflation rate of 7%. Since then inflation and returns have dropped but the principles still hold true. The new types of managed funds such as split trusts that have the ability to maximise growth at the expense of income (a kind of internal negative gearing) should be capable of doing better than 14% if inflation is 7%.

At an average inflation rate of 7% a year, $24 million dollars in 60 years time is worth over $414,000 in today's money which cannot be regarded as "worth little", particularly for a total investment of $37 000. Under present laws little capital gains tax would be incurred if a progressive realisation of the investment commenced at age 60.

The chart below illustrates the principle and is based on the figures used in the example. Obviously future earnings can never be guaranteed, **but** I will guarantee that anybody who practises this strategy over the long term will finish up with a lot of money.

Few people will make the effort to try it out yet the truth is that it DOES work and costs only $2.73 a day. Why not give it a go?

STATION NO.	GROWTH	VALUE OF TRAIN	STATION NO.	GROWTH	VALUE OF TRAIN
1	140	1 140	31	62 747	510 937
2	300	2 440	32	71 671	583 608
3	482	3 922	33	81 845	666 453
4	689	5 611	34	93 443	760 896
5	926	7 537	35	106 665	868 561
6	1 195	9 732	36	121 739	991 299
7	1 502	12 233	37	138 921	1 130 221
8	1 853	15 086	38	158 231	1 288 452
9	2 252	18 338	39	180 383	1 468 385
10	2 707	22 045	40	205 637	1 674 472
11	3 226	26 271	41	234 426	1 908 898
12	3 818	31 089	42	267 245	2 176 143
13	4 493	36 582	43	304 660	2 480 804
14	5 261	42 843	44	347 312	2 828 116
15	6 138	49 981	45	395 936	3 224 052
16	7 137	65 255	46	451 367	3 675 420
17	9 276	75 530	47	514 558	4 189 979
18	10 714	87 244	48	586 597	4 776 576
19	12 354	99 598	49	668 720	5 445 296
20	14 083	114 681	50	762 341	6 207 638
21	16 195	131 876	51	869 069	7 076 707
22	18 602	151 478	52	990 738	8 067 445
23	21 347	173 825	53	1 129 442	9 196 887
24	24 476	199 301	54	1 287 564	10 484 451
25	28 042	228 343	55	1 467 823	11 952 274
26	32 108	261 451	56	1 673 318	13 625 592
27	36 743	299 194	57	1 907 528	15 533 174
28	42 027	342 221	58	2 174 644	17 707 818
29	48 051	391 272	59	2 479 094	20 186 912
30	54 918	447 190	60	2 826 167	23 013 079

* Using the Noel Whittaker Wealth Creator on CD-ROM it is a simple matter to work out that if you started investing $2.73 a day in January 1980 into a share trust that matched the All Industrials Accumulation Index you would have accumulated $135 608 on 31st December 1999. That covers a 20-year period and indicates a much better performance than the 14% used in the table above. Naturally, past results are no guarantee of future performance.

4

Cash Type Investments

It's a kind of spiritual snobbery that makes people think they can be happy without money.

(ALBERT CAMUS: Notebooks)

Before we get into heavy issues such as property, shares and tax let's think about why it's important to keep some money in cash. In this chapter I'll discuss cash type investments, indicate the importance of the cash component in a balanced portfolio and then show you areas where cash can best be invested.

The purpose of cash investments in a portfolio is to give you the certainty of being able to get access to your money when you need to. Thus the requirements for cash type investments are:

(1) There should be minimal costs to invest or redeem. Once there are costs involved it takes time for them to be recovered.

(2) There should be no loss of capital no matter when the money is withdrawn; no waiting till "the market recovers".

(3) An investor who withdraws should not be penalised by losing earnings. No penalties for early withdrawal.

(4) The money should be accessible quickly.

Contrast these requirements with investments in property or shares. Here there are normally substantial costs of acquisition and disposal and neither capital growth nor liquidity are assured. We all know that shares can fall rapidly in value, while property is not liquid, can be hard to sell, and prices often stay flat for years.

People regard cash type investments, such as bank bills and term deposits, as very secure. They are easy to understand, your money is usually safe and there are no fees to deposit or withdraw.

However there is one major and often forgotten drawback. The $100 000 you have in the bank now may appear to be a lot of money, but think of the Rule of 72[1].

If inflation averages 5% a year your $100 000 will buy only $50 000 worth of goods and services in just 14 years. If inflation rises to 8% another nine years will see its buying power reduced to just $25 000. By leaving the money in cash form you have lost 75% of its value in around 22 years. That is far worse than any property or stock market crash; there is no risk free investment.

Fixed Term Or Short Term

So the purpose of cash type investments is to give you a place where you can invest money which you can access fairly quickly, at minimum cost, and with the certainty that the face value of your money will remain intact. The first decision you have to make is do you want your money at call, or are you happy to invest some of it for a fixed term, where you do not have access to it.

The main reason to invest money for a fixed term is because you believe the earning rate on that investment is going to fall and you can achieve a better rate by 'locking' the money up. There may be a price to pay. History has shown that few can accurately predict market trends and the price of investing for long fixed terms is that you lose the ability to switch out quickly if alternative opportunities come along.

The other reason to invest money for a fixed term is that you wish to defer interest by placing your money in the kind of deposit where the maturity date falls after June 30th and thus pays the interest to you in the following tax year.

> **EXAMPLE:** *It is April and you have $30 000 to invest for a short period. By placing it in a term deposit that matures, plus interest, on July 1st you have transferred three months interest from the present financial year to the next which gives you another year to pay the tax on it.*

Some Important Considerations

The big question to ask yourself is "How much money do I need to keep in the cash area?" The answer will depend on what you want the money to do and on two other factors, the "real rate of return" and your marginal tax rate.

---

1 The Rule of 72 is explained in Chapter 9 of *Making Money Made Simple.*

The "real rate of return" is the difference between the rate you earn on your money and the inflation rate. If the bank is paying you 6%, and inflation is 2%, the real rate of return is 4%. If the gap between inflation and interest rates grows, the real rate of return rises, and it becomes more attractive to leave money in interest-bearing areas. Conversely, if the real rate falls, cash-type investments become less attractive. We'll go into this theory of relative attractiveness in more detail in the section on shares.

Now think about the marginal tax rate – this is the rate at which the Government takes its cut of the interest on your money. A high income earner will lose 48.5% and a nil income earner will keep it all. Consequently lower income earners find interest-bearing investments more attractive than do high income earners.

> **EXAMPLE:** *Joan earns $70 000 a year, Tom earns $9 000 a year and both have $100 000 invested at 7%. Joan's yearly net return after tax is $3 605 (3.6%), while Tom's is $5 705 (5.7%). Notice that Tom's after tax return is 58% more than Joan's. Also, don't forget that Joan is going backwards if inflation is 3.7%, or more, so her real return after tax may be a negative one. Tom is making a small real return after tax provided inflation is less than 5.7% per annum.*

A good question to ask yourself is "Am I likely to have to withdraw this money within the next three years?" If the answer is yes, you should be investing in cash-type investments and at the same time taking care to place the funds in the name of the lowest income earner to save tax.

This advice must be tempered by the state of the share and property markets and by the certainty of your needing the money. If the answer was the one we hear almost every day, "I don't think I'll need it for a long while, I certainly have nothing in mind for it, but cannot be certain", you could consider putting some into shares or property if the market was depressed and looked like there was a good chance of a rise. If you decide to invest part of the money in property or shares understand that you are about to sail into uncharted waters and may have to moderate sudden spending urges if the market doesn't kick up as quickly as everybody expected.

The most important thing of all is to make sure your money is safe. There is no point in getting a high return if you cannot get your capital back. We now live in challenging times and it is important that investors go for strength and not put their savings at risk by chasing above average interest rates with an above average degree of risk. Those investors who were lured by the above average returns of the Estate Mortgage Trusts are now wishing they had chosen lower returns and lower risk.

Savings And Cheque Accounts

Everybody needs a working account — that is an account that receives your salary and pays the bills. There is no point in wasting money so why use a no interest bearing cheque account that charges you fees when you can use some of the low or no fee savings accounts that have a cheque facility and pay interest. In any event there is no excuse for leaving much money in your working account when the cash management trusts mentioned next will pay you competitive rates of interest and let you withdraw on 24 hours notice.

Cash Management Trusts

Cash management trusts (CMT's) are superb places to invest liquid funds. They have no entry or exit fees, invest in secure areas and your money is available at call. They often have useful features such as a free cheque book, and a telephone withdrawal facility. Bear in mind they are intended to be a "reserve tank" from which you siphon large chunks of money as needed and are not meant to be a vehicle for paying the milkman. The best way to use a CMT is to hold the bulk of your spare cash in there and work in association with one of those free savings accounts I mentioned above that pay interest and have a bill paying facility.

If the balance in the savings account falls below $100 top it up with a cheque for $500 or $1 000 from your cash management trust. Similarly if your savings account starts to build up funds, transfer them across to the cash management account in $500 lots.

Cash management trusts are growing in popularity to such an extent that the major trading banks who once poured scorn on them are now setting up their own. However, check out the rates before you open the account, for some CMT's have a sliding scale of interest and don't pay you the highest rate till your balance reaches a certain figure. Others give you their highest rate on the whole balance, so be on your guard.

A CMT places its unit holders' funds in short term securities such as bank guaranteed bills. The CMT's claim they can obtain better rates than a private investor because of the size of the parcels of the funds they place, but the money market margins are small and most investors seem to get higher returns in bank bills. However, most CMT's offer a same day withdrawal facility and offer additional services such as a free cheque writing service. Bank bills don't come with these frills and when you invest in one, your money is tied up for the term of the bill. This is marvellous if rates are falling but frustrating if they are rising. My own choice is to use a CMT as I don't have the time to spend half a day on the phone battling various banks to squeeze another couple of points out of them.

Debentures

A **debenture** is a document issued by a company evidencing a loan to it. The loan is usually for a fixed term which may range from one to five years. Interest is payable at the rates stated in the prospectus and is fixed for the term of the debenture. Interest may be paid to you monthly, quarterly, half yearly, or yearly but there are also "compound debentures" which add your interest to the principal to allow it to compound. This accrued interest is paid to you together with the initial principal at the end of the investment term. The rate of interest will vary with the timing of the payment. The longer you have to wait for the interest the higher rate you get, so monthly is usually the lowest rate and the compound rate is the highest.

A **compound debenture** is a good method of compulsory saving but may cause you liquidity and tax problems as there is tax and provisional tax payable on the interest despite the fact you do not receive it till the debenture matures. You thus have to pay money out for tax before you receive it.

Debentures are popular but have varying degrees of security as their safety depends entirely on the ability of the company issuing them to repay your money to you. The main companies issuing debentures in Australia are finance companies who lend out the money raised to their borrowers.

I suggest you stick with the big name companies if you want to invest in debentures. They may pay a slightly lower rate than the secondary companies but the risk is lower. Remember "the greater the return the greater the risk".

I have never been keen on debentures although I am aware that they are a very popular investment. Certainly they are useful for locking in high interest rates but you lose all flexibility and in these volatile times you cannot afford to have your money locked up. I much prefer a combination of CMT's, mortgage trusts, and bank bills.

Bank Bills

These are good investments when rates are high and look like falling. The term is usually three to six months, which is not so long that you lose flexibility. The procedure to invest is simple (phone your bank) and your money is highly secure as it is bank guaranteed. An added benefit is that interest is paid at the end so you can take out a bank bill in March to mature in July and defer the income to the next financial year.

The banks will "bargain" on bank bill rates so make sure you shop around if you are considering investing in them.

Mortgage Trusts

The public reaction to the problems experienced by the Estate Mortgage Group showed that few people understood what kind of investment a mortgage trust is.

Let's learn some history. In past times many investors seeking a regular secure income would lend out money by private mortgage (through their solicitor) on an interest only basis. The term was usually three years, the interest rate was fixed, and the money was secured by a registered first mortgage over property. The solicitor was recompensed for his time by the fees he received for the cost of preparing the mortgage documents.

Restricting the amount of the loan to no more than 70% of the property valuation gave the lender assurance that the amount of the mortgage debt, at least, should be achieved if the borrower defaulted and the property was sold to recover the debt. The major drawback with this type of investment was that the lenders' funds were effectively frozen for the period of the loan unless the borrower defaulted or the lender could sell the mortgage to another party with money to lend.

Mortgage trusts are an extension of the private mortgage concept except that by using unit trusts a fluctuating pool of money is created. The cash in the pool grows from receipt of new monies, loans being repaid and from interest payments from borrowers. It shrinks when investors redeem funds, when it pays interest to investors and when it lends funds out.

Provided the new cash coming in is not less than the money going out, the pool remains able to repay funds to its investors on demand despite the fact it is lending out money for terms of at least three years. However, if many of the investors decide to ask for their money immediately, at the same time as new subscriptions dry up, the fund becomes unable to meet the unit holders' request for their money back. This is perfectly logical and should not be of surprise to anybody.

It need not indicate the trust is unsound, provided the loans are good ones, or that the unit holders' money is at risk, but it could mean the unit holders may have to wait for three to five years to collect their money unless the manager can raise money in the meantime by selling off the three to five year mortgages. There is no reason why interest payments should not continue in the meantime provided the loans are to credit worthy borrowers.

Be careful of exit penalties with mortgage trusts. Some mortgage trusts have exit fees which can be quite heavy so watch out for them and prefer a mortgage trust where there are no exit fees after 12 months at most.

As few advisers recommended Estate Mortgage to their clients Estate Mortgage had to rely on extensive advertising to attract new money. Many of the radio and television advertisements appeared to be aimed at people with no commercial experience and the newspaper advertisements were, in my mind, blatantly misleading. The term "Bank Guaranteed 18% Return" would indicate to most people that their principal was guaranteed, yet a close reading of the fine print showed this was untrue and the only guarantee offered by a bank was a certain rate of interest for a specific term.

A mortgage trust is different to a cash management trust. The former lends money out on a three to five year basis against the security of mortgages over real estate, the latter invests in highly liquid prime **short term** securities.

If you are investing in mortgage trusts, or any other managed funds, seek the services of an independent financial adviser with comprehensive research facilities. Those who ignore independent advice and invest on the strength of glowing newspaper advertisements may pay a heavy price.

Summary of Main Points

(1) There should be minimal costs to invest or redeem.

(2) There should be no loss of capital no matter when the money is withdrawn.

(3) An investor who withdraws should not be penalised by losing earnings so stay away from accounts that pay interest on the minimum monthly balance.

(4) The money should be accessible quickly.

(5) Beware of tying up your money for long periods.

(6) Watch out for exit fees on mortgage trusts.

(7) Spread your money.

(8) Don't chase higher than average returns.

5

The Nature Of Real Estate

Do you know the difference between education and experience? Education is when you read the fine print; experience is what you get when you don't.

PETE SEEGER

Real estate is one of the three major areas where the bulk of your money can be invested, so it follows that a sound working knowledge of real estate is ESSENTIAL for anybody who is serious about becoming wealthy.

The problem with understanding real estate is that almost everybody's knowledge is limited to **residential** real estate. They grew up in a house their parents owned, or rented, then bought a house or rented one themselves. In later life they probably bought an investment house if they could afford it. Consequently if they talk about the "property market" they are referring to the residential market in their own area.

In fact there is no such an animal as "the property market" and a person who talks of "the property market" is displaying their lack of knowledge about the subject. There are many separate property markets and they all go through booms and busts in their own fashion. It is impossible to make a valid comparison between the residential property market in Sydney, the commercial market in Perth or the industrial market in Adelaide. Simultaneously, one may be flat and another may be booming.

There are five basic types of real estate:

1. **Residential Real Estate** — this is the one you probably know best. It consists of houses, units and flats.

2. **Commercial Real Estate** — this is where you may work. It comprises office accommodation which can vary in size from a small suburban strata title office to a huge high-rise inner city office block.
3. **Industrial Real Estate** — this is the hub of the nation's industry. It makes up the buildings which are involved with manufacturing and distribution of goods.
4. **Retail** — this where you do your shopping. These properties can vary from the small shop which acts as your corner store to a massive shopping complex.
5. **Rural** — the larger tracts of land away from suburbia. They may be used to live on or for farming or grazing.

We shall learn in this chapter that each type of property has its advantages and disadvantages, but understand that residential property is affected mainly by interest rate levels, whereas non-residential real estate prices are more influenced by the state of the economy.

First we'll consider how real estate is valued for it is in the area of valuation that real estate is so different to shares.

There are two features of property which make it hard to value. The first is that no two properties are alike and the second is that properties are expensive, so tend to change hands infrequently. This makes valuation of property a difficult task and means that a valuation, at best, is an educated expression of opinion. Valuers have a saying "Valuation is an art and NOT a science" and a tolerance of 5% in a property valuation is acceptable.

Before we start let me tell you about a recent experiment carried out in Britain which illustrates the difficulty of obtaining an accurate valuation.

Ten of the top valuers in the country were sent to a suburb in London that was well away from the area of expertise of any of them and provided with as much data about comparable sales and capitalisation rates in the area as they asked for. The valuers were asked to value a number of properties using their experience and the data supplied. There was over 63% difference between the highest and the lowest valuations for any given property, not because the valuers were incompetent or that the data was wrong, but because so much of the accuracy of valuing depends on knowing the area. This clearly demonstrates the difficulty of valuing property but also explains why a person buying a property needs to put so much time into doing research BEFORE they start to look seriously.

Value is also greatly affected by special conditions that may be placed on the property. For example in Brisbane is a property listed by the National Trust. It has been valued at $8 million as a vacant site, $3.7 million if just the facade is kept and only $1.3 million if it has to be kept in its present state to satisfy National Heritage conditions.

Methods Of Valuation

THE COMPARABLE VALUE METHOD: Houses, vacant land, home units and identical factory units are usually valued by assessing their price in comparison with similar house properties in the same area. You phone the local agents when you decide to sell and they give you an estimated market price based on comparable local sales.

If you need a valuation for a deceased estate or a transfer between members of the same family this valuation will still be based on comparable sales in the area. The agent's local knowledge is important because some streets are more in demand than others, just as some suburbs have a prestige name.

Notice the main element that contributes to your value is the **prices of comparable properties** and that you have no control over them. Certainly you will obtain a premium for superb presentation and you may gain increased value by adding a pool or an extra room, although it is generally doubtful if the value added is more than the cost of adding it. The position, of itself, will have a large bearing on the value but you paid for this when you bought. Despite these other issues the value of the property will move in line with comparable properties in the same area; the other factors will determine whether it goes in the top priced homes for the area or the cheaper ones.

The other types of properties, including flats, may be valued by the following methods:

(1) Applying a capitalisation to the earnings (the cap rate method)

(2) Assessing the value on a cost basis (the summation method).

There is another procedure called the Discounted Cashflow Approach which is used when the property has a unique feature that does not allow the use of the traditional cap rate method. An example may be a sound property with a 10 year lease which has no provision for rental reviews. We will ignore it here; there are plenty of text books on valuation available for those readers who wish to find out more.

Applying A Capitalisation Rate To The Earnings

It's vital that you study this section until you understand what the capitalisation rate (cap rate) is and how it interacts with the income to produce a final valuation. It is not only the method used to value most non-residential real estate, it has also a close link to the ways shares are valued.

The cap rate is the price in terms of yield that a buyer will pay for the property and varies with the type of property and with the general level of interest rates. For example prime commercial property in the centre of Sydney may have a cap rate of five per cent. This means buyers are prepared to accept an EARNINGS return of only five per cent on the funds they invest to buy the property. Why would they accept such a low return when they could get twice as much in debentures? Because they believe the EXTRA GROWTH the property should achieve will more than compensate them for the low INCOME return.

In a period when interest rates are generally high capitalisation rates tend to rise for two reasons:

(1) The seller is now competing with high interest rates for the investor's attention because it is attractive to leave cash in bank bills or interest bearing accounts when they are paying 17% or 18%.

(2) High sustained interest rates can cripple negatively geared investors which forces them to dump properties on the market. This tends to depress prices.

Using The Cap Rate

To determine the value, you divide the capitalisation rate into 100, and multiply the answer by the earnings. It's not nearly as hard as it sounds.

EXAMPLE: *A small industrial shed has a net income of $50,000 a year. The accepted cap rate for that type of building in the area is 12.5%. Dividing 100 by 12.5 gives us a figure of* *eight, therefore the price is $400,000 being eight times the net rental of $50 000.*

100/12.5 = 8.   8 x $50 000 = $400 000

Look how the value drops if the cap rate blows out to 14% because of rising interest rates and pessimism in the economy.

100/14= 7.14   7.14 x $50 000 = $357 000

The owner could get the value back up by increasing the rent if the tenant could handle it and the lease terms allowed it.

Assume the rents increase by 10% to $55 000 at the same time as the cap rate goes up to 14%.

100/14 = 7.14   7.14 x $55 000 = $392 700

Notice the lower the capitalisation rate the higher the price. This is because a low capitalisation rate indicates the buyer will accept a lower income return in the expectation of higher capital growth than would be shown by properties giving a higher income return.

If the property has substantial tenants with long term leases, or is a quality building that has not yet been completely tenanted, the valuer may put a slightly lower capitalisation rate on it as an expression of the extra value provided by the existing or potential tenants.

The Summation Method

The summation method values the land and improvements separately and is used generally as a check valuation or where the property is unique such as a church or a large historic home on a huge block in the middle of a good suburb.

A summation valuation might state:

Land	
4 000m^2 at $100 per square metre	$400 000
Improvements	
700 m^2 at $450 per square metre	$315 000
less Depreciation at 10%	($31 500)
Fencing	$5 000
Total Valuation	$751 500

The problem with a summation valuation is that it fails to recognise that cost may not be relevant to value. One of the best examples may be the houses and shops in a remote country town that were erected by the mining company for its staff. If the mine closes down the properties are worthless despite the huge cost of building them.

Growth Or Yield?

The basic property choice is expressed in the formula:

HG/LY or HY/LG

which means you choose between a property that is High Growth coupled with Low Yield or High Yield coupled with Low Growth. This ties in with the cap rate method because a low cap rate indicates a low yield and expected high growth. Conversely a seller with a building for sale in the outback may be forced to offer a much higher yield to a buyer to make up for the lack of expected growth.

In other chapters I have pointed out the advantage of interest only borrowing because it allows a buyer to opt for a lower yielding property and thus obtain better capital gain. The HG/LY is a better proposition for high income earners because it means that bulk of the return is taxed under the capital gains tax rules which are milder.

Major Factors That Set The Price

Now we'll think about the factors that large institutional buyers consider when assessing the many offers to buy that come across their desk each week. Notice here the different approach to that adopted by the residential private buyer. The residential buyer is after a "good buy" and hopes the normal steady increase in house prices, helped along by the leverage of negative gearing, will produce a reasonable result over time. The institutional buyer is looking to improve the value of the property which we now know can be done in only two ways:

(1) Increase the income after all outgoings

(2) Reduce the cap rate

Therefore they are considering if the ingredients for long term growth are present. These may include:

- A secure tenant with a long lease with regular rent reviews. The value of the property will rise in line with the increased rents if the cap rate stays constant.
- A good location to continue to attract tenants which will keep the rents rising. A good location will enable rents to keep on growing because rentals are driven by supply and demand.
- An inherently good building which will not need a fortune spent on repairs or have continual management problems.

A property may have the potential for short term growth, mid term growth or long term growth.

An example of **short term growth** is when you come across a very ordinary property priced at 30% below the normal market price because the seller has seven days to raise the money or go bankrupt. This may enable you to buy it cheaply and make a short term capital gain. However, you are better off to take your profit and unload it quickly if there are no ingredients for substantial long term growth. By hanging onto it you tie up capital which you could use better elsewhere.

An example of **mid term growth** was the North Sydney commercial market in the early 1980's. New buildings kept coming on stream, the vacancy rates fluctuated and the usual prophets of gloom made dire predictions about over supply of office space. However, the potential for growth was present and it became one of Australia's most successful growth areas. Naturally it suffered in the 1990 crash, but there is no doubt of its inherent value because there are limited facilities to enable people to cross the harbour. North Sydney is now almost a city of its own on the other side of the harbour. It's a little like Kowloon and Hong Kong.

The case of the Sydney suburb of Chatswood demonstrates **long term** potential. For years Chatswood was a sleeper with the focus on retail shops but it had the fundamentals for growth, for it was situated at a major road and rail junction. The State Authority Superannuation Board became the catalyst for Chatswood development when it built a major commercial development which was promptly tenanted by the Australian Tax Office. This started the rush and Chatswood is now one of the largest regional centres in Australia.

Notice how location played such an important role in the growth of Chatswood and North Sydney. The factors that make for a good commercial location are nearness to transport, nearness to retail shopping and possible views which make for a pleasant environment.

For example, long term growth is now assured in the commercial property markets of Parramatta, North Sydney and Chatswood. Each of these markets is situated on a major train line, a major bus interchange and has a large regional retail base.

It's also important for large commercial buildings to be close to their competition in the traditional areas. Examples are Collins Street in Melbourne, St George's Terrace in Perth, and Queen Street in Brisbane; in Sydney banks and life insurance companies have traditionally placed themselves around Bligh and O'Connell Streets.

Trends In Real Estate

There is now a trend in industrial property to high tech industrial estates such as the ones now situated at North Ryde and Lane Cove in Sydney. Here the buildings do not look like industrial buildings. They are environment friendly and have a smaller site coverage, which means a better use of the landscaping. There are also greater staff facilities and it is now more common to find tennis courts, swimming pools and perhaps even a golf course in the large industrial parks.

The tenants in these complexes can expect to pay two or three times the rent of tenants in the ordinary industrial areas where such facilities are not needed.

As technological advances are made, more sophisticated facilities such as cabling and electrical support are needed in the bigger commercial and industrial buildings. Because of amalgamations and takeovers many businesses, such as law firms and accountants, need larger office floors.

Industrial Property

Apart from residential property this is probably the best area for people who wish to own their own real estate. There will always be a place for the ordinary industrial sheds which cater for the manufacturers and distributors who do not need high tech facilities.

The basic advantage of industrial real estate is its simplicity. There are no lifts or air conditioning to worry about, you do not have the everchanging tenant mix of shopping centres and there is very little to go wrong structurally or mechanically. Provided you pick a traditional area, and do not pioneer, you should be able to re-tenant again readily in normal times, but I suggest you have a good standby fund in case long vacancies do occur.

Retail Property

Retail property is a highly specialised area and involves constant management of the tenant mix as well as management of the centre itself. There was a proliferation of shopping centres built in Australia in the 1980's and it would seem that the rate of shopping centre growth is outstripping the shopping dollars available.

Shoppers are now regarding shopping as more of a family outing and the larger and newer centres are gaining business at the expense of the smaller and older ones. As a result I am cautious about exposure to much retail real estate, although I am still confident about the prospects for the shopping centres owned by the major property trusts because of the quality of services they provide.

The earnings of a centre are raised by:

- Extending the centre to provide extra facilities and to cater for an increased population growth in the area.
- Changing the mix of shops to satisfy the needs of the shoppers.
- Continual research to ensure the centre is meeting the demands of the shoppers and the tenants.

All these actions increase the performance of the tenants and hence the profitability of the entire centre. It is interesting to note that some of the most successful retail centre owners will not use rents based on a percentage of turnover. They believe that a higher base rent provides them with a rental income that is insulated from economic variations, and does not penalise the tenant who is increasing turnover. The unspoken reason is that they accept the fact that a lot of tenants will not admit to their accurate turnover, but keep two sets of books.

The land for large centres is scarce and is tightly held. Large retailers such as Myers or David Jones will often take out a 30 year lease with a 30 year option so the rental stream from the large "anchor tenants" is consistent and predictable. The rent from the small speciality shops is far less predictable as they tend to change hands, or go out of business regularly, especially in the smaller centres. The long leases that are a feature of the larger centres have given the values of retail property less volatility than commercial, industrial or rural property.

Some Case Studies

There are loads of stories about big money being made in real estate. Here a few of them:

CASE STUDY ONE: There was a heavily trafficked road that went through a developing suburb. A quiet road ran off it to a nearby housing estate and, at the junction, were two adjoining vacant blocks that were stony and unattractive with a strong backward slope. The year was 1980 and there were no buyers at their going price of $8 000 each.

A lateral thinker made an offer of $7 000 each for the blocks which was gratefully accepted. He then applied to the council to amalgamate the two blocks and re-zone the land for a small shopping centre. The backward slope was perfect for it allowed car parking under the shops at the rear, and the corner position gave good access.

A year later he sold the amalgamated and re-zoned site for $130 000.

CASE STUDY TWO: A young friend asked a real estate friend for advice on buying his first investment property. She told him to start work on doing the research on the market so he would be qualified to make the right decision. He eventually found a Public Trustee auction property that was in an excellent location on two adjoining small lots. The old house was tidy and situated on one of the blocks.

He paid $82,000 for the whole package and was able to sell the spare block on its own for $44,000 just after settlement, to make an instant profit of at least $25,000. Sometimes agents advertise property as being one large lot and don't realise that it is actually two smaller blocks. It's always a good idea for the potential investor to check out these properties, because sometimes, even though the home does encroach, it is possible to quite inexpensively remove the encroachment and sell off the spare lot at a good profit.

CASE STUDY THREE: A client of mine bought a small commercial building where the tenants had got into financial strife and were giving the absentee landlord lots of headaches. She bought the property for only $115 000, let the tenants out of their lease for a small fee (one month's rent) and sold the building vacant for $155 000 to an owner-occupier. It was worth $250 000 only a year later.

CASE STUDY FOUR: Two friends bought an old workshop, zoned business, in a good location some years ago for $118 000, and spent $40 000 on it to make it an attractive-looking building instead of a dirty old shed.

They became their own tenants and sold it two years later for $285 000 but stayed on as tenants. It sold again recently for just over $500 000.

The aim of these examples is to give you some ideas and to show you it can be done. However, remember it's not as easy as it sounds; you have to put in the time and accept the risks.

Success in property, whether you invest directly or through property trusts, depends on following the rules.

They are simple, and known to all good fund managers, but unfortunately are often ignored by people who invest directly in rental houses.

The **first rule** is to buy it right. It is well known that the foundations for above average profits are laid at the time the property it bought. What is not so well known is that good property is hard to come by. One fund manager told us that his office receives over 50 sale proposals a week. Few are worth inspecting so his buying staff are out looking for themselves.

People are often surprised when we tell them that it is generally too late to buy a property once it is advertised. Every real estate agent has a "good client" list who get first choice at the prime listings. Also in every real estate market are the "ferrets" who make a full time job of pouring over zoning maps, doing council searches, and scouring the market for undervalued properties. By combining skill and hard work they make consistent profits.

The **second rule** is to add value by rezoning or refurbishment. Here is where the passive investors separate from the active ones for the big money is made by those who have the ability to see a run down property as it may become, not just as it looks on first inspection. This is a skill that few possess.

The **third rule** is to manage actively, for it is active management that maintains the high rents that precede increases in value. Slack management means the property starts to get a run-down look about it. This results in a drop in the quality of the tenants which leads to the property becoming still more run down. The downward cycle continues as the tenant quality and the appearance gets steadily worse.

You will notice that most investors ignore all three rules. They buy a property because it looks nice, turn it over to an estate agent to manage and drive past it every six months to make sure it is still standing. It is no wonder that most investors in residential real estate receive only mediocre returns over the long term.

Property is a long term investment for most people. Certainly you hear stories about the quick kill — the property purchased for a song and sold for the great profit. When this happens it is due to luck or skill. Do you want to know which it is? See if you can do it consistently. If you can, it's skill. If you can't, it was luck.

The majority of us buy a property in the hope that it will rise in value. If we are lucky enough to buy at the start of a boom we may be rewarded by a huge capital gain. If we buy at the end of the boom we may experience no gain in value for three or four years.

There is never a guarantee that a property we buy will rise in value at any specified rate, or in fact rise at all. Its value may rise, stay flat or drop. It is the same if we invest in a property trust. The only difference is that we could expect to increase our chances by entrusting our property purchase to a skilled manager with a good track record.

The main factors in property are the location and the quality of the tenants. When times are tough it is the top quality tenants on the long term leases that can get you through the flat periods. If you are heavily negatively geared into a large property, and the tenant is unable to pay, you can well end up going broke yourself.

Summing Up

Real estate has been the way to wealth for many and its unique characteristics make it more "fool proof" than shares. It's hard to go wrong if you invest in quality property, either directly or through property trusts, and by using negative gearing you create a pattern of "compulsory saving" for yourself that speeds your wealth accumulation. If you do it yourself, just be aware you can greatly boost the returns by taking the time to buy right and manage properly.

6

Buying Real Estate

Nothing succeeds like address.

FRAN LEBOWITZ

This chapter concentrates on buying **residential** real estate, as it would take far more space than we have available here to cover the fine points of buying into the huge retail, commercial and industrial properties.

Let's assume you have made the big decision to buy a piece of property and are already familiar with the basics as described in this book. How do you feel now?

If you are like most of us you are excited about taking such a huge step and probably can't wait to sign a contract, complete settlement and show it off to your family and friends. This is all perfectly normal, and the way things should be, but now you should take a few deep breaths and review your plan of attack by analysing what you are trying to achieve and how you are going to get there.

First Checkpoint

What Are You Buying It For?

The answer will be to live in it, for an investment, or for a quick resale.

Buying It To Live In

Try to estimate how long you will be living in the property and what your future family plans are. Is this a stepping stone to a bigger and better house, or is it likely you will spend a large part of the rest of your life there? If you envisage a relatively short period of residence, and then resale, look for a property that has the potential for short term gain. The property to look for is one that is untidy and grubby but that is also well located, structurally sound, and not in need of extensive maintenance. The typical "worst house in the best street" syndrome.

These houses DO come on the market if you look for them long enough. You should not have a lot of competition. The traders won't be interested unless the presentation is so bad that the price is low enough to enable them to make a large short term trading profit, and ninety per cent of ordinary buyers will buy a house because of its good presentation. YOU have to find the ones with BAD presentation for most buyers will overlook these, thus giving you a chance to make an extra profit at little cost by simply improving the general appearance.

> **EXAMPLE:** *A divorced friend of ours with a limited budget found a great little house in a good location. The previous owner was an absentee landlord, the carpets were threadbare and covered with stains, the walls were dirty, the curtains were in tatters, there was no lawn and the garden was a mess.*
>
> *All she had to do to cause the house to rise substantially in value was replace the carpet, repaint the internal walls, make some curtains and spend a few weekends in the garden. When she sells it she will make thousands of dollars of tax free money.*

If the place is going to be your short term home consider resale over comfort; if you intend to be there for the long haul go for the features that will give you what makes you happy. These may include a large allotment, a workshop, an entertaining area or an ensuite. If there are likely to be children in the house keep in mind the importance of being near such facilities as schools, shops and transport but stay clear of a main road with a high noise level and dangerous and heavy traffic.

Buying It For An Investment

If you intend to rent it out go for nearness to facilities as well as closeness to areas where work is available. Tenants prefer fences and some sort of car accommodation so aim for that if possible. Most tenanted houses quickly become less than perfect in the garden area so DON'T buy a house to rent out on the basis of it having a well kept garden or because it is immaculate. Instead go for a low maintenance home such as a conventional low set brick.

Stay away from houses with pools. Few tenants will maintain them properly and there are many tenants who don't want a pool, particularly if they have young children. All a pool does is add to the cost of your investment and greatly increase your maintenance costs.

Buying It For A Quick Profit

You should not be doing this unless you have the ability, the time, and the persistence to see the project through. If this is your first attempt here are a few ground rules that may assist you:

(1) It usually takes longer to get from acquisition to receipt of the final sale proceeds than you expect.
(2) Costs ALWAYS exceed your estimates.
(3) It is much harder to sell a tenanted house than a vacant one.
(4) Few tenants will live in a house that is being done up.
(5) Most tenants don't like month to month tenancies.

You can summarise that by saying that the job will take longer and cost more than you estimate, and that you can't expect to get rent from the property while you are fixing it up. Therefore it is a matter of living in it yourself, and thus saving rent, or leaving it vacant.

When you find the house, be prepared to do a little feasibility study on the following lines:

DIRECT COSTS	
Cost of property	$100 000
Buying costs (say 4%)	4 000
Cost of improvements	12 000
Total direct cost	$116 000
HOLDING COSTS[1]	
Local Authority charges	1 000
Cost of money @ 8%	8 000
Total Holding Charges	$ 9 000
TOTAL COSTS	$125 000

Now make an estimate of the sale price after all your work has been done. I have assumed it is $145 000.

Sale Price	$145 000
less Selling Costs (assume 3%)	4 350
Net Sale Proceeds	$140 650
Less Total Costs	$125 000
EXPECTED PROFIT	$ 15 650

Do you think those figures look good? Maybe yes and maybe no, but consider that if the house does not sell as quickly as estimated it will be costing you almost $833 a month to hold it. This is based on 8% of $125 000 ($10 000 a year) which is the total amount spent when you have bought it and done it up. I have used 8% as a

1 These assume it is nine months from the date you pay for it till the date you get the money from sale in the bank. Believe me, this is optimistic.

conservative borrowing figure, but even if you are not borrowing you are losing the earnings the money could be making elsewhere. You are fooling yourself if you cost out a project and don't include the cost of the capital you are putting in.

If the house does not sell, in just 18 months your profit is gone and then you start LOSING $833 a month.

You can alleviate the situation by putting in tenants once the renovations are finished, but even if they pay $150 a week you are still going backwards at $183 a month. Be aware the presence of tenants is likely to hinder a sale even if you are lucky enough to find tenants who would go to all the trouble of moving to a new place knowing that in 30 days they might be asked to leave when the buyer comes along.

It is important you do this feasibility study BEFORE you sign any contracts to buy a house to re-sell quickly. Many people have discovered that doing up houses for a quick profit is much harder than it looks, and you will notice in the example above that total improvements of only $12 000 increased the house price by $45 000 or 45%. This is optimistic but, frankly, the project wouldn't be feasible if the profit had been much less.

The ONLY way you will learn for yourself is to have a go. Just make sure you keep DETAILED records of all costs, not just for the Tax Office but for your own knowledge.

Second Checkpoint

Whose name will it be in?

If there is to be more than one owner will it be held as joint tenants or tenants in common?

This will be covered in detail in chapter 23, but you should get your mind clear on it before you have to instruct preparation of a contract. Usually husband and wife would choose joint tenants and other buyers would go for tenants in common. The family home should NOT be in the name of a company or a trust, and negatively geared investment properties should be in the names of the highest income earner.

Third Checkpoint

How will you finance it?

In the chapters on negative gearing and borrowing you will learn the right type of finance is crucial to maximising the dollars you can make on a real estate transaction, and in the chapter on negotiation you will discover the value of making an offer with your finance approved, so you are nearly as strong as a cash buyer.

The major difference between financing the family home and financing a rental property is that the interest on the family home is not tax deductible, so it should be paid off first. For the family home prefer a lender who has an offset account facility and make every effort to pay off the loan as quickly as possible.

Usually the appropriate finance for investment property is an interest only loan in conjunction with a separate plan to build other assets.

Buy Or Rent?

A common question has become "Is it still worth buying a house?" To find the answer do your sums, in the manner that follows, using your own figures. Assume your dream house costs $120 000, rent is $140 a week and the cost of finance is $8 400 (7% per annum). If you add $2 000 at least for ownership costs it is clear that it will cost $10 400 a year to own the house.

Deduct from this the annual rent of $7 280 (52 x $140) you save by buying, and the answer is $3 120. If the house does not increase by $3 120 in the next year you are better off to rent, and bank the money that would have been spent on loan repayments, rates and maintenance.

The figures look different if you have a large deposit or can pay cash. Buyers who can pay $120 000 cash for the house must consider the effect tax will have on the $120 000 if it is invested in interest-bearing accounts at 5%. Tax may take as much as half of the $6 000 interest leaving them with a net $3 000. If they buy the house for cash they save $7 280 in rent, but lose interest (after tax) of $3 000, and have to expend $2 000 on rates, insurance etc. For them the difference between owning and renting is marginal and is almost certainly outweighed by the security of owning their own home.

Buy Land Now Or Save For A Deposit

If you can't afford a house it is tempting to say "Let's go and buy a block of land". The big question is whether that is the right thing to do. Let's fall back on our old friends the pencil and the calculator again, and do some more figuring. We'll have to make some assumptions, as is the case with any sort of forward planning, so we'll assume there is a couple involved and each party earns between $20 000 and $50 000 a year. This places them in the 30% marginal tax bracket.

Assume the land will cost $90 000 and they have saved $12 000, which will provide a $9 000 deposit and $3 000 for acquisition costs. A loan of $81 000 over five years at 8% would require $2 538 a month in repayments, and they may be liable for $50 a month in rates and weed control. If they can earn a net 4% a year (6% less tax at 30%) on their savings, and bank the $2 588 a month they would be paying for the land and maintenance, they will have over $110 000 saved in three years.

The land would have to appreciate by 7% a year to do as well. Here is a case where you have to make up your own mind as to the likely land price increases over the period. Land prices tend to stay flat and then jump suddenly so it may pay to bank your money, follow the land prices and jump in and buy when the prices seem to be taking off.

Another factor to take into account is where you are living now. If you are paying rent of $650 a month, a commitment of $2 588 for land would take your total payments to $3 238 a month. This would pay off a house mortage of $278 000 in 15 years, so it could be better to buy a cheaper home instead of renting and paying off the land.

The Emotions Of Buying Or Selling

Most people go through a stage that has been described as "temporary madness" when buying or selling a property and those who don't prepare suffer the worst. Let's face it, a property is probably the most expensive item most of us buy or sell in our life time. It is a big step for anybody irrespective of whether it's a young couple buying their first block of land or somebody older who has finally got enough to go for the dream home.

When such a big event is happening in our lives we are hit by conflicting emotions. Some of these will be positive and some will be negative. There may be the satisfied feeling of a goal about to come true, and there may be exhilaration that at last we are going to have a piece of property of our own.

There is almost certain to be some doubt as to whether "we are doing the right thing", there may be fear at the thought of the huge loan we may have to commit to, and there may be the worry that a better buy is lurking around the corner and will appear the moment we sign the contract in front of us. If there is a boom happening at this time the buyers will be frightened of losing the property to somebody offering more money, and the vendors are almost certain to feel they sold too cheaply. Is it any wonder we suffer "temporary madness".

Buyers' Remorse

Forty-eight hours have passed since the buyers signed the contract and they are entering the next stage which is called buyers' remorse. By now some of their family members have told them they should have bought somewhere else, or that they have paid too much or that now is the wrong time to buy.

To make matters worse they have almost certainly glanced through a real estate magazine or a newspaper and noticed a house advertised that sounds a better buy than the one they were so enthusiastic about. They have also had a preliminary interview with the lending institution and have met a curt staff member who has taken a negative view of the property they are trying to buy, as well as their chances of getting a loan. The buyers who were in the clouds two days ago are now in despair. Who can blame them?

One of the secrets of success in life is knowing what is likely to happen and getting prepared for it. The way to stop all the problems I mentioned above is to understand why they occur, and take steps to stop them before they happen.

Much of the trauma can be taken out of buying a property if you check out your borrowing capacity before you start to look at any properties. If possible obtain a letter from the lending authority confirming approval of a loan to a certain figure. This does two things:

(a) It makes you a powerful buyer as you can show the agent or vendor your approval letter. You have become almost the equivalent of a cash buyer and we all know that most desperate sellers will accept a lower price if they know the contract won't fall through because the buyer cannot get finance approval.

(b) It removes worry and uncertainty about getting the loan approved after the contract is signed.

Once the amount of your finance is certain you know the price you can pay and you can concentrate on finding the best property for you in that price range. This will take some time, and some leg work, but it will pay dividends because:

(a) You won't be talked into signing a contract to buy some overpriced property just because you like the look of it.

(b) You should know a true bargain when you see it and, since your finance is approved, are in a position to make a low but realistic offer. You certainly won't be distracted by one of those advertisements that are designed purely to attract inexperienced buyers.

Buying The Property

By this time you should know both the price you can pay, the approximate location where you want to buy, and should have looked in enough agents' windows to have an idea of the general price range in the area. Now you can start a "project book". Pretend you are doing a school project and you have chosen as your subject the suburb in which you intend to buy.

Start the project book with a brief history of the suburb, the demographics (break up) of the population, and the population trends. The local library is the best place to start discovering the history, and the office of the State or Federal member of Parliament should be able to give you a population breakdown by age, sex, and income.

You probably wonder why you want the background of the community for it may be of little value when you are buying a house. Throughout this book I am encouraging you to think for yourself and put the time into analysing data; finding out the history of a suburb is one of the best places to start as it is involves gaining knowledge which you will use to advantage when the negotiations start.

An age breakdown lets you know whether you are moving into an area where young families predominate, which is important if you have a young family yourself, the income level helps to provide a genuine indication of the status of the suburb, and growth trends are a reliable indicator of future demand in the area.

Your "report" should list all schools, transport, shops, other recreation areas, what the local industries are, whether bad smells waft across at certain times, where the dog pound, sewage treatment works and the gravel pit are located, and any other items such as regular flooding that you believe will affect the demand for property in the area. When this is done, and it shouldn't take more than a couple of weeks, you can start to visit homes open for inspection, attend auctions and generally start to get to know the local agents. It is likely they will have additional information for your project book.

You are bound to find at least one agent with whom you establish a rapport and this person or persons will be a useful guide to help you with your house hunting. If you stumble across an untidy home that appears vacant while you are driving around you may ask the agent to try to find the owner for you and see if they will take an offer. There is a good chance the agent will know the property, but there is also a possibility that nobody has bothered to follow it up. Many bargains have been found in this way.

Some Useful Rules

1. **Once a "dog" always a "dog".**

There are some homes that are always hard to sell. It may be the result of their location, appearance or construction (or a combination of all three) but they are just plain difficult to get on contract. You can probably buy one of these cheaply but remember it will be just as hard to find a buyer when YOU come to sell.

2. **You always buy and sell on the same market.**

Many existing home owners want to sell their present home at the top of the market, and buy another next day at the bottom of the market. That is obviously not possible. If you want to move **do it now,** why wait and deny yourself the pleasure of the new home?

3. **Another good buy ALWAYS comes along.**

Don't be pressured into signing a contract because this bargain "will never come again". Take your time and sign up when you know, from your research, that you have got a good buy.

4. **All sellers think their property is worth more than it is.**

This happens throughout the world, so don't be frightened to make a low offer as long as your own research has confirmed it's not too unreasonable.

5. **Most people don't take the time to acquire the knowledge about the area or the market.**

This is your chance for a sprint along the road to wealth. Obviously anybody who puts in the hours to do the groundwork will end up well in front.

6. **Property has the capacity for capital gain or capital loss.**

A nil risk means no profit, a medium risk means medium profit and a high risk could mean a high profit (or loss). The choice is yours.

7

Selling Your House

Set thine house in order.

ISIAH 38.1

Throughout this book I am giving you knowledge that is not known to 90% of the population and I am showing you simple techniques that, if followed, will put you in the top 10% and keep you there. The reason the road to success is so lightly travelled is that most people never do the things that need to be done, either from lack of knowledge or from lack of motivation.

In the 1970's I owned a chain of real estate agencies and spent most of my time selling and appraising residential property. I discovered that less than 10% of sellers gave more than the most scant attention to the task of presenting and marketing their property for sale. They did not seem to know, or care, that you can add thousands of dollars to a property's value by the right marketing and presentation. The great news is that it doesn't take a lot of money and, as it is usually a private residence that you are selling, the extra money you get is TAX FREE. Can you think of an easier way to make tax free dollars?

Let's analyse the basic proposition on which a real estate agency operates. The premise is that every year in a neighbourhood a given number of homes will change hands for reasons as diverse as death, divorce, debt, transfer, retirement or having a new baby. Some of the sellers will be highly motivated and keen to sell, while others will start off just "feeling the market" and then increase their desire to sell as the pressure of time takes it toll. The couple who have just heard of a likely job transfer may start off "feeling the market" but develop strong motivation when the wife and children take the husband to the airport, and realise they are unlikely to see him again until the house is sold and the family reunited in the new home.

Beware The Pressure Of Time

The pressure of time is the worst of all and it is therefore vital that you try to avoid being caught in a time trap.

> **EXAMPLE:** *A couple had a successful business and were used to making fast decisions. They saw an auction advertisement for a house on the river that looked just what they had always wanted. They went to the auction, got carried away in the spirit of the bidding, and signed a 30 day unconditional cash contract. They intended to sell their house to pay for the new one, and were happy to pay the cost of bridging finance for a short time as they believed their house would sell quickly.*
>
> *They then discovered a problem. Their present house had a lot of features such as a tennis court and a heated pool, but it was not in a "high price name" area. It was a great house, and they had been happy living in it for many years, but they had lost touch with the modern buyer who was not going to pay the price they wanted to be in that suburb.*
>
> *It was a classic case of over-capitalisation. It took nine months for them to sell that house and the eventual price was less than half their original listing price. In the end the pressures of time got too much and they let it go for a song.*

Typical situations that create time pressures are:

- You are forced to sell by the bank because you can't keep up the payments.
- A divorce settlement has to be arranged.
- You are building a home and it is only partly constructed. You need to sell your present house to provide the money to finish the new one.
- A job transfer has split the family.
- The seller has signed up to buy another property (as in the example above) and MUST sell within a fixed time period.

If you think about the above cases you will see that almost all of them could be avoided. It is risky to push ahead with building until your own house is signed up on an unconditional contract, or to sign up for another while yours is still unsold, or to leave it to the last minute to find your mortgage payments have gone way outside your capacity to pay.

Buying Before Selling The Present One

Clients regularly seek advice on immediately buying a home to live in, and selling the existing one at leisure. When this idea is put I always ask "Which house will you live in?" The answer is invariably "In the new one". I then paint a mental picture of what will happen to the existing home.

The special intangible qualities vanish immediately the furniture goes, and in less than a month what was once a warm cosy home degenerates into a cold empty house with a corresponding heavy drop in value. The furniture will be gone, so there will be the inevitable marks on the walls where the furniture used to be, and there will be the uneven patches of wear on the carpets as the worn trafficked sections contrast with the still new sections that were always covered by the furniture. After a short while cobwebs will start appearing everywhere, and the garden will either get a weary look from lack of attention or the owners will get a weary look from maintaining two homes.

In a matter of a month or so you could lose 10% to 20% of your selling price.

Homes sell on atmosphere and the best way to achieve the right atmosphere is to sell it with the family, and all their treasures, still in it.

Setting The Price

The average house changes hands every seven years so most of you will find yourselves in the situation where you have to put your house on the market. It will be a bit scary if you are a first time seller but remember your main objective — to sell it on the most favourable terms for yourself. In the chapter on negotiating you will discover that this need not necessarily mean the highest price.

After you have made the decision to sell, your next job is to find out a fair market price. The best way to start is to contact the main local real estate agents and invite them to come around. Probably you have found regular leaflets in your mailbox from the most active local agents as there is always a shortage of good saleable properties, and one of an agent's hardest jobs is keeping up a supply of property to sell. Choose agents who have highly visible offices in your area, who have a high presence by the amount of their "For Sale" signs and who advertise heavily in your local paper. These are the proven active ones; they are most likely to attract buyers who may be interested in buying your home.

Tell them you are THINKING ABOUT putting your house on the market and ask them to give you an idea of what is a realistic market price. Don't let them trick YOU into setting the price. If they ask you what price you are seeking tell them you have no idea. Remember that there are different price levels that range from the **forced sale** price at the **bottom** of the market, to the high price that sellers may claim they want if they are not serious about selling. These are the sellers who "may move when Bill retires in three years time, but would sell now if we get our price".

A good agent will quote a price range instead of a specific price. For example "I believe this property is worth between $135,000 and $155,000". When they give you the price range ask them to justify it by compiling a CMA (Competitive Market Analysis.) A sample is on the next page and you will see it is is a document listing details of homes, similar to yours, that are currently on the market and details of similar homes that have sold in the last three months. Don't use an agent who won't provide a CMA.

Your next task is to look over the "competition" because your home is competing for the buyers' attention against all the other similar homes for sale in your area. The CMA should contain addresses so, as a first step, drive past the ones that have been sold. Do this with an open mind, for the problem with valuing property is that no two properties are alike. You may drive past a house which looks just like yours, and which sold at a high price six weeks ago, and not be aware that there is a heated pool in the back or that the seller has spent thousands on a bar and billiard room.

The prices of the sold ones are past history. You will get a better appreciation of value if the agent takes you through the ones that are still listed for sale because they are your real competition. Most agents will do this readily.

When setting the price you should be aware that it is the buyers, and not you, who decide what they are going to pay for your house. Far too many sellers add up what they have spent on the house, or in more extreme cases what they need to clear their debts and have enough over for another house, and regard this as the selling price. Your home is competing in price with other similar homes in the area, and the amount you **need** to get, or the amount you paid for it, **is of no relevance whatsoever.**

XYZ REALTY
Competitive Market Analysis

Analysis of Property at 10 Barcoo Drive, Hereville

Owner Bill and Mary VENDOR Date

Current Listings – Listed within 60 Days

Suburb	Address	Price	Comments
Hereville	16 Barcoo Dr	$120,000	L/s Brick, Neat yard
Hereville	28 Kennedy Dr	$125,000	Busy road, nice IG pool
Nearville	112 Jones Rd	$120,000	Close schools/shops
Nearville	113 Main St	$105,000	Untidy, on busy road

Sold in Past 3 Months

Suburb	Address	Price	Comments
Hereville	12 Barcoo Dr	$115,000	Big block, pool
Hereville	29 Ash St.	$110,000	Quick Sale
Nearville	38 Blaxland Tce	$105,000	Untidy. Bad position

Listed in Past 6 Months — Still for Sale

Suburb	Address	Price	Comments
Hereville	88 Barcoo Dr	$130,000	Neat and Tidy
Nearville	145 Jones Rd	$140,000	Big home – over capitalised

Our Recommended Sale Price $115,000 to $120,000

Signature

XYZ REALTY

Do It Yourself Or Use An Agent?

Now that you have taken the time to establish the approximate market price of your house, you have to decide whether to sell it yourself or to engage an agent to do it. In my experience you are much better to use an agent for the following reasons:

1. The way to get the best price for your home is to expose it to as many potential buyers as possible. An agent has access to a continual stream of buyers who are attracted to the agency by its advertising. The only way a private seller can attract a buyer is by erecting a "For Sale" sign on the front of the property or by placing advertisements in various newspapers. These have a much smaller impact than the on-going marketing of a top agent.

   Another problem with advertising the house yourself is that you usually reach a stage where you have spent several hundreds of dollars on advertising, have still not found a buyer, and then have to start from scratch and make the decision again about using an agent, or spending more precious money on advertising.
2. Most buyers prefer to deal with real estate agents. Think about how you would feel if you were the buyer. It is a far less stressful experience to go to a real estate office and be driven around various properties for sale, than to have to knock on the door of a strange house and introduce yourself as a buyer.
3. An essential part of the selling process is the payment of a deposit by the buyer. Buyers know that a deposit placed in an agent's trust account is far safer than a deposit given to a stranger, and many are reluctant to hand over a deposit to a private vendor in case the sale does not proceed and they cannot get a refund of the deposit.
4. You will see in a following chapter on negotiation that it is far easier to negotiate through an agent than to negotiate face to face.

EXAMPLE: *You are trying to sell your house yourself and some buyers inspect it and appear to show interest. They ask you the price, you tell them it is $175,000, and this does not appear to concern them. They then depart saying "We will get back to you soon".*

Do you ask them for their telephone number so you can contact them, or do you think would be rude? How would you feel if you asked for the telephone number and they answered

"We would rather not give it out"? What do you do when four days have passed and you have not heard from them? Even if you do have their telephone number you are going to appear to be a desperate seller if you call them back. The moment they hear your voice you have effectively dropped the price.

5. It is a little more secure to deal through a real estate agent. I know that agents don't do identification checks of buyers but they usually have at least a telephone number before they take them out looking. How do you know that the "private buyer" who knocks on your door is not a burglar checking out your house for a possible robbery?
6. This is an ethical matter but I believe that ethics are important in life. Real estate agents are paid only when they effect a sale on your behalf. I suggest it is unfair for anybody to use all the free services that a real estate agent can provide, and then take over the selling of the property so the agent has no chance of earning a commission.

Listing The Property

I hope that by this stage you have established a fair market price and have decided to list your property with an agent. The next questions are "Which agent and which type of agency?"

When choosing an agent look for the traits you would welcome if you were a buyer. If the agent arrives and he or she is grubby, or chain smokes, or drives a filthy brokendown car it is unlikely that buyers will want to spend much time with them. Look for an agent who is active in your area, who has been at least a year in the industry and who can answer all your questions quickly and accurately. If the agent makes grand promises, or doesn't take the time to find out all the features of the property, choose somebody else.

Beware of an agent who overvalues your property. You should have a good indication of its value by now, but unfortunately there are some unscrupulous agents who will try to "buy the listing" by putting an inflated value on it just to beat the competition and then telling you a few weeks later that "the market has gone flat". A competitive market analysis should be the best guide to the right price.

The agent who tells you what you want to hear rather than the truth does you no favour. By the time you have had the house on the market for months the property has become stale in the agents' minds and you have missed sales at the real value while waiting for the dream figure predicted by the "nice agent!"

The above comments about price do not apply in "boom" periods when prices are rising rapidly, for price is then almost impossible to gauge. Agents know a boom is on when they hear that the house they confidently valued at a maximum of $175 000 a week ago has just sold for $200 000. I believe auction is by far the best way to sell in boom times, for the best way to get a high price is to have buyers fighting each other for your property.

There are four basic listing methods:

(1) List the property with several agents (an open listing).

(2) Give one agent an exclusive agency or a sole agency.

(3) Multiple Listing.

(4) Auction.

Open Listing

An agent gets paid only when a sale is made so if you list the property with five agents, four will receive no payment for any work they do. It's a bit like going to five doctors, asking them all to look at you to see what is wrong, and telling them that you will pay only one of them. They probably won't work hard on your case and neither will any real estate agents who realise that they have only a one in five chance of getting paid.

The argument put by some agents in favour of open listing is that you have more chance of selling your home if many agents have it listed. This is wrong because most buyers check out every agent in the area in which they intend to buy. Buyers have one major fear; that they will sign a contract and then discover they could have bought a better house around the corner. Believe me, if active local agents have plenty of "For Sale" signs throughout your area the buyers will check them out.

You could try open listing the property with a few agents for a couple of weeks to see which one performs the best. If you do that please allow only ONE "For Sale" sign on your property. Nothing looks more desperate than a house with a dozen signs in the front yard.

A Sole Agency

In a sole agency you appoint one real estate agency to act for you and undertake to pay them a commission if the house is sold by them in the agreed listing period. Don't tie your property up for too long but 30 days is certainly not long enough for the agent to do the property justice and anything over 90 days is too long. I believe that 60 days is about right but be guided by what is customary in your area.

It is vital that you clarify what will happen if you find a buyer by yourself in that time. Some agents are happy to allow you to try to find a buyer and will not charge you any commission if you do. However, if there is no specific provision in the listing contract that covers this you may find yourself liable to pay commission to your listing agent if you find a buyer yourself. Ensure this point is covered in writing, and be aware that a buyer who knocks on your door as a result of the agent's "For Sale" sign, is NOT a buyer you found yourself.

You should also remember that a listing agreement is a binding contract between you and the real estate agent (your listing agent). Don't fall into the trap of having to pay double commission if another agent sells it without reference to the listing agent. Make sure you refer any buyers, as well as any offers you may receive, to the listing agent.

CASE STUDY: *A couple listed their house for sale and signed a sole agency agreement in which they undertook to pay commission to their listing agent if the property was sold in the listing period. During that period a real estate agent who was not a member of the Real Estate Institute saw the FOR SALE sign on the house and brought a buyer around who subsequently signed a contract to buy it. The couple asked this second agent what was the position regarding commission and he advised them that he would be "working something out with the original listing agent".*

This did not happen and he kept all the commission for himself. The original listing agent then successfully sued the couple for commission on the sale, so they ended up paying a commission to BOTH agents.

If the second agent had been a member of the Real Estate Institute his unethical conduct would have been dealt with by the Arbitration Committee, and a fine imposed upon him. The commission would have been awarded to the listing agent so the seller would not be liable for two commissions. In this case he was not a member of the Institute so the owners had no redress. This proves the importance of referring ALL offers to the listing agent and of dealing only with members of the Real Estate Institute.

Multiple Listing

Another form of sole agency is Multiple Listing. In this case you appoint a sole agent who circulates details, with a photograph, to all fellow agent members of the Multiple Listing Bureau in your area. The commission is split between the selling agent and the listing agent. It is important for you to check that the system is used by all the reputable agents in your district so that they will all have access to the listing.

Generally, it's not a good idea to multiple list your property with an agent from out of the district where the property is situated. Understandably, the local agents won't drive ten miles to get the key, they'll put the listing in the "too hard" basket and the sellers miss out on the chance of a sale, all because they used an agent from outside their area.

Both sole agency and multiple listing are fine if the listing agent is competent and hard working, but both methods are a complete waste of time if the agent doesn't do the job properly. This is why it is essential to have faith in your agent before you sign any sort of sole agency agreement.

Auction

Another form of sole agency is auction. This is also a controversial method of selling, but can be highly effective in the right market and with the right property. The great feature of auction is that people who bid at auction make UNCONDITIONAL offers so if your property is sold "under the hammer" the sale is fairly certain.

The first step is to sign an auction agreement in which the agent agrees to auction the property in return for your granting a sole agency which is usually for 90 days, 30 days prior to auction and 60 days after it. The agent then prepares a marketing program for your approval and the action starts.

The property is extensively advertised (at your expense), the agent will hold "Open House" days and on the appointed day the auction will take place. Often the activity generates buyers who make offers prior to auction, and you are at liberty to accept these offers and cancel the auction, if you and the agent decide this is the best course.

Where should the auction be held? This depends on the property. If it is on a busy noisy road, or smells and smoke from the local factory drift over the yard, have it in the agents' rooms. However, prefer to have it at the property if the house has romantic features such as great views or a glorious garden. The problems with having the auction on site are that wet weather can ruin the auction and that neighbours can create a nuisance. An agent told me about an auction where the buyers were put off by the loud rock music the neighbours had decided to play while the auction was going on. It has happened that unscrupulous neighbours have loudly "knocked" a property on auction day because they wanted to buy it themselves at a cheap price.

On the auction day you and the agent decide upon a reserve price, the lowest price you will take, which is disclosed to the auctioneer just before the auction starts. Don't set the reserve before the auction day because most buyers inspecting the property in the weeks before will ask the agent "What's the reserve?". If no reserve has been set the answer can be an honest "I don't know". The idea of an auction is for the buyer to set the price which will hopefully be more than the seller hoped to get. Once you let your price be known to the world, the only way the price can move is down.

The auctioneer may not sell the property for lower than this reserve price so you won't be trapped into selling at a lower figure than you approve of. If the auctioneer receives bids lower than your reserve, and they are getting near your reserve, he may halt the auction for a conference with you to seek further instructions. If you wish you may then instruct him to lower the reserve.

After that only two things can happen.

(1) The bidding may reach your reserve and the auctioneer will accept the highest bid. Your property is sold!

(2) The bidding will not reach your reserve and the property is passed in. The highest bidder then has the right to negotiate with you.

Many properties fail to sell at auction so don't be discouraged if your property is passed in. Some properties sell prior to auction and most sell in the period after it because of the interest generated by the marketing program. The auction day itself is just one part of the whole auction process.

The aim of an auction is to have buyers fighting each other to buy your property, which is why the state of the real estate market and the type of property must be considered when deciding to use auction. I believe auction is the **only way to go** if the property has unique features such as being of historical significance, being in a prime location such as on a river or a beach, or if it is situated in a sought after area. Auction is good for any property in boom times when buyers outnumber the properties for sale, but if the house has no special features and the market is flat, or worse, depressed, all an auction will do is bring out the vultures who are looking to grab bargains from people who are in financial problems.

The Marketing Programme

Now that you have selected your agent and your method of selling, you must confer with the agent on the marketing programme. Prepare a list of features such as a larger than average block, or proximity to schools and transport and special advantages of the neighbourhood and give the agent a copy of it.

Then ask the agent for suggestions for ways to make your house more presentable. This usually entails washing the house down, attending to minor repairs such as leaking taps, holes in the fly screens, faulty switches and touching up worn paint here and there. Bear in mind there is nothing will frighten off a buyer as much as a savage dog next door that tries to bite them over the fence, or the smell of your own animals in the house.

I have inspected several houses where the owners kept several large dogs in a small allotment and the bare earth from the animals running around, together with the stench and mess of their droppings, took many thousands of dollars off the house price. If you are after a quick sale, and you have dogs, consider putting them in a kennel until the contract is signed.

It is important that your agent give you a written report setting out what you are required to do and what they are required to do. Certainly no commission will be payable to them until a sale is completed, and so all the work they do until that time is at their own risk. However, you will be expected to pay for any advertising and this may include costs for signs. At this stage clarify the rate of commission with the agent, so you can allow for it when working out your budget.

The agent should prepare a schedule which will include suggested advertising and its cost, who will pay for this advertising, tentative dates to open the house for inspection and any other proposed actions such as a brochure mail out.

On The Market

Having a house on the market is a trying experience. You have to keep it in pristine condition from dawn to dark because you never know when the agent will bring buyers along, and there is the continual emotional strain of wondering IF and WHEN a buyer will make an offer. The agent should be your partner in this experience so make sure you speak to him or her at least every second day to review progress and to discuss feedback.

It is important to consider the effect having a home "on the market" can have on family life if things don't go smoothly. When putting a price on the home, consider what you would pay for it if you were a buyer rather than what you would like to get! Enrol ALL the family in the sale process, sharing the chores that create the right presentation. If price and presentation are "right" it will be a quick sale resulting in much family joy, but if price and/or presentation are wrong, the penalties are high. Eventually you will hate the place and believe that everyone else does too, the family will be at loggerheads, and you'll sell the property for far less than its real value after a thoroughly unhappy experience.

If the agent is not in regular contact with you, or if there is just no action, I suggest you have a discussion with the principal of the agency to find out whether the problem is a lazy salesperson, a bad market or because your house has some undesirable features that nobody has mentioned to you.

Summing Up

Use an agent.

Beware the pressures of time.

Use only members of the Real Estate Institute.

Beware of auction in bad times but favour it in boom times.

If you choose to auction on site beware of what can go wrong.

You don't set the price, the buyer does.

Houses sell on the three P's; Presentation, Price and Position. The only two you can change are presentation and price.

8

Negotiating Techniques

He is free who knows how to keep in his own hands the power to decide.

SALVADOR DE MADARIAGA

When you are buying or selling shares, it's only a matter of deciding the price range that fits your decision and instructing your stock broker to buy or sell. If you don't like the current buy or sell price, your only alternative is to stay out of the market. When you buy or sell real estate the situation is entirely different — you have to negotiate.

Large sums of money can be saved, or made, by skilful negotiation, yet few people I know have made the slightest effort to learn basic negotiating techniques. In line with our goal of giving you an edge on the competition we'll start by discussing negotiation in a general way and then show specific examples as they relate to buying and selling property.

Basic Negotiating Techniques

First I'll give you a definition of negotiation which will probably sound strange to you but, if you really understand it, will give you the edge in every negotiation situation. "Negotiation is the technique of finding ways to fill the needs of the other party." Think about it as we progress through this chapter.

Before a negotiation can start there must be at least two parties who each wish for an outcome. The outcomes need not be in conflict. For example, Dad might want the car washed, and Daughter might like to borrow it on Friday night. You can see a

"Competitive negotiation!"

mutually rewarding outcome there. Be aware too that "collaborative negotiators" who seek a mutually rewarding outcome achieve more success than "competitive negotiators" whose only goal is to beat the other party.

There are three ingredients that are present in every negotiation and often a successful result will depend on which party can use them best. They are:

(1) Information (2) Time (3) Power

Effective negotiation involves preparation. Before you can get down to the hard business of negotiating, you should think about the adequacy of the information you already have, what time pressures are likely to arise and where the power will come from. Poorly prepared negotiators almost always fail to achieve their objectives, which is why I stressed the importance of preparing a "project book" on the area in which you wanted to buy.

It is interesting that the supply of these three factors is a bit like happiness. Most people think that others have more than they do and this is often wrong. When you go into a negotiation as a property buyer it is likely the sellers do not have nearly as much **information** about their property as you think they have. The sellers may say they are in no **hurry** to sell and yet be hiding the facts from everyone; the use of **power** by a short term cash offer may result in a large price drop.

Often you will feel insecure about negotiating when buying property. The price of the item is generally huge in relation to your resources, the act of buying property is something that few do on a regular basis, the particular piece of property is unique so arriving at a price is difficult, and the motivation to sell varies between vendors. It is like being out on the open seas in a small boat with just your luck to trust to. The only life buoy you have is preparation.

At this stage I'll assume that you have looked around and found the property that you wish to buy. The price fits your budget, the location suits your needs and the style of the property meets your requirements. By now you should know the market well enough to know what the property is worth. If you don't, you should spend more time investigating all the facets discussed in previous chapters.

However, there is another party in this process — the seller. If you are reading this chapter as a seller, remember these techniques work for both sides.

Principle One: Look For "Win/Win"

Stephen Covey, in his best selling book *"The 7 Habits of Highly Effective People*[1]*"*, stressed the importance of creating a win/win situation. In any negotiation the best outcome is one that leaves both sides with a feeling that they have not just accomplished their objectives but have also done so with dignity and integrity.

History abounds with stories about lose/lose negotiations that devastated the participants and often others as well. The result of the 1989 pilots dispute in Australia was hundreds of pilots out of work, the airlines nearly crippled, and a multitude of small and large businesses in bankruptcy. You could hardly call that a successful negotiation.

Few people understand the importance of creating a win/win. When I was doing some landscaping at home, I wanted to erect a large shed of the type that is built to specifications in the factory and then assembled on site. There was one small problem, the company selling the kind of shed I wanted had just gone into receivership. Our landscaper did not want to give the company the 50% deposit in case they could not complete the project, and the company was not prepared to start the shed without a deposit in case we defaulted. Both sides had a valid viewpoint and nobody would budge.

1 Published by Simon and Schuster and released in Australia in May 1990.

That was until I entered the negotiations personally. I phoned the General Manager of the shed company to discuss the matter and we agreed that we wanted to do business. I said "What if I give you a cheque for 50% deposit and post date it to the day you believe you can deliver the finished shed. If you deliver on time you can bank it, and if you don't I can stop it". He thought that was a great idea and much to the amazement of both my people, and his, everything proceeded smoothly.

The secret of "win/win" is to understand the motivation of the other party, which is why having information is so important. Maybe the sellers are an old couple whose family have grown up and left home, with the result that the parents now wish to move to a smaller house. They may be much softer with their price if the buyers are a young couple with small children, than if the buyers were investors who intended to rent out the property. If the young couple are the buyers, the sellers get a reasonable price plus the feelings that the house will continue its happy tradition, and the buyers have the joy of continuing the happiness as well as buying well. That is win/win.

Principle Two: Information Is Vital

We agree that creating a win/win situation is important, so it follows that both sellers and buyers need as much information as possible about each other's motivation and not just about the property. As an example consider the depreciation allowance on buildings. Few people, including real estate agents, understand it.

> **EXAMPLE:** *Suppose you are selling a $130 000 house to an investor and it qualifies for a 4% depreciation allowance on buildings. This allowance will create a tax deduction of around $4 000 a year for the buyer for many years to come. If the buyer is in the top marginal tax rate, as most investors are, the building will give out the equivalent of a $1 930 tax free cash bonus every year. That is like having around $30 000 cash in the bank.*

It is hard to put an exact value on it, but it certainly makes the property more attractive to an investor than a property that does not qualify for the allowance. It should also make it more desirable to people who intend to live in it. Even though they can't use the depreciation allowance themselves, the average house changes hands every seven years and the next buyer might be an investor.

This is where the information and the power combine. When the buyer says "I can get a similar house up the road for $10 000 cheaper" and you respond with "Do you know that house was built before July 1985 and does not qualify for the depreciation allowance". The response is likely to be "What's this depreciation allowance?" and you are well on your way to a successful negotiation.

Information about the reason for selling gives you power if you are buying, for it enables you to formulate the type of offer you can make. It is just as important to know the buyer's motivation if you are a seller; maybe the buyer is a front for a developer and your property is a key site, perhaps they need a home in your area to be close to a relative. All this input enables you to try to find the win/win situation.

Principle Three: There Is Much More Than Money In The Price

The biggest mistake made by non-professional negotiators is to believe that price solves everything.

Think about the following:

(a) **The seller is desperately short of money and needs an urgent sale.**

The factor here is **TIME** more than money. The buyer who has this information, and who has the **power** to come up with the cash in seven days, may get a lower price than one who needs 30 days.

(b) **The sellers are building another house.**

The factor here is **CONVENIENCE.** What could be better for the sellers than a contract which allows them to stay in the house until their own house is completed. It's going to cost over $1 000 to move to rented premises for the intervening period, and the waste of time in a double move is huge. Imagine if the buyers had the **information** that the sellers were busy business people and time was extremely important to them. I wonder how much they would drop their price for the benefit of staying in their own home for a few months after settlement to allow their builder to finish.

(c) **The buyers have to be near their aged mother, and also need room for their boat and caravan. You have the only home in the area that is on the market that fits the requirements.**

The factor going for you here is a **SCARCE PROPERTY,** and a captive buyer who may be prepared to pay a high price for what you alone can offer. Naturally the key factor here is that you know the buyers' needs, and also know that there are few homes around that meet those needs. Information is the key that gives the power.

(d) **The sellers are moving into a unit and have a large collection of tools, pot plants and other assorted useful but bulky items that would cost a fortune to replace, but that would bring little at a garage sale.**

The factor here is **FREE EXTRAS.** You may well save thousands of dollars buying these items if you offer a reasonable asking price for their house, but negotiate to have all the extras thrown in for nothing. Better still agree the normal price first, and then go for the extras at the last moment.

(e) **An elderly widow is moving out of her home to enter a nursing home. Her main aim is to retain some assets for herself and her beneficiaries. She does not want income.**

The factor here is that **CAPITAL** is more important than **INCOME.**

You may get one or two years interest free terms for a higher price.

(f) **A couple are in conflict, they are embroiled in blazing rows and the house is neglected and looks like a battlefield.**

The factor here is **ESCAPE.** In many cases they will take almost anything to get out of the situation. Once you have this **information** you can move in with a low short term offer, and they are likely to be glad to take it. They have lost both time and power.

(g) **The sellers wish to move but are extremely cautious. They fear that they may sell their own home, and then be unable to find what they want.**

The factor here is **SECURITY.** You may get a sizeable price drop in return for a clause in the contract that enables them to back out without penalty if they have found nothing suitable within 30 days. Naturally you have to be prepared to lose the sale if they don't find something else suitable, but this is highly unlikely.

Notice in all the above illustrations that price is NOT the governing factor.

Principle Four: Always Keep A Third Party Handy

The reason why it is so hard to sell your own property is that there are few things harder than negotiating face to face. "What's the lowest you will take?" followed by the response of "What's the lowest you will go to?" is hard to handle.

It's far better to have an absent third party such as a spouse, a board of directors or a builder friend to use as a negotiating lever. A real estate agent may perform this role if you are using the services of one, but I suggest you still use a real, or fictional, third party.

Then when you hear "What's the lowest you will take?" your answer is much more powerful. "I don't know, my wife (banker, lover, builder, husband, mother-in-law) has a lot of say in that decision. Why don't you put an offer in writing and I'll discuss it with her (him, them etc)."

You have just tossed the ball right back into the other person's court. Of course they are keen to buy the property otherwise they wouldn't make those statements, so now they have to come up with their first offer.

Of course they might have read this book too, in which case their response might be "I'm not in a position to make an offer until I talk to my wife (banker, lover, builder, husband, mother-in-law), who has a lot of say in that decision. What if you give me an approximate figure to discuss with her (him, them etc)". Ouch, you just got the ball back!

Luckily few people are educated about negotiation but if you did get that response you could come back with "Look at these figures of recent sales in this area. Based on these we believe a fair price is $150 000. What do you think?" This assumes, once again, that you have put the time into getting the information. If you are trying to negotiate by the seat of the pants you deserve what you get.

The real estate agent is well placed to ask the parties "How much are you really prepared to pay?" but at times it is necessary to negotiate against real estate agents who may be trying to close the sale quickly and move onto the next sale. Then you go back to "I have to ask my etc". Remember the agent is the VENDOR'S agent, not the buyer's agent, so if you are the buyer play your cards close to your chest and don't tell the agent too much.

Principle Five: Split The Difference

You want $200 000 for your property and all the buyer wants to pay is $180 000. The next step is for somebody to offer to split the difference but it should not be YOU; the first one to offer the split puts themselves in a weak position. If you are the seller and the buyer wants to "split the difference" by offering $190 000 your response is "I don't know, my wife (banker, lover, builder, husband, mother-in-law) has a lot of say in that decision. Why don't you put an offer in writing and I'll discuss it with her (him, them etc)".

The figure of $190 000 is now in the buyer's mind, and when you get the written offer of $190 000, you are perfectly placed to respond with "Let's split the difference at $195 000!".

Michael Klug[2], who is one of Australia's foremost authorities on negotiation, points out that the majority of property prices are eventually settled on a "split the difference" negotiation. This is why it pays to start with a low offer. If the vendor wants $150 000 and you offer $140 000 you may end up splitting at $145 000. However, if you start at $130 000 you may end up with a negotiated price nearer to $140 000.

Principle Six: Try Not To Be Negotiating Over One Factor Only

Everybody likes to have a win, and the more options you can have on the negotiating table the more chance you have of satisfying everybody. Often a party to a negotiation can be distracted into over concentrating on one point at the expense of others. Consider an offer that included a purchase price of $150 000, 90 days for completion, the lawn mower, and the dining room light fittings that the sellers received as a wedding present.

I have seen sellers become so rigid about not including the light fittings that they agree to everything else without a murmur. People are basically decent, and few like to respond by refusing EVERYTHING on the offer statement. The more items that are up for negotiation the better chance you have of agreeing to a mutually satisfactory solution.

Principle Seven: Don't Negotiate For The Sake Of Negotiating

Don't negotiate if you feel uncomfortable about it. You've spent weeks checking out the neighbourhood, you have found the house that you want, you know from your research that the price is right, the people selling it have a genuine reason for selling and you have a rapport with them. If this is the case why not pay the fair price instead of trying to engage in time consuming negotiations that may result in somebody else beating you to it. This is why the information gathering process is so important.

---

2 Michael Klug is a partner of Clayton Utz, Solicitors.

There is one problem with protracted negotiations. The property remains on the market and there are always buyers out there looking. Each party is open to the risk of losing the other party to another transaction. It is not easy to locate just the property you want, or to get the terms you want when you are selling, so be aware that there is a time to say YES.

Principle Eight: Don't Fall In Love With The Property

The reason many people pay too much is that they get carried away by emotion. The process goes like this:

STEP 1: They make the BIG DECISION to buy and then can't wait to do it (excitement).

STEP 2: They check out a few advertisements, spend about two weekends looking, and then suddenly find the DREAM HOME which they CAN'T WAIT to own (more excitement).

STEP 3: They are inexperienced in the market so tend to offer too much, but enjoy being mixed up with all the rigmarole of the offer documents (more excitement).

STEP 4: They wait in nervous anticipation for the sellers' reply to their offer (high emotion).

STEP 5: The seller comes back with a higher counter-offer and by this time they will sign almost anything (more emotion).

STEP 6: They apply for finance and nervously await the decision (high emotion).

STEP 7: They receive finance approval, move in and have a house warming party (more excitement).

STEP 8: The excitement fades as normal living takes over, and slowly a realisation comes that they may have paid a shade more than the property is worth, and that it has a few undesirable features they never noticed till after they moved in.

They made the mistake of FALLING IN LOVE WITH THE PROPERTY and had NEVER been seriously negotiating. They lost the three essential elements of:

(1) **Information** — they never had much.

(2) **Time** — they gave it up for impatience.

(3) **Power** — they never used it.

This is the danger of falling in love with a property and of not doing sufficient research.

Principle Nine: Don't Knock The Property, Or The Vendor

The seller wants $200 000 and you only want to pay $170 000. Don't tell the seller the house is overpriced, instead use this technique "I like the property but my budget can't go over $160 000". The agent will say the vendor won't take that price so you say "Let's put up an offer just in case" and insist on presenting a written offer with a deposit.

The vendor will probably choke at the offer, and might come back with a counter offer at $190 000. In response you can "possibly find another $5,000" and offer $165 000 by which time you may be well on the road to closing negotiations at between $170,000 and $175,000.

Principle Ten: Keep Your Emotions Under Control

If the stakes are high, and both sides are emotionally involved when negotiations are going on, there is a period of near insanity. Understand that your adrenalin will be flowing as you wait anxiously for the auctioneer to start the auction for your house, or when you have made an offer and hear that somebody else has made a higher one on the property you want. This is normal so be prepared for it.

As long as you have done your research you should know if the value is right. If you are a buyer, and have not fallen in love with the property you want to buy, you will be prepared to walk away from an asking price that is too high and wait for a better deal. If you are the seller, and have vetted your buyer properly, the contract should not fall through because of lack of finance.

Summing Up

There are no guarantees in life. Even after you have done everything right the first outcome may not be successful. There is no point in blaming buyers or sellers or the economy if things don't go as planned. In my experience there is always another buyer or property around the corner and sometimes the eventual outcome is better than the first would have been.

9

Buying Real Estate With Friends

We need more understanding of human nature because the only true danger that exists is man himself.

C.G. JUNG

Investment decisions are becoming more challenging for two main reasons. First, the laws are now far more complicated. Second, the price of property has risen so much that a deposit on an investment property is beyond most people's resources.

Nevertheless, many investors still lack an understanding of both property trusts and the sharemarket, and only feel comfortable with direct ownership of real estate which may well be out of their reach. Therefore it frequently happens that those with some spare money to invest consider pooling it with friends, or with members of their family, and going into a real estate joint venture.

Going into a joint investment does not just happen when the parties feel their individual resources are too small to allow them to act individually. Often these ventures start because members of the family think it would be fun, as well as profitable, to undertake a project together, or because one of them acquires some money as a result of a windfall gain, such as a legacy or lottery win.

In my experience, such activities are fraught with danger and the outcome is often the end of the friendship between the parties as well as the loss of a large sum of money. When things start to go wrong they often go horribly wrong, and the original good intentions, trust and tolerance are quickly forgotten. Time Magazine quoted the American policeman George Napper who let forth with the now famous lines "When you're up to your ass in alligators, it's hard to remember that your purpose is draining the swamp!"

In his famous book *"The Richest Man in Babylon*[1]*"* George Clason tells the story of a farmer who could understand the language of animals.

One evening, he heard the ox complaining to the ass about the difficulty of his lot. "I work hard all day pulling the plough from morning until night. No matter how hot the day, or how tired my legs, or how the bow doth chafe my neck, still must I work. But you are a creature of leisure. You are draped with a colourful blanket, and do nothing more than carry our master about where he wishes to go. When he goes nowhere, you do rest and eat the green grass all day."

Now the ass in spite of his vicious heels was a goodly fellow and sympathised with the ox. "My good friend," he replied, "you do work very hard and I would help ease your lot. Therefore will I tell you how you may have a day of rest. In the morning when the slave comes to fix you to the plough, lie upon the ground and bellow much that he may say you are sick and cannot work."

So the ox took the advice of the ass and the next morning the slave returned to the farmer and told him the ox was sick and could not pull the plough. "Then," said the farmer, "hitch the ass to the plough, for the ploughing must go on."

The ass had only intended to help his friend but he found, himself doing the ox's work. When night came he was bitter and his legs were weary and his neck was sore where the bow had chafed it. The farmer lingered in the barn-yard to listen. The ox began "You are my good friend. Because of your wise advice I have enjoyed a day of rest." "And I," retorted the ass, "am like many other simple hearted ones who starts to help a friend, and ends up by doing his task for him. Hereafter you draw your own plough, for I did hear the master tell the slave to send for the butcher were you sick again. I wish he would, for you are a lazy fellow." Therefore they spoke to each other no more — thus ended their friendship.

The moral of the story is — if you desire to help a friend, do it in a way that will not bring the friend's burdens upon yourself.

---

1 Clason G.S. 1926 *The Richest Man in Babylon,* Bantam Books 74, 75.

A phone call I received on a talk-back radio program in Sydney is typical. A woman in her 50's said she had received $100 000 from a legacy and was considering going into a land development project with her relations. After some questioning she admitted that her own home was her other main asset, she knew nothing about land development, and the relations had no experience in that field either. They had bought a block of land, with what appeared to be considerable possibilities, and were seeking finance to develop it.

Unfortunately the finance companies they approached did not share their enthusiasm, and would not grant a loan for the development. Thus arose the need to enlist finance from a family member. The family felt the finance company had failed to recognize the potential in the project, and had not given the loan application sufficient consideration.

One of the benefits of reaching the ripe old age of 50 is that you develop some warning bells and at this stage mine were ringing loudly. Finance company staff are not stupid and their job is to lend money. It was obvious in this case that their experience indicated that the project was not viable. The result was that my inquirer, who had no experience in this area, was being asked to put money into a venture that experienced lending executives regarded as hazardous. They would not commit their depositors' funds to it, yet the caller was prepared to put her life savings at risk. She was truly being asked to carry someone else's burden.

All development projects are risky but land development is one of the riskiest of them all. Land is particularly sensitive to economic conditions and it often takes up to 18 months to bring a project to completion; by this time a booming market may have turned into a non-existent one. The owner may then be stuck with a large debt, unsaleable land, no income to pay the monthly interest bill, and enormous charges for rates and land tax. For many it has been a rapid ride to financial oblivion.

One of the major difficulties can be caused by differences in the temperaments of the parties involved. Some investors are aggressive, some are timid, some like to make decisions quickly and others like to mull over them for days. Put two different investment personalities together and you have a recipe for strife.

CASE STUDY: *Mary and Helen were single sophisticated women in their late 20's. They decided to cash in on the property boom by buying an investment house for $95 000, putting in $10 000 each and borrowing the balance. The first problem arose when they came to finance it. Mary was an aggressive investor who wished to borrow on an interest only basis using a five year fixed interest mortgage — the method used by most serious investors.*

Helen was a less adventurous borrower who felt people who borrowed on an interest only basis never got anywhere because the debt did not reduce. She plugged for a short term principal and interest loan. Mary stood firm and Helen reluctantly went along with the interest only loan.

Then came the decision of who was going to manage it. Helen wanted a real estate agent to do it, because she felt nervous dealing with tenants; Mary believed this is a total waste of 10% of the rent and persuaded Helen to agree.

Mary was an ambitious person and found her work load was increasing. She began leaving more of the rental management and maintenance to Helen who started to resent doing the lion's share of the work. Friction started to build, and the situation worsened when Mary was transferred to an executive position in Sydney, leaving her friend with the job of all the management.

By this stage Helen had met her dream man and had far better things to occupy her spare time than being involved with property management. She and her fiancee decided to buy a house to live in but, to find her share of the deposit, Helen had to sell the *investment house. Only then did she realise there would be a penalty of three months interest ($2 500) for paying out the loan before the end of the agreed term. Mary was not happy either. She was liable for a large sum in capital gains tax because of her large salary. It was the end of a good friendship.*

A similar problem would arise if one of the women lost her job and could not make up the monthly contribution required. The one who is unemployed is likely to insist the house be placed on the market so that she can fulfil her obligations, but this may coincide with a time when the market is in one of its long flat spells.

Unfortunately real estate is an investment that usually needs time to produce a large profit. A forced sale, too soon after purchase, could result in a loss.

People's situations never stay static. The high income earner of today may be unemployed tomorrow, the single person with no thought of marriage may be walking down the aisle within a year.

Problems arise when owners display dissimilar attitudes towards tenants. Many people with business experience have a different outlook on life to people who have never been in business. Often a business person wants to get a repair done as quickly as possible and employ a tradesman they have used before. A non-business person may think this is all too quick and easy, and want to call several quotes.

CASE STUDY: *The Browns were energetic business people whereas their friends the Greens were plodders who liked to take their time before making any decisions. The Browns decided it would be a great learning experience for the Greens if the four of them bought a rental house. The Greens were happy to be involved, so a house was bought. The two couples decided to manage the property themselves.*

The first tenant was a workmate of the Greens who was accepted as a tenant on their recommendation. When he skipped owing a month's rent, and leaving over $1 200 of damage behind, the Browns enquired about the bond. To their amazement they discovered the Greens had not worried about asking for a bond because he had seemed such a decent fellow.

Then came the repair decisions. The Browns liked to co-operate with tenants to keep the property in tip top condition. The day the hot water system broke down they were ready to buy a new one immediately.

Alas, the Greens had other ideas. They were disillusioned with tenants after their first experience, and believed that landlords should be as tough on them as possible. They wanted to call several quotes to repair it. This was going to take a week, but they were not concerned that the tenants had to have cold showers for that time. Unfortunately it was the Browns who had to listen to the complaints from the shivering tenants.

Joint ownership also costs investors flexibility.

CASE STUDY: *Ron and Anne worked for the same company and bought a property in joint names as an investment. They ploughed all their spare cash into paying it off, and were almost debt free, when Ron unexpectedly received an opportunity to go into a promising business venture. He wanted to mortgage his share of the property to borrow the funds for the capital he needed, but there were immediate problems.*

Anne regarded his venture as risky and would not consent to a mortgage over the property. The result was that Ron could not raise finance because he could not find a lender who would accept a second mortgage over half a property. It was a case of miss out on the venture or sell the property.

Summing Up

One of the keys to investment is flexibility. In most cases smaller investors who think they need a partner are far better off buying shares or putting their money into equity or property trusts. An initial investment of $1 000 is usually sufficient to start off an investment in a unit trust and subsequent investments can be as small as $100. Withdrawals of capital in whole, or part, can generally be effected in less than a month.

For those who like direct ownership, even at high interest rates, a lending institution is the best partner, provided you have the cash for the deposit and can handle the gearing. Provided you honour your commitments the lender will leave you alone.

10

Property Trusts And Syndicates

Be wary of the man who urges an action in which he himself has no risk.

JOAQUIN SETANTI

Let's think a little longer about property. We know there are only three places we small investors can put most of our precious dollars. We can put them in interest bearing accounts and suffer the ravages of inflation and taxation, we can go into the share market with its exciting ups and downs, or we can go for stodgy old property that has been the only real security for prudent lenders for decades.

Certainly the bank account fills the need for a method of keeping some cash on hand for immediate access, and the stock market enables us to enjoy the tax benefits of franked dividends and be part of the growth of Australia's major corporations. However, the fact remains that we need the stability of property to balance up our portfolio.

Now we face an obstacle. Property prices have jumped so much that many of us are hesitant, or unable, to sign a contract for a $125 000 rental home if it means putting down $35 000 deposit and borrowing nearly $100 000 (including buying costs).

We also know that residential yields are so inadequate that $400 000 of debt free property in our old age won't give us much more that $400 a week to exist on, after we pay rates and maintenance and cope with the hassles of tenants when we should be playing bowls. We've looked with envy at the higher yields and better tenants obtainable in prime commercial, industrial and retail property but we really don't have a few million spare right now to buy any.

What is the solution? We have a need and a desire to be in good property but don't have the means. As I explained in the previous chapter buying with other people raises fresh problems. Anybody who has ever owned property in conjunction with anybody else, for example by being in a body corporate, is fully aware of the difficulties of joint ownership.

For a time property syndicates appeared to fill the need. However, they were an imperfect solution because they had a short fixed life, and, if you needed to cash in part of your investment, there was only a limited market for your share.

Then what seemed like the perfect answer appeared — property trusts. Thousands of investors, just like you and me, could pool our dollars and become unit holders in a unit trust that could then buy the type of property that was out of reach of any of us individually.

Listed Or Unlisted Property Trusts

It is important you appreciate the difference between a listed trust and an unlisted trust and you may find it easier to refer back to this chapter after you have read the sections on Shares and Managed Funds.

They are similar inasmuch as they both use a unit trust as a vehicle to pool investors' savings and invest them in large properties. The difference occurs in the way the units are valued and bought and sold.

In a **listed trust** the units are bought and sold on the Stock Market at the prevailing market price. Thus, the value of your investment is determined by what a buyer will pay for your units. Therefore a unit in a listed trust is akin to a share and you have the ability to cash in your investment in whole or part and receive the proceeds without delay.

In an **unlisted trust** the units are issued by the fund manager. If you want to withdraw your money you apply to the fund manager who will try to redeem your units based on an independent valuation of the underlying assets held by the trust.

Because of the popularity of the major **unlisted** property trusts, the continual inflow of funds was enough to cover redemptions of anybody withdrawing their money, as well as enabling the trusts to acquire an increasing portfolio of quality real estate. Investors became used to expecting that their money would be available on demand.

Until the property crash in 1990 the majority of unlisted property trusts showed good consistent results. The respected research group Assirt reported in July 1990:

> *"There are 56 existing funds which have a five year performance history to the end of June 1990. This represents a full economic cycle for property. It includes the quiet times of the mid eighties and the soft market of 1989-90. 75% of those funds achieved an annual compound return of greater than 13% and there was not one property trust whose return did not keep up with inflation. You would have to go a long way to find a better long term investment in this period, particularly given the fluctuations in interest rates and the sharemarket crash which occurred during this period."*

Unfortunately there was a basic flaw in a system that allowed the unit holders to withdraw their money at will, for one would believe that a property trust would keep the bulk of its assets in buildings; if you wanted to be in a cash investment you would choose a cash management trust. But how can a trust that has the bulk of its assets in landmark buildings be able to repay all its unit holders on demand.

"Stick with the listed property trusts," said the stock broking fraternity. "They give investors the ability to have a slice of prime property together with the added benefit of being able to sell their units in a free market." The idea might have sounded fine but it didn't work quite so well either. The investing public took one look and said "Looks like a share, feels like a share, it IS a share" and have treated units in listed property trusts as shares ever since.

As proof, look at the graph which shows the All Ordinaries Accumulation Index, a measure of the price movements of Australia's leading shares compared with the Property Trust Accumulation Index, which measures the movement of the major listed property trusts for the period July 1, 1979 to June 30, 1990. You might see more that a passing similarity in price movements.

Now we come to the problem of valuation. A large commercial, industrial or retail building is valued by applying the net earnings to the capitalisation rate. For example, if the net income is $200 000 and the capitalisation rate for that type of property is 8%, the value is 100 divided by 8 x $200 000 or $2.5 million. As the net earnings are a finite and verifiable figure, any variations in valuation must come through a change in capitalisation rate.

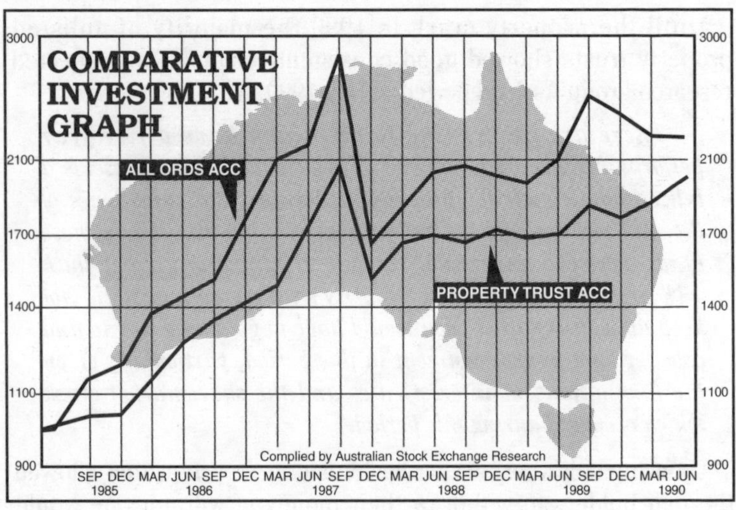

This has been the method of valuing unlisted property trusts, which is poles apart from that used by the "market" when valuing listed trusts. As the graph shows, the value of buildings as measured by the listed trust prices rises when the stock market is booming and falls when it is flat.

The capitalisation rate method of valuing property assumes there is a willing but not anxious seller, a willing but not anxious buyer, no special influences in force and a reasonable time for completion of the contract.

However, there is a problem if some of the unit holders who own the property with us panic about the economic situation, and demand the return of their investment capital immediately. Do we all agree to dump the property and sell it at a fire sale price for a quick sale, or do we put a freeze on redemptions to allow time for a meeting to allow competing interests to put their points?

The problems rapidly rose to the surface in July 1990 when the troubles of Estate Mortgage, Pyramid Building Society and OST combined to create a crisis of confidence. There were many investors who did not appreciate the difference between a mortgage trust and a property trust and rushed to withdraw their funds from the unlisted property trusts; there were others who had nowhere else to go for funds as the rest of what they had was frozen in Estate Mortgage, OST and Pyramid.

These created a run on the unlisted property trusts which resulted in the Australian Securities Commission publicly authorising the trusts to suspend redemptions for six months in need. Naturally this statement generated more fears, the volume of redemptions increased and within days four major property trusts had announced freezes on redemptions for periods of up to six months.

The Safety Of A Property Trust

A lot of the investor suspicion is caused by a lack of faith that anybody else can manage their investment, and a failure to understand the unit trust concept.

One day I was discussing property trusts with a client who said "I suppose they would be a sound investment as long as the fund manager doesn't go broke". This statement typified the general lack of understanding of the way unit trusts operate and helps to explain why many investors are wary of them. My answer was "Do you lose your rental property if the real estate agent who is managing it goes broke?"

There are three parties to a property trust investment — the investors who put up the funds, the trustee who holds the money and takes title to the property, and the fund manager who is responsible for acquisition and management. At no stage should the manager touch the invested funds or own the trust properties. This should help you to understand why the solvency of the manager is not a critical factor in the safety of a property trust. However, a manager with substantial assets is far better placed to cope with a rush of redemptions.

An investment in an unlisted property trust is similar to a direct investment by persons buying property on their own behalf. The main difference is that investors in the property trust are pooling their money with that of other investors to buy a property that would be out of the reach of any of them individually. The result should be a better class of property, in a prime location, with strong tenants on long leases.

What is a vital factor is the **ability** of the fund manager. It is the manager who must locate the properties, buy them at the right price and then manage them so as to achieve maximum returns for unit holders. The leading property trusts have a professional team of experts who have devoted their life to the real estate business. They are close to the markets and often are given first chance at the new listings by the real estate agents.

Investors should also scrutinise the assets held by the trust and carefully note the objectives of the trust and how it is going to attain them. The "least risky" trusts are those that buy quality buildings with strong tenants on long leases. The future cash flow is virtually guaranteed by the rental income, and capital growth should come as a result of the regular rent reviews if the capitalisation rates do not rise.

However, these assets are not likely to show dramatic rises in value. The big rises will come from trusts who opt for the riskier end of the market and undertake development or refurbishment projects. Some trusts have done well in this area, but investors should remember that the higher returns have been accompanied by higher risk.

Other high risk real estate investments are resort properties which are renowned for being subject to seasonal, as well as economic conditions, and hotels and motels, which depend on the skill of the management. You will find that few property trusts become involved in these areas and prefer the stability of retail, commercial and industrial real estate.

Residential property is in the low risk category because of the lower costs involved and because vacancies are usually easily filled. However, residential property requires active management, tenant turnover is high with a resulting higher vacancy factor and repairs are far more common than when the tenants are substantial businesses.

The Future Of Property Trusts

It now appears certain that listed property trusts will be the major indirect property investment of the future. While I have no objections to listed property trusts as an investment you must remember that, in exchange for ready liquidity, you pay the price of volatility.

Therefore you should look at an investment in a listed property trust as a long term one and not place funds in this area if you are likely to need them suddenly.

Summary

In the final analysis the safety of an investment in a property trust depends on the quality and mix of the underlying assets, and the skill of the manager. Unit holders in listed trusts are subject to the ups and downs of the stock market and enjoy high liquidity; holders in unlisted trusts suffer the possibility of restricted liquidity as a trade off for a reduction in price volatility.

11

Are Shares A Good Investment?

Let a man start out in life to build something better and sell it cheaper that it has been built before, let him have that determination and the money will roll in.

HENRY FORD

Do you remember the scene in *Sound of Music* where the governess Maria is trying to describe the intricate and gigantic topic of music to seven young children. She ponders for a while about the difficulties of explaining it and ends up by doing it in the song "Do-Re-Mi".

This is how I feel when I face the problem of trying to explain the stock market with only limited space to do it. Unfortunately there is no song that encapsulates the excitement and complexity of it! The stock market is the engine room of the nation, the barometer of its fortunes and the place where our major businesses raise much of the funds they need to expand.

The stock market is a market of opportunity because:

- It is a forum where our most important companies can raise the vital capital for their growth and so make life better for all of us.
- It gives us the opportunity to be part owners of those companies and share in the profits that growth may bring. We can do this by direct investment in shares, through equity trusts and through investment vehicles such as superannuation.

Despite those fine sounding words, if you are like most people I meet, your reaction to shares is:

Aren't they highly risky?

I bought some once and lost my money

I heard about a person who lost their life savings in shares

It is because of these views that many Australians are still reluctant to invest in the stock market. This is unfortunate because, despite the normal negative reaction to shares, they are one of the best areas of investment if you follow the rules. In *Making Money Made Simple* I provided some basic information as we traced the history of an emerging company and learned how to read the quotes in the paper. In this book we are going to go much further to give you an understanding of the way the stock market works.

What Is A Share?

When you own a share in a company you become a part owner of the company. It need not be a big organisation, the business may be a tiny private company where the managing director and his wife are the only employees. However, businesses grow, and as this growth occurs they need money for increased stock and debtors, for general expansion and for new plant and machinery.

This extra money may come from three sources:

(1) From profits that have been re-invested in the business instead of being paid out as dividends. This has limited benefit because retained profits are heavily reduced by company tax.

(2) From borrowing. However, borrowing causes an increasing interest bill and the company may reach a stage where further borrowing becomes self defeating. In any event expanding businesses often find it hard to obtain loans because of the lack of tangible security they can offer a lender.

(3) From injections of capital, or loans, from the owners' private assets. This may work well in the early stages but most expanding businesses continually need funds to grow and may often reach a stage where so much capital is needed that the owners cannot find it.

This is when they consider becoming "public companies" and raising equity participation from members of the public by inviting them to take up shares. This is why the word "equities" is often used as an alternative for shares.

Once a public company reaches a certain size it may apply to the Australian Stock Exchange for permission to be "listed" on the Main Board. Listing makes the shares more valuable because of the ease with which they can be traded. The prospectus issued by the company to its prospective shareholders must pass a rigourous inspection by the committee of the Stock Exchange, as well as the Australian Securities Commission, before listing is granted and it is a requirement that the capital of the company exceeds a certain level and that there is a sufficient spread of shareholders to provide a genuine market for the shares.

The Stock Exchange requires listed companies to produce half yearly and annual reports, as well as brief preliminary financial reports. This is to make sure shareholders are kept well informed of any activities which may affect the company's share price. An announcement that the reports have not been produced on time may be the first sign of a problem with a company's finances.

A Proper Market

You must understand the concept of a proper market if you are going to think like a serious investor. This is a place where the price paid is a true reflection of the value of the article. This requires a constant and plentiful supply of three essential ingredients — sellers, buyers and products. If one seller controls all the stock there can be no free market because the buyer has nobody else to make an offer to. If the volume of stock is infrequent or unpredictable there may be no market at all for most of the time.

The stock exchange is both a "primary market" where a company can raise its initial capital and a "secondary market" where shareholders can offer shares for sale and where buyers can make offers for existing shares.

The stock exchange should be the perfect free market. Nobody is forced to buy or sell and strict regulations require listed companies to provide prompt and accurate information to their shareholders. However, a free market needs more than honesty and information, it also needs inventory. It would not be much of a stock market if there was so few shares available that a buyer would have problems finding any to buy or where a seller is unable to find a buyer. The aim of the Stock Exchange listing regulations is to ensure an informed market is always available.

Shares listed on the Australian Stock Exchange are bought and sold under SEATS (Stock Exchange Automated Trading System), which enables stock brokers to buy and sell shares using video terminals in their offices. Clients can phone their broker who is able to tell them the current state of the market and execute a buy or sell order in seconds. This is far more efficient than the old system where orders had to be relayed to the trading floor.

Some Terms To Understand

Here are a few terms you will need to know:

Market Price: The current prices being offered by buyers or sought by sellers. There are usually three prices quoted, the buying price being offered, the selling price sought and the last sale price. A typical range might be

Buy \$2.20 Sell \$2.25 Last sale \$2.24.

Market Capitalisation: The number of shares multiplied by the last sale price — the total worth of the company as seen by the stock market. Naturally this figure changes every time the sale price changes (which is usually at least daily). The result is reflected in the relative positions of the top 150 Companies which are published weekly. One way of picking a share is to watch companies that are climbing up the market capitalisation ladder faster than many of their competitors as these are the ones whose share price is rising the fastest. This is similar to watching the price of a favoured racehorse shorten as the money goes on. Naturally, in neither case is a win guaranteed.

Bull Market: One that is booming.

Bear Market: One that is going down or is flat.

Earnings per share: The total earnings of the company divided by the number of shares. If the company is doing well this should continually increase.

Price Earnings Ratio: The price divided by the earnings per share. It may be referred to as a number of years earnings. Assume a company was earning one dollar a year and the market price was $5. The PE Ratio is five so a buyer at five dollars is paying five years earnings for each share. The PE ratio is one of the leading indicators watched by share analysts.

Equities or Stocks: These are alternate names for shares. I will use all three names throughout this chapter to get you used to them.

Net Tangible Assets (N.T.A.): This figure provides an indication of the worth of a company if it is wound up, all assets sold and all debts repaid. It is a somewhat impractical figure in view of the difficulty of calculating the value of plant and machinery, and because of the anomalies created by different accounting methods that often result in balance sheet values being vastly different to actual values if the company was liquidated. It should be used only for making comparisons between companies in the same industry.

Dividend Yield: This is the theoretical yield to a buyer based on the last sale price. It is theoretical because it is based on the last declared dividend, which may be different to the next one, and because it does not take into account brokerage and other buying costs.

> **EXAMPLE:** *The last sale price is $10 and the current dividend is $1 a share. The dividend yield is 10% because a buyer investing $10 would get a return of $1 or 10% of the buying price. If the price rises to $20 a share and the dividend stays at $1 the dividend yield drops to 5%. A low dividend yield may be an indication that the market believes the share has growth prospects; a high dividend yield may be a sign the market does not think the company will be able to maintain the previous dividend.*

The Index

The Stock Exchange indices are produced through an alliance with Standard & Poor's (S&P) and the Australian Stock Exchange (ASX). The main activity on the Australian Stock Exchange is reflected in the All Ordinaries Index (All Ords), which breaks down into the All Industrials Index and the Resources Index, which in turn break into various sectors. An understanding of the way the index works is fundamental to an understanding of the stock market.

One way to get the feel of it is to think of a large paddock called All Ords and see it subdivided into two smaller paddocks named All Industrials and All Resources. Both the All Industrials paddock and the All Resources paddock are broken up into serveral smaller paddocks.

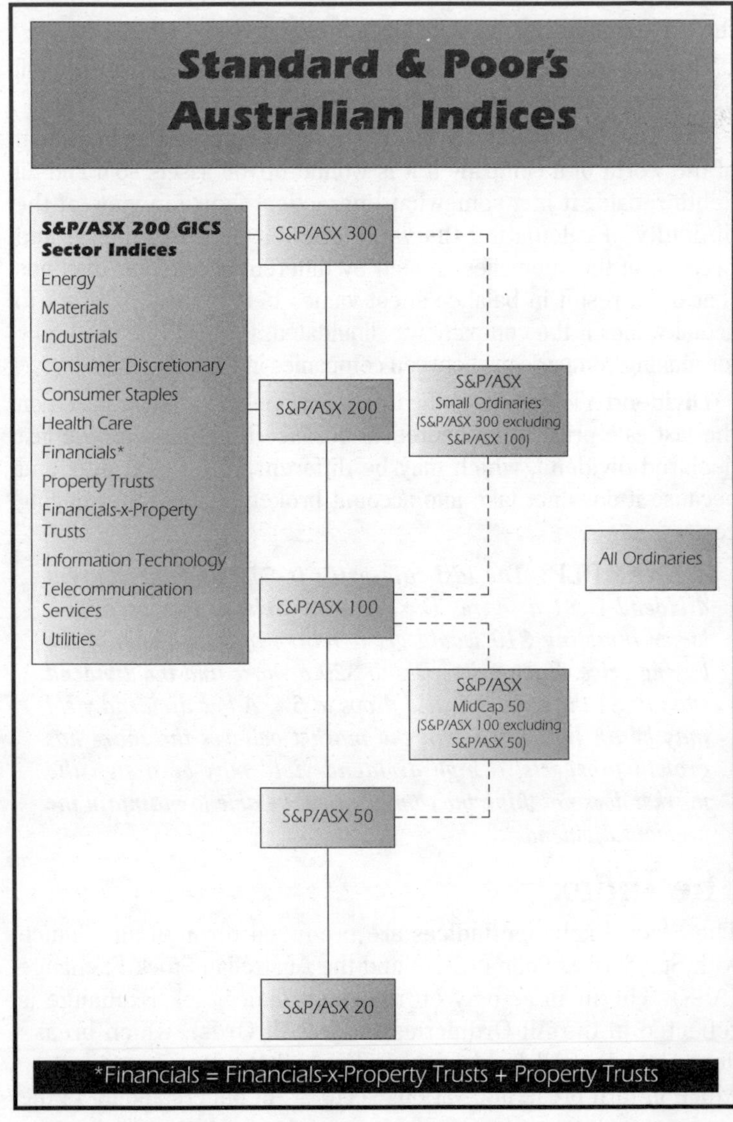

There are also several additional indices including:

- The S&P/ASX 20 index, which comprises the 20 largest stocks by market size.
- The S&P/ASX 50 index, which comprises the 50 largest stocks by market size.
- The S&P/ASX 100 index, which represents approximately 84% of the Australian market.
- The S&P/ASX 200 index, representing approximately 90% of the Australian market.
- The S&P/ASX 300 index, representing the top 300 companies.
- The S&P/ASX small ordinaries index, which represents companies included in the S&P/ASX 300 but not in the S&P/ASX 100 index. This represents approximately 7% of market capitalisation.
- S&P/ASX MidCap 50 index which comprises companies within the S&P/ASX 100 but not included in the S&P/ASX 50.

The All Ords is the premier index and represents the 500 largest companies on the Australian stock exchange. It is a measure of the price movements of the market as a whole and is calculated using the weighted average by market capitalisation[1] of many of the shares listed on the Australian Stock Exchange. Not all companies are included in the All Ords, but obviously the bigger the company the larger part of the All Ords it represents. For example, the top 10 companies represent nearly 45% of the market. This gives us an indication of how large these companies are in comparison to the rest of the market.

You will notice the two major sub-groups are Industrial companies and Resource companies. A resource company is defined as one that derives at least 50% of its profits from mining. At time of writing about 70% (by market capitalisation) of the All Ords is made up of industrial companies and the remaining 30% make up the resource sector. These proportions change continually.

The performance of industrial shares is more predictable than that of the resource shares. Resource companies are affected by metal prices and the performance of the Australian Dollar and, as a result, their prices are more volatile than those of the industrial shares. This also has applications on an international scale. The stock markets of Canada and Australia are regarded as two of the most volatile because they are more highly resource based than the other countries.

---

1 Market capitalisation is the total value of all the issued shares in a particular company.

Beating The Index

You should now appreciate the figures shown by the various indices contain most of the significant data about the stock market. They are accurate, always up to date and allow investors to make informed decisions about their future actions. As the individual indices include all the leading companies, it should follow that the performance of any of the leading companies must reflect in the index.

If you are investing in managed funds[2] such as equity trusts remember it is the aim of all fund managers to **outperform the index.** If fund managers could not do any better than keep pace with the index there would not be much of a job for them. They could simply buy shares that mirrored the index and their performance would match the index.

This highlights the problems facing a fund manager. The only companies suitable to buy are those with a large market capitalisation as there would be insufficient volume in the smaller companies to enable a buying order to be executed without putting undue upward pressure on prices. To do better than the index the fund manager has to select individual shares that are performing better than the index despite the fact that the chosen shares are part of it. Thus to beat the index the managers have to ensure the particular shares they choose represent a larger portion of their fund than they do of the index.

EXAMPLE: *In a newsletter a fund manager might say:*

XYZ Ltd is one of our major Australian equity holdings. We now hold double the All Ordinaries index weighting of XYZ stocks and intend to increase our holdings in XYZ over the coming months in line with our strategy.

Another way to beat the index, if it is falling, is to have a large part of the portfolio in cash as the value of the cash does not fall. Imagine that Equity Fund A was fully invested in shares, and Equity Fund B had half its assets in bank bills and similar fixed interest investments. Fund A would perform better if prices were rising and Fund B would win if prices were dropping. Be aware that it is almost impossible for any fund manager to be producing results that are vastly better than the index because so much of what they buy and hold is part of the index.

---

2 These are covered in detail later in this book.

Pricing A Share

In the real estate chapters I showed you how the price of most real estate was a multiple of the earnings of the property and 100 divided by the capitalisation rate. A way to determine what is a fair price for a share is to multiply its earnings per share (EPS) by the market accepted price earnings ratio (PE Ratio) for that sector.

You can see that the EPS is equivalent to the net rents and the PE Ratio is equivalent to the capitalisation rate. Be careful of the major difference. Because capitalisation rates are expressed as a percentage and PE ratios are expressed as a number, high capitalisation rates mean lower property prices but high PE's mean higher share prices.

It's difficult to obtain much concrete information about what a PE ratio should be for any particular stock. Certainly there is a link to interest rates as high interest rates tend to make shares less attractive when compared to fixed interest investments, so PE ratios should decline if interest rates rise. Yet, PE ratios are higher when the market is booming as there may be a general feeling that the upsurge has a long way to go and that company profits are on the increase.

The experts watch the trends of the PE ratios and look for companies that seem to be out of kilter with the rest, but the task is made difficult for amateur investors because "normal" PE ratios vary between sub sectors of the index. You may get excited when you discover a bank share has a lower PE ratio than some other shares you are looking at, but this excitement needs to be tempered with the knowledge that bank shares traditionally have lower PE's than some other sectors. Thus your "find" may not be a bargain at all but merely a share priced on the same level as its peers.

In summary the PE ratio is similar to the property capitalisation rate. It is an indication of what the market thinks about the future prospects of the economy as well as the growth potential of an individual property or share.

Shares And Interest Rates

To be a serious investor you must understand the connection between shares prices and interest rates. Changing interest rates affect the stock market in three ways:

(1) **THE EFFECT OF INTEREST RATES ON CORPORATE EARNINGS.**

You now know that a share's price bears a strong relationship to a company's present or expected earnings. If interest rates rise the cost of funds borrowed by the company also rises, which reduces profits (earnings), but in addition the higher cost of money reduces the ability of the customers of the company to buy. This is likely to cause a drop in sales which may result in a drop in earnings. For example, if the Government caused a rise in home loan repayments by pushing up home interest rates the average household would have less money to spend on items such as groceries, clothes and entertainment.

You can see it is logical that falling interest rates are favourable for the stock market and rising rates are likely to be accompanied by a price fall, either because the market anticipates the effect or because of the drop in earnings caused by higher rates. The next two factors should put it in clearer perspective.

(2) **THE EFFECT OF INTEREST RATES ON COMPETING INVESTMENTS**

The three major investment areas, cash, property and shares, are constantly competing with each other for the investors' dollars. Rising interest rates do two things. First, they depress property and share prices so these two areas become less attractive. Second, they make interest bearing accounts more attractive because the net return rises and the **relative performance** of interest bearing accounts compared to property and shares is better. At this stage market sentiment feeds on itself because investors become wary of shares and property as prices start falling and flee to the perceived safety of interest bearing accounts.

(3) **THE EFFECT OF INTEREST RATES AND BORROWING FOR SHARES**

Many serious investors borrow to buy shares and these loans are usually secured by liens[3] over scrip. If interest rates start to rise and share prices fall, the lender might insist the borrower reduce the loan or increase the security. This is called a "margin

---

3 A scrip lien is a mortgage over scrip (share certificates).

call". Usually shares are sold to meet the margin call, which creates further selling pressure. At the same time other investors with loans for shares will be reassessing their positions because of the increasing costs caused by the higher interest rates.

In the next chapter we shall compare the two major capital growth investments — shares and real estate.

Summing Up

The stock market is the barometer of a nation's economy.

It depends on a vigorous and free market to balance buyers and sellers.

When you own a share you become the part owner of a business.

The Index measures the activity of our major companies.

12

Real Estate versus Shares

The season of failure is the best time for sowing the seeds of success.

PARAMAHANSA YOGANANDA

By this time you might be opening your mind to the opportunities of the stock market, but deep down you may still feel better with real estate. People tend to invest in what they know about. Therefore it is not surprising the investment most people feel comfortable with is real estate, or to be more accurate, residential real estate.

There is a perceived security in being able to drive past your investment house and note that it still looks in good order. However, to ignore shares is to ignore one of the best performing investments so let's continue our journey by discussing the way shares differ from rental houses.

First Difference: Shares Are A Liquid Investment Therefore They Can Also Be A Volatile One

There is no perfect investment, every one has its advantages and disadvantages and the irony is that often the advantage also contributes to the disadvantage. For example, property has a certain stability about it and you are unlikely to see it rise or fall 30% in a day. However, you can't sell the back bedroom if you need a little bit of money, and you are hard pressed to achieve a sale in a few minutes. Moreover you can't pick up today's paper and get an accurate indication of what you can sell it for.

The outstanding advantage of shares is their liquidity which provides great flexibility. If you own 1 000 shares in BHP and you need $1 000 in a hurry you have only to phone your stockbroker and place a sell order for 100 shares. The sale is normally consummated in a matter of minutes. It is this flexibility, this ability to sell or buy in small parcels, that makes share prices so volatile.

Second Difference: Shares Will Always Give You A Genuine Market Value

Contrast 10 investors who each own one of 10 similar properties with 10 investors who each own $300 000 worth of shares. The property owners will tend to sit tight if recessionary times come along. They don't want the expense of selling those large properties and then buying them back before the next boom comes so they hold on until the sun shines again. They know that no recession lasts forever.

In contrast the share owners may "trim their sails" because their shares can be sold in small lots. Maybe they will weed out the ones that did not live up to expectations and sell some that performed well to reduce the average cost price. This is called "taking profits". Some may even sell all their shares if they thought the outlook for the next couple of years was particularly bleak and will not start to re-buy progressively until prices start rising. This selling pressure has a downward effect on the market and prices of individual shares fall. The prices, and the overall number of shares sold, are quoted daily so everybody knows precisely what is happening. There are few secrets in the stockmarket.

The property owners tell themselves the price of their real estate has not fallen, but if any of those 10 property owners tried to sell on this depressed market they might change their tune. Of course they don't sell and, for them, the illusion continues that the property market is doing better than the sharemarket. Even a forced sale at a low price may not bother them much. There is always the justification "My property is different".

It is vital you understand completely this major difference between property and shares. Shares are a "no illusion" investment and their prices are quoted every day. This is totally different from real estate where you don't know the final price till you have listed the property, negotiated the price, and exchanged contracts. Then there is a chance that the buyer will not proceed.

Third Difference: A Good Share Has A Greater Potential For Gain Than A House

A share's price is a multiple of its earnings. It therefore follows that the increase in a share's price should be somewhat in line with the increase in the company's profits. A well-managed growing company has the potential to increase its earnings by 20%, 40%, or 100% in a year. Think of a number. For example, in the 1998/9 year alone, Flight Centre and Qantas increased profits by more than 53% and 26% respectively.

It would be impossible to get that sort of return out of a building; property is different. We are accustomed to the regular booms when the price may rise 30% in a year, but if you look at the overall trends you will find the average annual increase is not much more than the CPI. This is logical because a house must be built with labour and materials bought at current prices, which tends to keep house price costs in line with inflation. Nobody would be able to afford to buy homes if prices grew way out of line with home buyers' earnings.

When you add the greater potential for capital gain to the higher likely earnings from shares you can see why shares have outperformed residential property over the long term.

> **EXAMPLE:** *If you had invested $1 000 in 1960 into a fledgling company called Westfield and reinvested all your dividends and taken up all your issues, you would now have over $150 million. Yes, $150 million.*

Naturally that is a rare success story but it shows the huge potential of a share market investment.

Fourth Difference: The Price Of Shares Is Outside The Investor's Control

You can't do much about changing the price of your BHP shares, the market does it all for you. However, there is plenty you can do about changing the price of your property. You can neglect it and watch it go slowly to rack and ruin, or you can put the time into managing it properly and keeping it well maintained. If you do this you will achieve far better income and growth than a passive landlord.

This is why property may be an exceptional investment for those people who have the time, the skills and the inclination to add value and manage intensively and why it is a mediocre investment for many who buy a rental home and virtually ignore it.

Fifth Difference: A Large Part Of The Income From A Share May Be Tax Free

Thanks to our imputation system, dividends from shares that pay franked dividends are either tax free or taxed at a low rate; it depends on your marginal tax bracket. Consequently the after tax yield from shares is higher than that from property unless there is a large tax free component of property income from building and depreciation allowances.

In the chapters in this book on negative gearing you will see that the figures for negative gearing look better for shares than for property, provided you can tolerate the increased volatility of the stock market.

Sixth Difference: Property Has A Degree Of Permanence, A Share May Not

If we ignore earthquakes and severe flooding, property is a permanent asset. It cannot be created like a company can, nor can it be wound up and liquidated if it is unable to pay its bills. It will merely change hands. Eventually there comes a time when the building is worn out and a new one is built on the same land. The cycle goes on.

When you buy a share you are buying an interest in a business and we all know that businesses can go broke, become redundant or be taken over. Without doubt many of our larger companies have been progressing solidly for over 100 years and many have large and valuable real estate holdings but big ones have still be known to topple. This is why diversification is so important. Luckily shares can be bought in small parcels, or through equity trusts, which enables even a small investor to diversify easily.

Seventh Difference: It Is Easier To Borrow Against Real Estate Than Shares

It is the uniquely permanent nature of property that has made it the preferred security for lenders because history has shown that prime real estate seldom suffers huge price falls. However, many lenders will require mortgage insurance to be taken out if the loan to valuation ratio is over 66% so a provision for a fall in the value of the property by a third is already covered.

The corporate collapses in Australia in 1989 and 1990 have now made lenders more wary of real estate as a security because of the difficulty of striking a valuation that will stand up in times of economic hardship. There is little joy in trying to sell a vacant commercial, retail, or industrial property.

Eighth Difference: The Stock Market Offers Better Diversification

You can't buy a rental house in most places for much less than $75 000 and even if you invest in real estate through property trusts you would be unlikely to have your money spread over more than six properties. A person with $10 000 to invest may buy $500 worth of shares in 20 separate companies and placing just $1 000 in an equity trust may provide a spread of over 50 companies in a range of industries.

The 23 sub groups of the All Ords Index show how large is the range of areas in which a small investor can have an interest through shares. Even further diversification can be obtained by investment through shares listed on stock exchanges in other countries.

Ninth Difference: Property Requires Regular Management and Maintenance

Once you buy a fully paid share you can rest secure in the knowledge that you won't be called out of bed in the middle of the night to attend a burglary, you won't get a large bill for land tax and your budget won't be shattered with huge repair bills. These are the frustrating incidents that every landlord copes with.

Shares carry different risks and the main one is that the share price might start on a continuous downward slide. When that happens you have the agony of trying to decide whether to buy more to average your cost down or to cut your losses and quit.

A Day With The Fund Managers

As part of the research for this book I spent nearly a week in Sydney with some of the top fund managers, the individuals who handle millions and sometimes billions of dollars on behalf of superannuation funds, private individuals and unit trusts. As you can imagine, looking after hundreds of millions of dollars of money that belongs to other people is a huge responsibility and they take it very seriously.

They live on a mega diet of data that pours non stop into their offices. The day starts with a meeting to discuss what has happened around the world overnight for most of the major world financial markets are behind us in the international time zones. The world starts each day in New Zealand and the clock slowly turns as the rest of the world wakes up. By the time it is 4 p.m. in Sydney, the time in New York is 1 a.m.

The meetings are routine, unless some international crisis has triggered some feverish activity, and involve exchanging market gossip that is filtering through the grapevine, discussing the financial stories in the morning papers and sharing other ideas that may have cropped up.

The mail arrives, usually in huge stacks that contain financial magazines, more newspapers, economic commentaries from institutions such as banks and stock brokers all over the world and newsletters. A junior member of the staff will open it for distribution to staff members after which most of it will end up joining piles of similar material on the research analysts' cluttered desks.

The telephone calls start pouring in from the stock brokers' offices. The first broker has heard that the fund is keen to buy bank shares and has just had a large parcel offered for sale, another provides information about the prospects of a company in which the research team has shown interest, a third broker is letting it be known that his firm has 100 000 BHP shares for sale. Fund managers take a cautious and rather cynical view of stock brokers' opinions and realise that some brokers are specialists in certain companies. As a result the degree of weight given to a stock broker's information will vary with who is giving it and what it is about.

So the day goes on, no sense of panic, no sense of rush, just a lot of people manning telephones, getting and giving information and watching the ever present computer terminals.

The computer terminals are the heart of the operation. At a flick of a switch you can check up on the present state of such diverse indicators as the All Ords, the Tokyo stock market, or the state of the Australian dollar. Key in the code for a particular share and in less than a second you have the present market prices, sales volume, PE ratio, last sale price etc etc. Press another button and you can look at a graph of that share's prices over any given time frame.

The decreasing dependency on the post means more information comes by electronic mail. Many stock brokers now send their buy/sell recommendations and reports by computer so a push of another button will let you check out, on your own screen, all the information flooding in from the stock brokers' research departments.

The fund managers have a list of shares that receive special attention. Maybe the word is around that company A is having problems, perhaps a takeover bid is in the offing for Company B. Probably the research department has identified a share that has all the ingredients of a "great value buy" but the fund manager does not want to start buying until somebody else shows some interest. All these shares go on the "watch list" and several times a day this list is brought up on the screen to check that nothing unusual is happening to the prices of the "watched" shares.

While all this is going on the staff of the research department continue their never ending job of checking and adjusting asset allocations, looking for companies to buy by studying balance sheets and financial statements, and studying economic reports to try to predict which direction the market is heading.

As the middle of the day comes, thoughts turn to lunch. It might be a quick sandwich and a chance to mull over the morning's activities with colleagues, or it might be time to go to a luncheon in a stock broker's office or in the boardroom of one of the companies listed on the stock exchange. Information is the life blood of successful investing and what could be a better way to get it than by visiting the offices of the companies in whom you have an interest.

When they get back from lunch there are more screens to be checked, more research reports to read and more decisions to make. The pulse of the stock market never stops pounding.

In the next chapter we'll discuss selecting the right shares to buy and the risks involved.

Summing Up

Investing in shares is nothing like leaving your money in the bank, buying an investment house or having a bet (unless you are punting in the speculative area).

The advantage of share based investments is liquidity and flexibility.

The price you pay for this is volatility.

Historically the stock market has provided better returns than fixed interest securities or property and those who ignore the market are likely to pay the price in below average long term returns.

13

Selecting Shares

You can't expect to hit the jackpot if you don't put a few nickels into the machine.

FLIP WILSON

I was once a guest speaker at an art seminar where my topic was "Financing a corporate art collection". During question time one of the audience asked me how to go about identifying a promising young artist whose work would have large capital gain. As I tried in vain to find an answer another member of the audience saved me with the interjection "Surely that's like asking how you can pick a promising young race horse!" The answer also seems to apply to shares.

The fund managers I spoke to agreed there was no certainty they could pick a winner in the stock market. There were important selection criteria which were similar in many ways to that used when choosing property, but there is no **guarantee** that any given company will perform. This highlights the difficulties the private investor faces when trying to choose between individual shares.

You may buy shares directly in which case they are bought through a stock broker. Alternatively you may decide to leave the selection of stocks to fund managers and invest in equity trusts, or do a combination of both and have some money in shares and some in equity trusts.

To help you understand about picking shares we'll start off by learning how the fund managers do it and then we can use their ideas to help you to invest on a personal level.

Top Down Or Bottom Up?

Just as different investors have different goals, so do fund managers have different approaches. It's important that you realise this if you are seeking diversification in your equity trusts, managed bonds or superannuation. There is no point in investing your funds with four managers if they all have the same portfolios, or the same investment philosophy, for there is no spread. It is similar to individual investors who have all their money in rental houses, or in shares in one sector of the market — they have no spread either.

Fund managers approach share selection from a "top down" or "bottom up" approach, and often combine the two.

When adopting a top down approach they look "down" on the world, country or economy as a whole and consider the factors that interplay to affect the financial system. Once they have digested this knowledge they make a decision about what percentage of their assets should be in shares. Then they decide what percentage of these shares should be in each index sector. The next step is to allocate an amount of money for investing, and go to the market to buy the shares.

For example, the fund managers might decide that now is a good time to buy shares in a certain country because the economy of that country was coming out of a recession. Company profits should rise strongly in the coming years with a corresponding increase in share prices. Perhaps their research tells them that the retail sector should boom because of tax cuts, falling interest rates, a wage rise and increased tourism. The top down approach identifies both the country, and the sector, to target.

The "bottom up" technique involves looking for companies whose shares are priced at a level that represents "good value" at present market prices. There are always some companies doing well no matter what the economy is doing, just as there are ones that will perform badly in boom times. The emphasis is more on the choice of individual shares rather than by sector or country selection.

The "top down" approach reminds me of people sitting on a mountain top looking out at the valley and making plans; the "bottom up" approach suggests people in the creek fossicking for gold. Naturally there is a degree of interplay between the two strategies, because the "top downers" have got to fossick for the right companies to buy once they have made their decision to enter a certain sector of the market, in the same way as the "bottom uppers" have to give regard to the general economic outlook.

It is interesting to note that an analysis of profits achieved by large equity funds showed that 90% of the profit performance came as a result of the fund manager selecting the right sector, whether by industry or country, and that only 10% was attributable to selecting shares in particular companies.

A Fundamental Or A Technical Approach?

Do you take a "fundamental" or a "technical" approach to share selection? The debate has raged for years and neither side will give much ground. When deciding whether to buy shares in a company the fundamentalists consider such factors as:

- Growth in earnings per share
- The company's position in its market
- The effect of competition in that market
- How the company is financed
- The calibre of the management
- The number of shares issued
- The size of the company
- The present PE ratio

If the fund manager is satisfied that the share stacks up in all the above areas, a decision to buy is likely.

The fundamentalist looks for price earnings ratios that are low relative to the market and the sector. The word "relative" is important for in the early 1980's most PE's stayed around six or seven, but by the boom of October 87 were moving between 15 and 20.

Technical researchers look at charts that track share prices over various periods and make their decisions mainly on the basis of what they read from those charts. This approach is discussed in more detail later in this chapter.

Notice how both these approaches differ from that used by private investors. Most private investors make their decisions based on the following information:

- The Managing Director has a high media profile and is always in the news.
- Tips from friends.

- Tips from stock brokers.
- There is a share boom going on and they want to be in the action.
- Recommendations in newspapers and magazines.
- Good reports in the media about earnings or growth.
- A new issue of shares receives coverage in the media and the prospectus looks impressive.

Notice that selection by these methods is undisciplined, has no underlying method and is disorganised. In my own filing cabinet is a folder full of scrip that testifies to my own "sins" in this area. Typical of these are the shares I bought for $5.60 (now worth $1.80) that I acquired after having lunch with a stock broker, there are the shares I grabbed because they were about to pay a special dividend. Then there are some speculative mining shares I bought years ago based on a tip at a luncheon I went to. That is one of the problems caused by spending so much time looking after your clients that you neglect your own affairs. It is also the reason most of my investing in the share market is now done through equity trusts.

What Type Of Company?

Australian listed companies fall into two main types. The big ones that make up our top 300 companies and the smaller ones that represent the balance.

Fund managers prefer the larger companies, not because they will necessarily outperform the smaller companies, but because there is always a "market" in their shares enabling them to be bought and sold. The fund managers usually have large chunks of money to invest and there is no point in deciding to invest $100 000 in buying shares in a particular company if there are only a few shares available. In that case a buying order as large as $100 000 would sent the price rocketing.

I remember the time I owned 5 000 shares in a small company and decided to buy another 5 000. The quotes were 40 cents buyer and 45 cents seller (last sale 41 cents) when I phoned the broker to invest another $2 000. Within minutes there had been a sale at 45 cents so my tiny amount of buying pressure had pushed the market up 10%!

The shares in the bigger companies can be sold quickly too. During the 1987 share crash many investors panicked, and sold what they could as quickly as possible. There were no buyers for the second rate shares so all investors could sell were the best ones. At the end of that day all they had left was a portfolio of shares that nobody had wanted to buy.

There is no evidence that smaller companies will do better or worse than the large ones just because of their size. Investors in the smaller companies may benefit if the company is taken over and they receive a good offer for their shares, but many smaller companies find it harder to raise capital, are often more affected by competition and many of them are badly financed.

The ideal company for a fundamentalist to buy shares in is one that has over $100 million of market capitalisation, is well managed, sensibly financed, has good growth prospects and whose PE ratio is below the average for the sector. Most of the research analysts' time is taken up in trying to find such gems.

How Do You Choose?

How does the average investor select the right share to buy? First decide on what you are trying to achieve. Is it income, or growth, or are you just in there for speculation.

INCOME: If income is all important you should not be concerned with volatility because fluctuations in the price of a good share should not affect the dividends. Accordingly you should seek shares in substantial companies that have low debt and a good consistent earnings record. I suggest you stay in the Industrials sector as these shares have more predictable earnings. Prefer shares that are paying franked dividends so you can enjoy the advantage of the tax credits.

GROWTH: Remember the old property adage — low growth/high yield or high growth/low yield. Both the property and the share markets mark down the yield when high growth is expected, so if growth is your aim you will have to settle for a lower dividend yield. You can spot companies the market believes will give high growth by their high PE ratio or their low earnings yield.

SPECULATIVE STOCKS: Picking these is like trying to pick a 50 to 1 winner at the races. You can opt for an equity trust that specialises in speculative stocks or you can talk to your broker and seek some recommendations. You could also go to the library and look at some of the tips offered by the newsletter writers, or if all else fails try hanging the financial page on the wall and throwing darts. The essence of the 50 to 1 shot is that **nobody** expects it to win, so don't try to pick speculative stocks using any sort of logical system. If they could be picked as easily as that they wouldn't be giving such spectacular returns.

After you have determined your objective you may adopt a top down type approach and look at the economy as a whole, to try to work out which sectors are likely to perform the best. For example, if the economy had been in recession and a building boom was imminent, you may choose to target the building material sector.

The next step would be to obtain a print-out of detailed information on all stocks in that sector. This can be done using the resources of the stock exchange library or simply by telephoning your stock brokers and asking them to prepare a list with recommendations.

Once you have decided on the sector in which you are interested and obtained a list, you should go through this list to find shares that appear undervalued. These are indicated by a high dividend yield or a low PE ratio. Mark them first, then examine them in detail to discover why the price appears low. Has the market overlooked them or is there something the market knows that, at this stage, you don't?

Some investors consider the net tangible assets of a company when assessing its growth potential. I have reservations about this approach because the net tangible asset approach is applicable only to winding up, and the anomalies of accounting reduce my faith in published asset values. Certainly it should never be ignored as it becomes of significance if a takeover offer is in the wind, but take care that you don't put too much emphasis on it in normal circumstances. The use of dividend yields also has some limitations if you are primarily seeking capital growth as dividends are income not growth. PE ratios are one of the better methods for stock selection particularly if you can obtain accurate forecasts of future earnings.

The best places to go to get information about the company would be your own stock broker, or the library at the stock exchange. Sight a copy of the last annual report of the company, available at the stock exchange research service which also produces a detailed yearly report extracted from the company's annual report. This service will include any announcements made by the company since the annual report was released.

These reports cover many pages and include the history of the company, names of directors, names of key staff, number of employees and the financial statements in standardised form for the last seven years and also full details of date and amount of dividends paid. Reports for individual companies can also be purchased from the stock exchange.

By this time you will have narrowed your search down to a few companies and you should now seek a stock broker's report on each one. These are usually prepared by the broker's research department after a member of the research team has visited the company concerned.

If you are satisfied with your research, and the stock broker has answered all your questions satisfactorily, you may make a decision to buy the stock.

Now you must decide your buying strategy. Do you try the dribbling technique of investing part of your funds now and some later, which is similar to averaging, or do you put all the money in immediately? If the price has been moving up sharply while you have been doing your research it may be prudent to make the whole investment immediately. If there has been little upward movement in the price recently I suggest you go for the dribbling approach and invest only a small part of your money right now. Then wait and see what happens.

You may have to take the "technical" approach if the price has been moving down while you were are watching the share prior to investing. You have to satisfy yourself why this price drop is happening so your first step should be to track the price against the performance of the sector index and see how the price of your share is performing relative to the index. My advice would be to hold off investing any money until the downward trend had stopped.

Keep in mind your purpose in buying a particular share. For your own learning purposes I strongly recommend you write down your reasons for buying the share on a piece of paper and staple the piece of paper to the scrip. This will prove invaluable to you in the future if you analyse it in the light of what actually happened instead of what you hoped would happen. If you bought for long term growth you should not be disturbed if the price falls after you buy it, or if the price stays flat for the next 12 to 15 months, as long as your ongoing monitoring of the situation tells you that the reasons for buying the share are still sound.

Are Shares Risky?

Every investment carries a risk and one of the secrets of successful investing is to understand the risks in each investment so as to prepare yourself for them. A share buyer faces certain risks as does any other investor and we'll consider these next.

RISK ONE: Losing Most Of Your Money

There are many companies whose share price jumps on rumours or because they are seen to be expanding at an exceptional rate. Companies like Ariadne and Qintex are examples. Because of their rapid growth they become the darlings of the media and their activities constantly make the headlines. People hear stories of fortunes being made by investors who bought shares in these companies, and decide to grab a bit of the action themselves.

There is a famous saying in the investment world "No tree grows for ever" and the investors who jump in at the end of the boom often suffer huge losses. Investors who follow the basic rule of diversification will put only a small percentage of their assets into these types of shares and will thus protect the bulk of their assets.

Solution: You can make a fortune buying shares in the high risk entrepreneurial companies, provided you sell at the right time and leave somebody else to carry the bag when the price drops. Unfortunately God did not give humans the ability to pick markets accurately so luck plays a large part in knowing when to buy and sell. It's fine to put some money into this area of the market as long as you only use money you can afford to lose. You may make a lot of money, and you will gain a lot of experience.

RISK TWO: Volatility

It is the nature of shares that prices can rise and fall rapidly; this is called volatility. The extent of this volatility can be seen on the following chart which shows the difference in the high and low points of the All Ords for each year for the last 25 years.

When you look at these huge swings you can see how much more volatile is the stock market than the bond market or the property market. They highlight how important it is that investors in the stock market accept the fact that **the value of their investments will fluctuate as much as 100% in a year** and be prepared for it.

RISK THREE: Under Performance

This is probably the most common risk. You do your homework, you buy the shares and the market does not share your

PERCENTAGE VARIATION BETWEEN THE ALL ORDS HIGH AND LOW POINT

(Rounded to the nearest whole number)

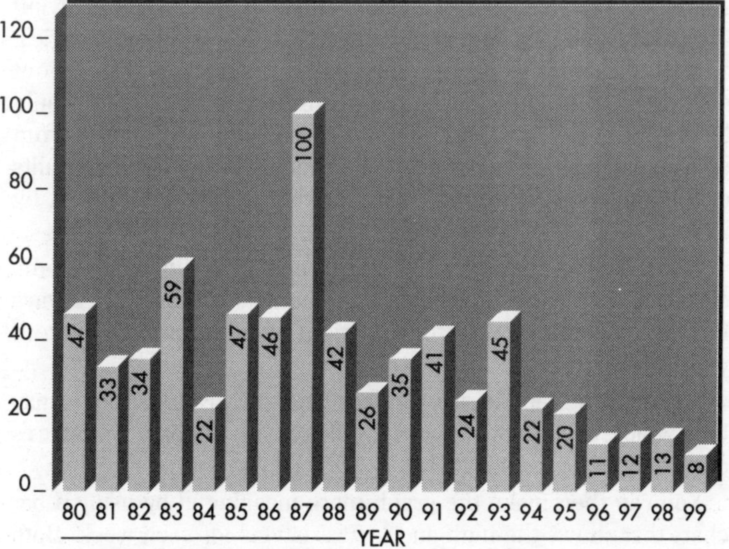

Compiled by Australian Stock Exchange Research

enthusiasm for them. The dividends come regularly but the price sits like a becalmed sailing boat or it drifts downward.

Solution: If you followed my advice and wrote down the reasons why you bought it you should review them to see if you made some basic error of judgment. Assuming your premises are still valid the next step is to talk to your stock broker to find out how this particular share has fared relative to its sector index. If it is doing better than its index congratulate yourself, you have beaten the index. However, there is little satisfaction in beating the index if that means no more than the price of your share has not fallen as fast as some others. This is the time to go back to a top down approach, in conjunction with your broker, and re-appraise the economic situation as a whole together with the prospects for the chosen sector.

Technical Analysis And Charting

Imagine how wealthy we would be if we could accurately predict the future. If only we knew tomorrow's race results or the Lotto numbers, or could buy shares in the absolute knowledge that they would increase in price next week. Of course that is fantasy and this is why there is such controversy about the effectiveness of "technical analysis" or charting.

In these chapters I have shown you the amount of time spent by share buyers in analysing PE ratios, tracking indices and studying the past results and future of companies. This is all quite logical and would seem to be the only way a person could go about picking shares. The chartists take a different view. They would have us believe they can sit in a room, totally removed from information such as the state of an economy or the trading results of a company, and predict what its share price will do just by looking at charts of previous share price activity.

Now I am not pouring scorn on this notion. We know, as do the chartists, that it is not possible that chartists can be right always but the question is "Can they be right enough times to make it worthwhile."

A chart is a graph of share prices over any given period. It may be a simple line graph (Figure 1) connecting the prices of shares or of an index.

You can then make the graph more meaningful by using a bar chart that shows the high and low variations for each week. Both the high and low point for the week are marked on the chart and a line is drawn between the two prices. This lets you see how volatile is the price. Another variation is to put the volume of

COMPARATIVE INVESTMENT GRAPH

ALL ORDS.

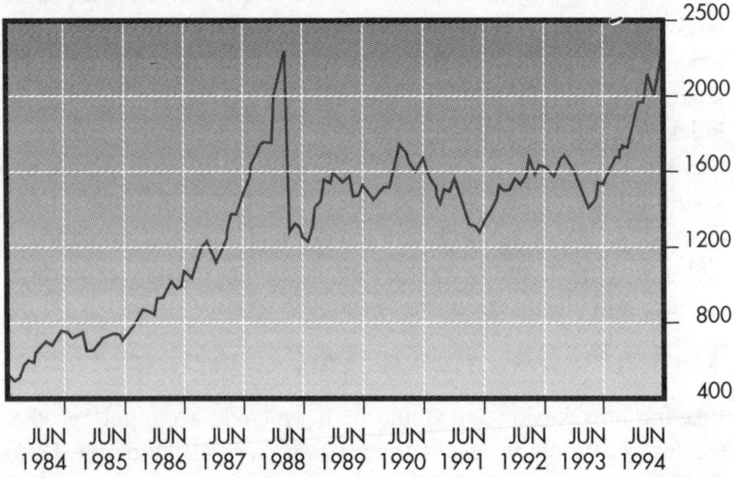

2500
2000
1600
1200
800
400

JUN 1984 JUN 1985 JUN 1986 JUN 1987 JUN 1988 JUN 1989 JUN 1990 JUN 1991 JUN 1992 JUN 1993 JUN 1994

Compiled by Australian Stock Exchange Research

Figure 1

COMPARATIVE INVESTMENT GRAPH

THE BROKEN HILL PROPRIETARY COMPANY LIMITED

Compiled by Australian Stock Exchange Research

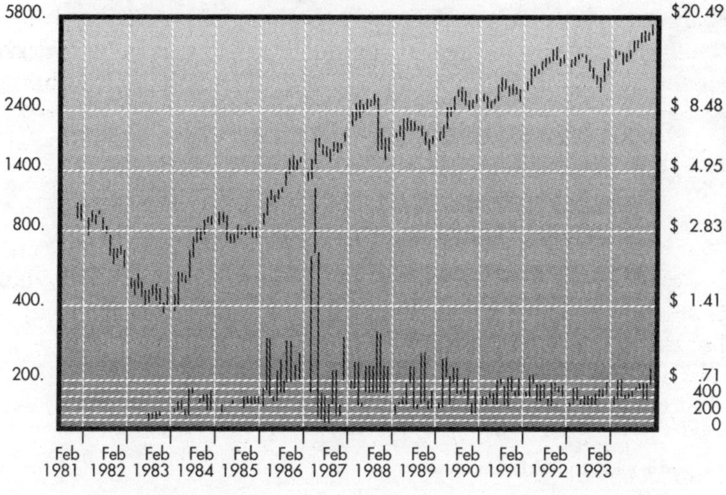

Monthly last Prices/Indices indexed to 1000.00 on 12/80

Prices adjusted for issues

Figure 2

turnover on the bottom of the graph (Figure 2) as unusually heavy volume is generally a sign that something is happening in the market for that particular stock.

Trendlines

Anybody can draw charts similar to the above. The difficult job is to interpret the information that is given. Usually the chartists start off by drawing in trendlines. These connect the lowest or highest points on the graph. As you can see on the final chart (Figure 3) there are major trends (the long upward line) and there can be minor trends (the smaller lines) that can go in different directions to the major trend. The chartist is concerned with both, but obviously the major trend is the most important.

The main aim of the chartist is to find shares to buy that are moving upwards (uptrend) or to sell out once the upward trend line has been broken and goes into a downward movement (downtrend). This sounds simple enough and the most remarkable conclusions can be made **in hindsight** but it is far harder to interpret the directions at the time.

If we look at the graph of the All Ordinaries Index in the year of the 1987 crash we can see that the massive fall happened without warning although some chartists claim that the "head and

COMPARATIVE INVESTMENT GRAPH
ALL ORDS.

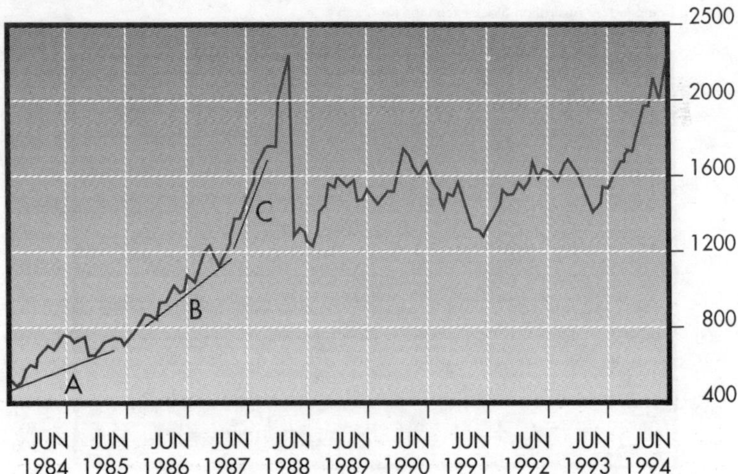

Compiled by Australian Stock Exchange Research

Figure 3

shoulders" pattern at 1750 in the middle of 1987 was a clear indicator of the forthcoming disaster. The same logic could have been applied to a similar formation when the index hit 1250 in 1986 when the market did not collapse, but the chartists could argue that the situation was different in 1987 to 1986 as the trend line in 1987 had grown much steeper.

I would never buy a stock without looking at its chart and would not buy one that was in downtrend. That is as close to following charts as I will go. Maybe I will change my mind in the future — meanwhile I suggest you borrow a book on charting from your library and make up your own mind.

Summing Up

The approach of most people to selecting shares is haphazard.

Share prices can be highly volatile.

As a general rule you will do better if you pick the right sector than if you pick the right share.

Record your reasons for buying a share and review them regularly.

Use charts with caution but don't ignore them.

14

Traded Options

See it big and keep it simple.

WILFRED PETERSON

Your interest in the share market will grow as your knowledge and understanding increases. As you become a reader of the financial pages you will notice advertisements claiming high returns from option and futures trading. You may also notice huge lists of "Call Options" and "Put Options" in the same part of the paper as the shares and unit trust prices are listed. Is this type of investing suitable for you? Read on, by the end of the chapter you should know.

First you will have to know what an option is. It is simply a document that gives you the right to buy or sell something for a given price on or before a specified date. In Chapter 31 I recommend the use of options to safeguard the rights of the surviving owners of a business if one owner dies. The survivors can "exercise" their "option" to buy the deceased's shares at a pre-arranged price.

Similarly you may pay $5 000 for the right to buy the property next door at any time in the next year for $200 000. If you do not take up (exercise) your option the transaction is over and the vendor keeps your $5 000. Neither of you has any further liability to each other.

Contrast this with a "futures" contract which I covered in detail in *Making Money Made Simple*. When you sign a futures contract there is a firm agreement for a sale at a future date at a set price. The buyer must pay, and the seller must deliver, on the due date.

The main options used in the share market are Exchange Traded Options which are traded through the Australian Option Market, part of the Sydney Stock Exchange. A traded option differs from the traditional options mentioned above in that it can be bought and sold like a share. Consequently a traded option may have several owners in its lifetime.

You do not have a traded option facility with most shares as the range available is restricted to major corporations such as BHP and Boral. However, the number of companies with a traded options facility available is gradually increasing, and if you look at the call and put options in the daily paper you will see which companies are included.

Types Of Options

There are two types of traded options.

(1) A **call** option which gives the holder the right to **buy** the share.

(2) A **put** option which gives the holder the right to **sell** the share.

Suppose XYZ Ltd shares were selling at $19 and **call** options to **buy** XYZ Ltd shares at $18 in four months were selling at $1.68. A **put** option to **sell** XYZ Ltd at $20 in four months was $1.50. Notice XYZ Ltd shares have to rise to $19.68 in four months for the person who bought the call option to be in front after paying the cost of the option.

Terms To Know

Premium is the cost of the option. This is determined by market forces.

Contract is the smallest amount you must deal with. It is usually for 1 000 shares.

Taker is the person who buys the traded option. The seller is the **writer.**

Exercise price or **Strike price** is the price at which the taker of a call option can buy.

Expiry date is the life of the contract. The dates are set at three-monthly intervals and for share options the maximum life is nine months.

Using Options

Now that we have the basic principles let's see how it works in practice. We'll assume you have got $10 000 and you want to invest it in the stock market. The basic rule is that you first decide what you are trying to achieve. If you want the money for your children's education, or to have a world trip in 10 years, you would buy solid shares or a conservative equity trust. Forget about options.

However, if you feel like a bit of a gamble, options might be your thing. Suppose you have a strong feeling about XYZ Ltd and have decided you want to invest your $10 000 in it. The present price is $10.00 a share. You notice a six month call option at $11.00 is $1. You may now buy 1 000 shares in XYZ for $10 each or buy 10 000 call options in XYZ at $1 each.

Six months have passed — what is your position? Suppose you picked a winner and XYZ shares are now $15. You now have a potential profit of almost $40 000 because you have the right to buy 10 000 shares at $4 below their market price. You have turned $10 000 into $40 000 in just six months.

Unfortunately it didn't turn out that way. Bad economic news arrived from America, and XYZ released a mediocre report for the half-year. The price of XYZ had fallen to $8.50 after the six months had passed. Your option contract is worthless, after all who wants to pay $11 a share when they be bought freely for $8.50. You have lost your $10 000.

It was a pity you chose the options that time. Just a year later XYZ had staged a strong recovery and the shares were $12. If you had invested your $10 000 in the actual shares it would now be worth $12 000 and you would be receiving franked dividends every six months.

You should now understand that options give you the ability to achieve much higher returns. However, you are depending on substantial market movements to make that profit. If they do not eventuate you may lose all your investment. It's a bit like a bet on a horse race. Fortunately you cannot lose more than your initial investment plus transaction costs. This is where option trading differs from future trading where you may lose far more than your original stake.

Now we'll consider put options and how they can be used to protect your portfolio. Think about that $12 000 we might have in XYZ Ltd. If you have a gut feeling that a crash is about to happen within six months you may buy **put** options giving you the right to sell XYZ for $12 in six months. These may cost $1 each. If there is a price plunge you have protected yourself because you have effectively sold for $11 ($12 less the $1 option cost). Of course you could have bought call or put options without owning any shares.

The Dangers

If you decide to become involved in the option and futures markets make sure you take the time to learn it thoroughly and practise by spending a few months doing simulated trading on paper before putting any money up.

There are some risks. For example, if you sell a **call** option you may be asked for physical delivery of the scrip on the exercise date. If you did not have it in your possession you may have to buy it. Imagine you had a call option giving the taker the right to buy XYZ at $10 next June. If the price rose to $15 during the course of the contract and the taker demands the actual scrip you would have to buy it on the market at $15 if you did not own it. In this case you took on a liability without knowing how much you could lose. It could be far more than the contract price.

Certainly there are ways sophisticated traders can cover themselves against similar situations but I mention the above example to make you aware of the potential for loss if you do not understand what you are getting into.

Conclusion

All I have done in the space available is give you a glimpse of the excitement, risks, and possible profit in the options market. If you decide option trading may be suitable for you start off by obtaining some literature from the Stock Exchange. Just remember the old investment adage "the higher the return the higher the risk".

15

How Managed Funds Evolved

A good scare is worth more to a man than good advice.

(E.W. HOWE: Country Town Sayings)

If you pick up most newspapers today you will notice a spate of articles on personal finance as well as regular question and answer columns on the same topic. There will also be a myriad of advertisements from licensed securities dealers offering financial advice and from fund managers offering a range of investments.

It is also sad, but true, that some investors have had bad experiences with financial advisers, managed funds and fund managers. The following letter that was sent to me by a doctor is typical:

"I note your advice in the Sydney Morning Herald that one should seek out a competent independent financial adviser.

Theoretically that is good advice. The practical question is where does one find such an individual. How is it possible to know that anybody is 'competent' or that advisers are 'independent', given the inducements and commissions offered by a battery of corporations and financial institutions.

Some of these individuals who claim loudly to be independent, charging only a fee for service, are in fact also taking back door commissions. How is one to know? What is one to do?

The total of fees and commissions are generally outrageous. This lure has drawn all kinds of frauds and hacks, if not outright cheats into the 'industry'. If they are not that they appear to have inadequate back up services to enable them to monitor all the investments on offer."

Whew! Obviously the doctor has had some bad experiences with financial advisers. Unfortunately this often happens to members of the medical profession who are so busy keeping up to date in their own field that they have little time left to study financial matters. As a result they become easy targets for salespeople posing as financial advisers.

It is difficult to answer a question like that in the limited space I have here because such a huge range of issues are involved. Nevertheless, in the next three chapters I shall explain the history of the industry and hope it gives you the background knowledge to sally forth with confidence into the world of managed funds, fund managers and financial advisers.

The Dawn Of The Industry

Financial affairs were simple in the "good old days" in the late 1950's when I worked in a bank. Half yearly bank fees were Ten Shillings or a Pound depending on the account activity and "exchange" was charged on all out of town cheques to compensate the bank for the loss of interest while the cheques were in the mail bag. In those days we still used inkwells and cheque-books had a blotter in the front of them to dry your ink.

Life was uncomplicated then. Inflation was minimal, interest rates were low and credit cards and personal loans were unheard of. Surplus funds were invested in a savings account or an interest bearing deposit. In those days few needed financial advice and often the bank manager could offer some fatherly counselling based on his (females did not have a say then) experience with his customers. Hardly anybody had superannuation, most of us had a small life assurance policy and the goal of most people was to get married and have a family.

Then technology began its impact on our lives. Improved communications enabled us to see world events as they happened, computers gave us the power to store and retrieve information at lightning speed, and the pill gave women the ability to control their fertility and to plan a career instead of treating a job as a temporary position until Mr Right came along.

Greater social awareness led to massive jumps in the quantity and costs of services provided by Governments and technology and larger numbers looking for work created chronic unemployment. Our attitude towards our bodies improved and fibre diets and sun tan lotion came in, while cigarettes went out. Now the young leave school at a later age and the elderly live longer.

Certainly these were all steps for the better but there is never change without drawbacks. The price we paid was that life began to get complicated.

Business grew more sophisticated as the numbers of products and services grew. Suddenly institutions found they had to upgrade their services to maintain and expand their client base or be taken over by their competition. Consequently the range of choices open to people increased dramatically.

Governments were swept along in the change and did what all governments do in these circumstances. They kept passing new laws and changing old ones. Many of these laws involved raising new taxes to provide the funds to cope with the public demands for more services from government.

The Enemy Inflation

In December 1972, after decades of conservative government, the Whitlam Labor Government was swept to power on the theme "It's Time" (for a change). It was dogged by a combination of high hopes and little experience and soon found itself in the middle of a unprecedented threat — an oil crisis. A new age of inflation had commenced and in the September 1974 quarter an inflation rate of 19.2% was announced.

Interest rates rocketed. Companies issuing debentures were offering around 9% in 1973 — within a year the rate had almost doubled to 15%. Many people who had invested in debentures had locked in funds for long periods and found themselves stuck with the lower rates and consequently a rapidly declining standard of living.

Remember how I have stressed the importance of flexibility when designing an investment portfolio. Those debenture holders who opted to tie up funds for long terms were now learning the pain of ignoring this principle.

The public was already facing more complicated tax laws and a growing number of services to choose from in all areas. Now it faced one of the worst enemies of all, roaring inflation. To counter inflation or just because of greed, fear or inexperience, many chased the highest interest rates on offer. Alas, there were no risk free escape routes. When Cambridge Credit crashed and took millions of dollars with it, investors found, to their horror, that putting money willy nilly into debentures did not necessarily guarantee its safety.

Other painful lessons were being re-learned. The years 1973 and 1974 saw the greatest stock market crash since 1929 and investors saw, once again, that what goes up can also come down.

Pensions came back into the news. In 1976 the Fraser Government came under pressure from the Country Party (now the National Party) who in turn were under pressure from asset rich but cash poor farmers. Reluctantly it scrapped the means test on welfare benefits and replaced it with an incomes test. The definition of "income" was a loose one and accruing capital gain was not included as income. There was no capital gains tax to worry about in those days so, to maximise their pensions, retirees looked for assets that produced low income but substantial capital gain.

This was probably the birth of financial advising as we now know it. A fledgling industry commenced to assist pensioners to maximise their pension entitlements.

Enter The Advisers

Now the financial advisers have joined our story. As you follow the history of the industry in this chapter you will see a quick but natural evolution in line with changing times and attitudes. Notice the **basic areas of investment have stayed constant** — they remain cash, property and shares. What **has** changed is the technology available and the role of Government. The natural consequence is a huge increase in the range of investment vehicles being marketed and it is this range which confuses the investing public. Insurance bonds, roll-over funds and property and equity trusts may be household words today but, in the 1970's, were almost unheard of.

The first unit trusts started in Britain in 1868 and began in Australia in 1936 when Australian Fixed Trusts launched their "fixed" equity trusts. These trusts were "fixed" in three areas. The life was set at 10 years, the sum raised was stated at the outset (usually a million pounds) and the funds were invested in a fixed portfolio of shares. A major drawback was the lack of flexibility.

The 1970's brought the investing public's notice to the power of the combined savings of a large number of people with small amounts to invest. Australian Fixed Trusts had introduced the first unit trusts to Australia in 1936 but it was not until Hill Samuel (now Macquarie Bank) launched the first cash management trust that the concept took off.

A cash management trust was a vehicle that gave small investors the ability to pool their funds under the control of a manager and achieve much higher earnings than they could have done individually. Because the cash management trust invested in prime securities, such as bank bills, investors' funds were not at risk. Because the money is available on short notice they did not suffer the inflationary dangers of locking up money for long terms.

The finance company debentures mentioned above appeared in the late 1950's and gave investors the opportunity to earn higher rates than they had obtained previously. However, they were controversial because of the high rates charged by the finance companies to those who borrowed from them. I well remember a client of the bank saying "I think these new finance company debentures are a bit immoral[1] but they certainly pay nice high rates of interest."

To take advantage of the introduction of debentures Australian Fixed Trusts introduced a "balanced trust", being a mixture of debentures and shares. These funds had a disastrous time in 1961 when the Menzies Government hit us with a credit squeeze which flattened the stock market and sent many companies issuing debentures (for example H.G. Palmers and Stanhill) to the wall. Consequently the Australian public decided to forget about trusts and the stock market for the time being and fled back to the perceived security of banks.

However, down phases don't last forever, and late in the 1960's we had another stock market boom. Remember Poseidon etc. AFT jumped back on the bandwagon with a whole array of trusts catering for the resources sector of the share market and, in November 1970, launched their first property trust in 10 years. The share market had its predictable boom followed by a bust and by September 1974, AFT Equity Trust Units that were selling at 54 cents in January 1973 had slumped to just 27 cents.

Shares and share trusts were back out of favour again but the cycle always continues. Now it was the turn of property trusts. I have already mentioned that in 1976 the Fraser Government had introduced a mild form of incomes test on pensions which did not treat accruing capital growth as income.

1 This reflected the community belief of that time that finance companies charged exorbitant rates of interest.

"What better investment could one get to provide this than a property trust?" said the new breed of advisers. They were the obvious choice for most pensioners who did not have the resources, experience or temperament to cope with owning rental property. The retirees agreed. Get ready for the property boom!

One problem for the promoters of unit trusts was finding people to invest in their products. There had been limited protection for investors for many years and one of the main safeguards was a prohibition on promoters advertising to the public for funds without issuing a prospectus. Aggressive advertising using such terms as "94% a year returns" was by then illegal, so some promoters took to marketing products through financial newsletters where glowing claims could be sandwiched in with the editorial.

Others formed syndicates and marketed to their own client base or obtained leads through seminars. The Balanced Property Trusts Group formed a "Pensioners Education Association" and gave "independent advice" by recommending pensioners invest in Balanced Property Trusts. If you wanted spread you opted for three or four different Balanced Property Trusts!

These marketing efforts were highly successful and unit trusts grew rapidly in popularity. In late 1981 Bruce Bird left AFT to form the Clayton Robard Group (now Tyndall). This was followed soon after by the formation of the Armstrong Jones group in Perth, Growth Equities Mutual in Perth and then by the launch, in Sydney, of the Australia-Wide group and Advance Asset Management. The funds industry was off and running — just a few short years ago.

Independent(?) Advisers

Notice that most of the marketing of the investments was done by commission salespeople calling themselves "advisers". This is not to say that the majority of advisers were dishonest or that the products were not appropriate for the people who put funds into them. It is merely a recognition of the fact that they did not receive any income unless they persuaded you to invest in their product. A situation like this will always lay itself open to charges of bias.

AFT continued to grow and by June 1984 had a sales staff of almost 300 "advisers" and nearly a billion dollars under management.

In July 1984 a change of staff at top level in AFT led to intense discontent among its sales staff. Frustrated at what they saw as lack of direction from the top, and at their inability to handle some of the top line investment products being offered by companies such as Armstrong Jones and Advance, they resigned en masse and went into business as truly independent advisers. This is the point where the "independent advisers" emerged in force.

This mass defection greatly increased the number of independent investment advisers but also caused a loss of funds to AFT as some of the now "genuinely independent" advisers recommended to their clients that they switch some of their money out of AFT to give greater diversification.

The wheel kept turning and problems began hitting the property trust industry. The shallowness of the Balanced Property Trust Group came to the surface when it collapsed, taking with it the life savings of many thousands of pensioners who had relied on their "independent advisers[2]". The Telford group made a rescue bid for Balanced and sunk themselves in the attempt.

Worse news for the industry was to come. In December 1986 AFT reported that six of its 15 property trusts had produced a consolidated loss of $14 million after a revaluation of all properties.

By now you should be starting to understand how the growth of the industry occurred in parallel with the times in which it operated. You will soon discover how the industry grew more sophisticated with experience.

The birth of independent advisers was triggered by the actions of the Fraser Government and their products grew in line with market needs and sentiments. By the end of 1981 the public were getting used to managed funds such as equity trusts and property trusts and fund managers were springing up to fulfil the demand. The public had also discovered that stock markets could plunge and that badly run property trusts could cost investors their savings.

The Hawke Government

Another wave of growth came with the election of the Hawke Government in 1983. Hawke was a very different Prime Minister to his predecessors Whitlam and Fraser. There was none of the exuberant excesses of Whitlam or the bumbling inaction of Fraser — he led a Government that was going to move carefully and stay in office for a long time.

---

2 Note that few, if any, genuinely independent advisers had ever recommended Balanced.

One of the Hawke Government's first tasks was to reform the superannuation system which, until then, had been virtually restricted to male white collar workers. Following the recommendations of the Campbell Report, laws were passed to stamp out the rorts which had flourished for years. To help the ordinary worker to provide for retirement, and hence not be a drain on the welfare system, the unions were encouraged to accept a compulsory contribution to superannuation in lieu of a 3% wage rise that would be quickly frittered away.

Another priority was to deregulate the financial system and bring Australia into line with the rest of the developed world. The Australian dollar was floated and, since that date, the value of our dollar has been printed daily on the front page of the major newspapers. Exchange control restrictions were relaxed to encourage investment by foreigners in Australia. This also enabled Australians to take advantage of opportunities overseas and paved the way for the introduction of international equity trusts that invested in share markets around the world.

The Labor Government, like all Governments, was looking for ways to raise more revenue. In 1983, in tandem with the superannuation changes, a decision was made to raise the tax on retirement payments from an effective maximum of 2.5% to a massive 30% plus Medicare levy. Treasurer Keating was aware of the need to avoid the Fraser stigma of retrospectivity and applied the tax only to that portion of a retirement lump sum that related to post July 1983 service.

As part of their policy of encouraging retirees to preserve their lump sums instead of wasting them and then going on welfare, the Government introduced roll-over funds. Invest your retirement pay-out into one of these and you could defer your lump sum tax and earn interest on it until you turned 65. The complications were starting in earnest!

Meanwhile, to stop people exploiting the pension rules, a modified assets and income test was introduced. However, there was a large problem finding a definition of income. Is income simply the amount that is assessed by the Tax Office? The Government said "no" and gave the Department of Social Security a different set of rules to the ones the Tax Office used. Just to make it more confusing they gave the Department of Veterans Affairs, who provide similar pensions, a different set of rules again.

Getting It Right!

Understand that there are two major factions in this industry. One is the Government, that is forever making policy and then drafting laws to put the policy into effect. The other is made up of the financial institutions, solicitors, accountants and financial advisers who are forever looking for **legal** ways to help their clients optimise their financial affairs. For them the Hawke Government provided a bonanza.

This is how it works. The Government thinks of a bright idea and one of the Ministers will release it as part of an Economic Statement, a Budget or from the steps of an aeroplane as he or she leaves for overseas. It is then analysed by the advisers, accountants and lawyers who work daily with the practical aspects of sorting out what the Government has proposed.

Naturally all the anomalies, and the cases that nobody has thought about, spring to light and the Government reacts by starting to patch up its proposed legislation. More anomalies come out, more patches are applied and eventually we get to a situation where only a few know what the real position is. The man or woman in the street doesn't have a hope of understanding what the experts are arguing about and is likely to encounter severe problems if they don't consult an adviser.

Roll-over funds are a good example. When they were introduced the main vehicles were Approved Deposit Funds (ADF's) and Deferred Annuities (DA's). A loophole was found. You had to exit an ADF at 65 but could stay in a DA until death, after which time the money could be re-rolled to your family. On January 12, 1987 this loophole was plugged, which created two classes of roll-overs — pre January 1987 and post January 1987.

Capital gains tax was introduced in September 1985 and the lawyers are still battling with the fine points of it. Imputation of dividends was welcomed in July 1987 but, despite its obvious benefits, recent research shows that less than 4% of the population understands it.

While all this was happening we were having a stock market boom coupled with an investment advisory boom. The public was confused by a never ending stream of new laws, together with the multitude of associated new products that were designed to cater for them. Many of them were stock market based and produced extraordinary returns which led to large financial institutions placing a spate of full page advertisements in the papers trumpeting returns of 40% PLUS. Few noticed the fine print that said "Future returns may bear no relation to the ones quoted above".

The cycle kept moving. Treasurer Keating made his famous "Banana Republic" statement in 1986 and our dollar collapsed; this boosted further the returns of those funds that had an off-shore component.

As usual all good times come to an end; in October 1987 we came back to earth with another stock market crash which shook the world.

You can usually find something good in most disasters and, after the crash of 1987, many salespeople masquerading as advisers who had got involved in "financial planning" to take advantage of the boom left it — hopefully never to return. The responsible ones who were left started to pick up the pieces to build a strong industry to cater for the majority of investors who could no longer cope without sound impartial advice.

Help from the Hawke Government continued. In May and September 1988, in August 1989, June 1992 and in September 1993, it brought in the most detailed, intricate and far ranging changes to superannuation, lump sum tax, and pensions in the history of Australia. The complexity of the changes was so great that many of them took years to be become law. Meanwhile the members of the financial advisory industry continued to battle to keep abreast of the everchanging scene, secure in the knowledge that it had long got past the point where the general public could ever understand it.

Conclusion

On our journey through the short history of the financial advisory industry we have seen how managed funds, such as unit trusts, grew in popularity, and how truly independent advisers replaced the adviser/salesmen as the product range grew.

As this was happening the increasing number of continually changing Government regulations made it impossible for most people to handle their own financial affairs properly while the never-ending up and down cycles of all the investment avenues have created growing fear in the minds of the investing public. In the next chapter we'll look at how the crisis of 1990 affected the lives of all Australians.

16

The Crisis Of 1990

It can't happen here is number one on the list of famous last words.

DAVID CROSBY

The crash of 1987 happened in a few hours; the crisis of 1990 built up as slowly and surely as a runaway car gathers pace as it starts to roll slowly down a slope. It was a compelling combination of events that combined to wreck havoc on Australia in general and Victoria in particular.

There was a general nervousness as we approached 1990. An American economist Ravi Batra had received world wide publicity with a book *The Great Depression of 1990*. The book attracted little notice when it was first released in 1985, but it was regurgitated in 1988 in the aftermath of the 1987 stock market crash. While it was not taken seriously in the financial world, it certainly set the nation talking. Over and over people would ask "Do you think there will be a depression in 1990?".

The Australian financial scene had been a friendly one in the late 1980's as banks flexed their muscles after deregulation and rushed to lend money to anybody who wanted it. The property boom of 1988 followed the stock market crash of 1987 and in late 1988 any Australian who had been lucky enough to buy a home was feeling wealthy.

It all changed in early 1989 when the Labor Government slammed the brakes on an over-heated Australian economy by a ruthless application of monetary policy — winding up interest rates. Home loan interest rates went up to 18% and many small businesses began paying up to 25% on their overdrafts. Home prices in many States started to drop because of slack buying demand and pressure on sellers who were forced to quit their homes as a result of the high interest rates.

Next came a national airline pilots dispute which saw over 1600 pilots resign in August 1989. The Federal Government brought in the Royal Australian Air Force and also used foreign planes with foreign crews, but this was a stop gap measure and provided only a limited service. Each side underestimated the will of the other and the battle went on for months. It almost crippled the country's tourist industry and a succession of new hotels went into receivership as rocketing vacancy rates made a mockery of their budget forecasts.

The position was exacerbated by the continual wet weather which saturated the East Coast of Australia for the first four months of 1990. This created conditions that made it impossible for builders to complete sufficient work to enable them to submit a progress claim, so they were unable to pay their suppliers. To compound the problem, the high cost of money took its inevitable toll and soon big names like Hooker, Girvan, Bond and Qintex started going to the wall.

The banks who had fallen over themselves to lend in the previous few years found themselves with an increasing number of bad debts on their hands. They panicked, went from one extreme to the other, and reined in lending. This hit the construction companies who were already starting to feel the pinch from high interest rates biting into their costs as well as reducing the demand for their products. As the construction companies started to go into liquidation more bad debts were created which made things worse for institutions such as banks, certain building societies and mortgage trusts.

Victoria was the State that was worst hit. Its State Government had embarked on ambitious projects that were now in trouble. The Victorian Economic Development Corporation collapsed. Tri-Continental Bank, the merchant bank arm of the State Bank of Victoria, announced massive losses. When the State Bank broke the news of its own huge losses the fear started to grow.

Rumours had been rife about the Estate Mortgage group in the advisory industry and these started to become public in late 1989 after a Sydney financial adviser circulated a newsletter to clients claiming that Estate Mortgage was a "high risk" investment. Finally the Estate Mortgage Trust group announced it was suspending redemptions to unit holders. This brought forth the wrath of the thousands of small investors who had invested with Estate on the basis of its glowing advertisements.

As the worry spread, the word got out that Pyramid Building Society, the biggest in Victoria, was in trouble. The strategies used by Pyramid were unorthodox; they offered the highest interest rates to depositors, their lending margins were slim and their main income came from hefty establishment fees. The inevitable run started, and on February 12 and 13, 1990 over $31 million was withdrawn. To stop the run the Victorian Treasurer, Rob Jolly, assured depositors their money was safe with Pyramid.

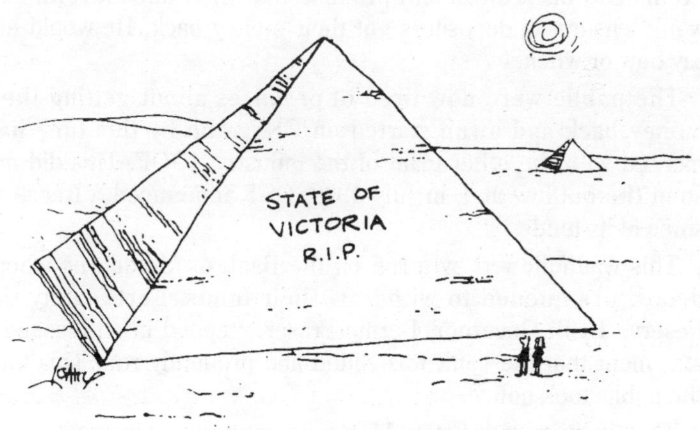

The building societies in the other States had got together in the early 1980's and formed the National Deposit Insurance Corporation (NDIC) to represent them. The NDIC is funded by a levy on each building society and monitors their capital adequacy, provides stand-by lines of credit in case of a run and insures the deposits of private investors. Unfortunately Victoria was the only State that refused to join, on the grounds that it did not need the NDIC. In hindsight this was a sorry decision.

In May 1990 the giant OST Group, which held over a billion dollars of savings in several friendly society funds, announced that its major borrower, the Dreamworld amusement park, was suffering liquidity problems. OST urged its investors not to panic. It quickly emerged that OST had made a $152 million loan and guarantee to a single borrower — Dreamworld. This sum represented 32 per cent of the OST Accumulator Bond Fund and 11 per cent of the OST Mortgage Bond Fund.

Meanwhile Pyramid was still troubled by rumours, and another run started. On June 22, Pyramid Building Society temporarily closed its doors with the announcement that its depositors, on whose behalf it held over $1.4 billion in funds, might receive only 60 cents in the dollar. The group had incurred huge losses by imprudent loans for construction. The Victorian Premier, John Cain, refused to honour what the depositors regarded as a Government guarantee from his own Treasurer, Mr Jolly, and announced the depositors would have to fend for themselves.

Pressure from both inside and outside the party forced the Premier to back down and promise that the State Government would ensure all depositors got their money back. He would not say how or when.

The public were now tired of promises about getting their money back and a run started on OST, who by this time had merged with the other giant of the industry, IOOF. This did not stem the outflow and, in July 1990, OST announced a freeze of some of its funds.

This was followed by a run on the Bank of Melbourne where depositors queued to withdraw their funds. Fortunately the Reserve Bank Governor, Bernie Fraser, stepped in and issued a statement that the bank was sound and prudently run. This time the public took notice.

The situation with Estate Mortgage got progressively worse. At first unit holders were told they would get “all their money back” but by late July 1990 the headlines were screaming “Only four cents in the dollar for some investors”. An analysis of the six trusts showed that those in the Income Trust Number One were worse off, with returns expected to range between four cents in the dollar and 37 cents in the dollar.

At meetings around Australia, unit holders in Estate Mortgage were told of the group’s unstable loan portfolio, with exposure to construction loans of 37% and to tourism, time share and retirement developments of 31%. Unit holders learned that at least 66% of the loans made by Estate Mortgage were “non performing”.

The poor selection of investments, the weak borrowers, the sick property market and the high interest rates had all contributed to the problems of the group. It was announced that Estate Mortgage had been capitalising the interest on some of their loans and were paying interest to unit holders from funds received from new investors, not from their borrowers.

Unfortunately the general public loses reason when bad news is constantly in the media and money started fleeing to the perceived security of banks. Unlisted property trusts started to receive an unusually high level of requests for redemptions, at the same time as their inflow was dropping off. This was caused by a general fear among small investors who just wanted to see their money in the bank, as well as a realisation among the more informed ones that the property market was in trouble, and there was currently more potential in shares.

Owning units in an **unlisted** property trust is like owning a piece of property in partnership with other people. However, despite the fact that property is a long term investment the unlisted property trusts had been so successful that most managers in the past had been able to offer to investors the opportunity to redeem their units within 60 days.

Investors had become used to treating them in the same way as they might treat a savings account yet the underlying character of property is that it is not a liquid investment. On July 16, 1990, after talks with the Unit Trust Association and the Trustee Companies Association, the Australian Securities Commission moved in as a defensive measure and gave property trusts the right to suspend redemptions for up to six months to protect the interests of all investors in the trust.

The purpose was to enable any trusts who suffered a panic run to ride out the storm, and not be forced to sacrifice properties at the expense of the silent majority who were with the investment for the long term. Naturally this action led to more rumours, and more requests for redemptions, and on July 17, 1990 the huge Aust-Wide Group announced a 60 day freeze on redemptions.

Two days later came a notice from the highly respected Heine group of a six months moratorium on redemptions. The Sydney-based Mirvac quickly followed and then Perth-based Armstrong Jones, the largest in the industry, called a national unit holders meeting using closed circuit television to announce a six month freeze on redemptions. Thus, by the end of July 1990 almost half a million Australian households had, at least, part of their funds frozen.

The giant hangover from the party of the 80's was about to begin.

17

The Players In The Game

Man has a limited biological capacity for change. When the capacity is overwhelmed, the capacity is in future shock.

ALVIN TOFFLER

The stock market boom of the mid 1980's coupled with the major changes made by the Hawke Government caused unprecedented growth in the investment advisory industry. Funds managers raced to bring out new products. In 1983 there were less than 100 products to choose from — by the end of 1987 there were more than 4 000 different products available!

Financial advisers were battling to keep up with the ever-changing whims of Government, let alone stay abreast of the vast array of products. Fund managers, all fighting for a share of the rapidly growing market, bombarded advisers with visits, glowing literature, cocktail parties and slide presentations. An array of magazines such as *Australian Business, Personal Investment, Money Management,* and *Business Review Weekly* sprung up to thrust more information at the investment industry and its clients. How could advisers cope with so much information? Enter the next players in our story — the research groups.

The Research Industry

The research groups evolved to fill the needs of financial advisers bogged down by the information explosion. How else, but by buying research, could advisers in Melbourne possibly satisfy themselves that a Sydney-based property trust had well-located buildings with good tenants, or that an equity fund manager was following a consistent investment strategy.

The research organisations set about publishing figures on the history, short as it usually was, about the major funds. They also interviewed fund managers in depth to find out their investment policies, monitored the funds to try to make sure the investment policy was being consistently followed, and often kept records on the performance of well-known people in the industry as well as details of their incentive packages.

On top of all this, many of them gave the funds ratings such as "A" or "E" or described them with brief paragraphs such as "mediocre trust with a holding of second rate property", "highly risky" or "first class consistent performer with a superb management team".

Naturally the emergence of research companies took a lot of the strain off the financial advisers, who could then spend more time trying to understand the complexities of Government regulations and explain them to even more confused clients. In fact at my own company, Whittaker Macnaught, we regard research as so important that we have gone to the expense of using three separate research companies as well as relying heavily on our own material.

The Dawn Of Reality

The crash of 1987 saw a drastic drop in new funds being launched and ushered in a new era of cynicism on the part of both financial advisers and research companies. To understand why you must be aware there are two main types of managed funds.

The first is the unlisted property trust where performance depends on the skill of the manager in selecting and managing properties. Until the crash of 1990 returns tended to be predictable and consistent. The second is the equity trust (share trust) where the ability to pick undervalued shares is important but where much of the short term performance is due to market timing, which is often a matter of luck. Equity trusts are the ones that show sharp volatility in returns as their performance depends largely on which way the share market moves.

During the 1987 share market crash some equity trusts that had been showing spectacular returns prior to the crash went into free fall losing up to 70% of their pre crash value. When the dust settled it was found that some equity fund managers had been carried away by the boom mentality. They had totally ignored their stated objectives and had invested heavily in second rate speculative shares which were worst hit.

Since then, the industry has stayed in a state of caution and only the naive advisers or investors take projections of future performance at face value or put much store in past results. The age of realism had arrived.

The Clients

The most important people are the clients, because the financial advisory industry would not exist if there was nobody to advise. Here are some of the people the staff of a large financial advisory office might encounter.

No single adviser would handle this number in a single day or even a week. Most of us find that any more than six new clients a week is overloading the stress levels as much of an adviser's time is spent, alone, thinking about alternative strategies for new clients. The rest of it goes on attending to existing clients, staying abreast of product changes and financial news and trying to keep up to date with the latest batch of laws from Canberra.

The first client may be a young widow still dazed from her sudden loss. If her husband was wise, or was lucky enough to work for a company with a good superannuation scheme, she is now in possession of a cheque for around two hundred thousand dollars. In a few short days the happily married wife with little money and a mortgage has been transformed into a shocked widow with more money than she ever dreamed of.

The first interview is a time for understanding, reassurance and possibly to explain briefly the choices open to her to fight the two enemies of tax and inflation. It's far too soon for her to make any long term financial decisions. She'll have only $140,000 left when the $60,000 mortgage is paid off, which will be barely enough to generate enough to pay the bills, attend to the children's' education and keep pace with inflation. Readers with little life assurance should note and take action.

* * *

An older couple might be next. He is about to turn 65. They are seeking the aged pension but are totally confused about money and how the latest set of pension rules work. To make it worse, well meaning friends have filled their heads with a lot of rubbish about the dreadful things the staff of the Social Security Department might do to them.

They relax when told that most of the department staff are helpful and friendly and breathe a sigh of relief when they find out the advisers' services include assisting them with the pension application and liaising with department staff on their behalf. The discussion turns to their elderly mother who is about to sell her home and go into a nursing home. How does she keep her benefits?

* * *

They might be followed by a couple in business. They have a superannuation fund, a family trust, a family company, a lot of assets and a lot of debt. They are mainly concerned about the administration of their superannuation fund and the best way to invest the surplus funds. To this end the adviser may consult his own in-house superannuation adviser or call in an outside specialist before arranging a conference with the couple's accountant to discuss the company structure in depth.

* * *

The next person in the door is a public servant who is about to retire with a large lump sum. Somehow his name has been leaked to what seems like every insurance salesperson in town and he has been bombarded with phone calls and letters. He is now saturated with advice and has just enough knowledge to be a danger to himself. Often the adviser will suggest he roll it initially into a cash type Approved Deposit fund with no entry or exit fees.

This action lets him settle into the retirement routine with a minimum of stress, and takes the urgency out of making long term investment decisions.

* * *

The clients who follow are many years away from retirement but have the foresight to be planning for it now. Thanks to the sophisticated software now available, the adviser has only to punch details of their ages, planned retirement date, income needed and their assets into a computer. In seconds they know whether they are on course now to retire comfortably or, if not, what extra dollars they need to invest to do so. Usually they leave with a new sense of purpose.

* * *

The next couple in the door are in their early 60's and are sick of that dirty word "tax". They are amazed when they find out that their tax can be greatly reduced, provided they are willing to venture further afield than their present investments which are entirely in debentures and term deposits. Spouse contributions into superannuation can radically change their situation.

The going is not easy. Terms like capital drawdown schemes, international investments, annuities, allocated pensions and dividend imputation may roll easily off an experienced adviser's tongue, but are a foreign language to a couple who were born over 60 years ago. The adviser talks and they nod with feigned understanding. However, they will probably find it all too difficult and continue to leave things as they stand. They'll be back next year when the big tax bill hits again and possibly break the ice with a tentative investment of a few thousand dollars.

* * *

Next the DINKS (double income, no kids) enter. They have high salaries, a high mortgage, a high standard of living and high ambitions. They are aware of the need to invest but know themselves well enough to realise the only way they will amass wealth is by having a commitment. Negative gearing is probably what they want and the adviser will discuss various negative gearing packages and explain the advantages and drawbacks in detail. This is probably a good time to mention income replacement insurance if they do not have any and recommend they take some out.

* * *

Lottery winners need financial guidance desperately. Overnight they may have become millionaires, yet deep down they feel no different. They will have a difficult time getting used to it and will often become the target of grasping family members, well-meaning friends and fast-talking salespeople.

EXAMPLE: *Mr and Mrs X were in their late 50's and had won $600,000 when they came to see our company. They had*

> *been battlers all their life and had used $150,000 of the money to pay off their children's many debts before they arrived. On their children's advice they had paid $250,000 for a home unit at the Gold Coast which was to be kept for all the family to use. We offered advice about safe ways to invest the remaining $200,000 but it was refused. They decided to "lend" it to Uncle Charlie so he could develop some land he owned. No bank or finance would lend Uncle Charlie a cent and they were going to make sure he got a "fair go".*

Lottery winners need to be saved from themselves as well as the other people but it is a sad fact that most people who win large sums have dissipated most of it within five years. They normally say "It just went — I have no idea where".

Space does not permit me to mention in detail other typical clients, such as divorced people with property settlement cheques, young people seeking superannuation and life insurance and those who want to maximise their returns from investment property. Suffice to say the financial advisory industry is now catering for a growing number of people.

The examples have some common threads. Large sums of money, often life savings, are involved and usually the people are not used to handling it. Many of the challenges they face are the result of increasing Government regulation which they do not understand at all, and many of the investment products recommended by the adviser have been developed only recently.

The Products

Understand first that a financial adviser is concerned as much with structure and putting investments in the right names as with designing a portfolio that suits the clients' needs. A bank bill might be a fine investment for a low income spouse but a poor one for the high income partner.

The primary tasks are to find out what resources are available, formulate a goal, make sure it is attainable and then recommend investments and a structure that will make it work. Unfortunately nothing is certain in this world and there are only two types of investments. One involves lending money to others by products which range from savings accounts to mortgage trusts. The other involves ownership in such areas as property, shares, precious metals, or works of art. Thus a person is a lender, an investor or a combination of both.

The "lender" investments are known as cash type investments as their value is certain, there is no capital growth and little or no fees are incurred when depositing or withdrawing. A savings account is a good example.

The other type of investment is concerned with capital growth but it is important to understand that capital growth is not guaranteed. Some investments can drop in value and take years to recover. When this happens the client will often blame the adviser or the fund manager. Anybody investing money in "capital growth" areas must be aware that wherever there is a chance of capital gain there is a chance of capital loss. Usually the funds that drop in value quickly are heavily invested in shares and thus suffer the same volatility as the share market.

Obviously this is not an area for the faint hearted nor for anybody who cannot see their way clear to leave the money untouched for at least five years.

The world is changing rapidly and the principle of shared ownership by managed funds is growing. The reasons are obvious. If many people pool their dollars they are able to buy a property, or invest in a diversified portfolio of shares that would be out of the reach of any one them. Provided an expert manager is chosen, the investments should perform satisfactorily.

You will find that almost every portfolio recommended by a financial adviser includes managed funds, as they are appropriate for almost everybody and offer a flexibility that is not available with direct ownership. The adviser may suggest a cash management trust or a bond trust for the cash component, a property trust to underpin the portfolio with the stability of property and an equity trust for the spice of the sharemarket. Add to this insurance bonds or friendly society bonds for situations where no income is required.

You can see there is consistency within the everchanging investment world. Investments will still fall into the three categories of cash, property and shares or into the two categories of "lending" or "owning". There are no risk free investments and no one path that anybody should travel. Flexibility and diversification remain the two essential elements; fortunately we now have the products to provide both.

18

Managed Funds Or Do It Yourself?

True, you can't take it with you, but then, that's not the place where it comes in handy.

BRENDAN FRANCIS

By now, I hope you have a solid understanding of the history of the vital and rapidly changing investment world. Now it's time to look at investing those precious dollars.

"I've got some money to invest, where's the best place to put it?" sounds a simple question but cannot be properly answered until the inquirer supplies a lot more information.

The first question to ask is what the investor is trying to achieve. The answers are all different and may be as diverse as:

To achieve maximum income, to minimise tax, to make the money grow, to get as large a pension as possible or to create a fund for retirement.

Different strategies are necessary to achieve each one of these goals. To understand why, you must realise that investments are generally regarded as being short term, medium term or long term. There are two additional categories into which they can fall — "income" or "capital growth".

It is human nature to want the best of both worlds but, sadly, there is no such thing as a free lunch. As I explained in the sections on property and shares a high income return usually means nil or low growth and high expected growth may be coupled with nil or low income.

When we talk about "capital growth" investments, we are referring to investments such as good property and good shares that should show a steady increase in value over time. However, bear in mind that wherever there is a chance of capital gain, there is a chance of capital loss. The October 1987 stock-market crash showed us how quickly, and how far, shares can fall. In the 1990 property crash many large non-residential properties suffered massive drops in value.

Investments in the "growth" areas may be made by buying shares and property directly, or by using equity and property trusts. In each case there are costs to acquire the investment and often costs to cash it in. These costs, coupled with the volatile nature of shares and sluggish nature of property, should make you cautious about investing in these areas unless you have at **least** a five year term in mind.

Here is an example of the folly of investing short term money in long term areas.

> **EXAMPLE:** *In July 1987 a couple received $180,000 from the sale of their house. They were uncertain about where to put it because they were thinking about buying another house. A friend had done well on the stock market and suggested they put it all into top quality shares. They took this advice and made the investments just before the 1987 crash. After the crash they took further advice from this friend, who suggested they hold the shares for the recovery. They missed out on the housing boom that followed the share crash. Talk about a double whammy!*

That example shows the importance of obtaining competent independent advice before making investment decisions. There is often a high price to be paid for failure to do so. The appropriate investment for those people was a cash management trust or an interest bearing account with a bank or building society. Certainly tax might have taken some of the earnings, but there would have been no loss of capital because of the costs of buying and selling or through market fluctuations.

During the 1980's we witnessed an explosion in the number of financial products and services available. There are now thousands of investments on the market with more coming out every week. Advertising for this proliferation of products has filled the gap created by the departure of the cigarette manufacturers but unfortunately there is no requirement that any carry a label *"Warning — this investment may be hazardous to your wealth"*.

The Major Investment Decisions

Most investors are totally confused by all this change but remember the "investment menu" concept. There are still only three areas where the bulk of your funds can be invested — cash, property and shares. Those who wish to invest face two main choices:

(1) What percentage of total assets should we invest in each of the three areas (the asset allocation)?

(2) Do we invest in these areas directly, or use managed funds such as unit trusts or insurance bonds?

There is no clearcut path that must be followed. Many people will vary their asset allocation continually in line with their belief in the way various markets are performing and it is also common for investors to have a "bit each way". They might own a negatively geared investment house and, at the same time, achieve a spread of investments, and a suitable asset allocation, by keeping the balance of their money in equity or bond trusts.

Managed Funds

I covered managed funds in *Making Money Made Simple* but let's revise the subject before we decide whether we prefer them to going it alone.

The two major types of managed funds are unit trusts and insurance products. Unit trusts are issued under a prospectus with trustee supervision and under the control of the Australian Securities and Investment Commission. The fact that a prospectus must be issued means more expense for the fund for a prospectus is costly to produce and has a life of only six months. They provide far more information to the investor than a life office brochure, however, this is not likely to influence the performance of the fund.

Life insurance products come under the control of the Insurance and Superannuation Commission, so investors do not have the added protection of a trustee nor do they receive the vast amount of information that is included in a prospectus.

Personally I don't regard the above differences as of great practical importance — the main difference between them is the tax treatment. A unit trust is not an entity for tax purposes and therefore pays no tax itself. It is merely a "funnel" that sends the taxable income to the unit holders by way of distributions. You will read more about this in Chapter 25 (Partnerships, Companies and Trusts).

Life insurance products, such as insurance bonds and superannuation policies, are tax paid investments and bonuses are declared only after the fund itself has paid its tax. You do not receive any income from life insurance products (unless you buy an annuity or an allocated pension) but almost all unit trusts will pay at least a small income which should be included in your tax return.

Fees Of Managed Funds

We all know that you get only what you pay for and can expect nothing for nothing. If you invest in a managed fund such as a unit trust or an insurance bond the fund pays certain fees to the managers, the people who run it. As you are a part owner of this fund it follows that you are the one who is ultimately paying for them.

Let's look at these fees in detail:

Entry Fees

Most managed funds still charge an entry fee and it is this fee which causes new investors the most concern. The fee varies with the time that a new investor could reasonably be expected to stay in the fund but you will find that funds whose main objective is to produce income have a lower fee than those that are expected to produce capital gain. Here are some examples:

Nil entry fee — Cash management trusts and debentures

2% entry fee — Income trusts

4% entry fee — Friendly society bonds, approved deposit funds and bond trusts.

5% to 6% entry fee — Insurance bonds and Equity trusts

Usually, a large proportion of the entry fee goes to the adviser who recommended the client place the business with the particular fund.

The fact that an adviser is entitled to receive a fee for placing business has led to allegations that advisers will recommend only funds that pay high commissions. I have discussed this criticism in depth in *Making Money Made Simple*. In any event some advisers are now rebating all brokerage to their clients and charging a fee instead. This fee is often worked on a sliding scale as a percentage of funds invested. For example it may be:

5% on the first $100,000

3% on the next $100,000

2.5% on the next $300,000

1.5% on the balance.

Investors need to watch these fees. Obviously it would be foolish to pay a 5% fee to the adviser when the total entry fee on a brokerage basis is 2%. Many advisers get around this apparent conflict by reverting to brokerage if the overall cost to the client is lower than the set fee plan I mentioned above. Don't be frightened to discuss the matter of fees with your adviser and raise any queries you may have.

Be aware that it takes a lot of money to run a proper financial advisory office and that an adviser has to be paid somehow. One of the main jobs of your adviser is to be there to provide you with on-going service and to do that, they will need to make a profit.

There is a trend towards no entry fee life assurance products but often the lack of an entry fee is paid for by higher internal charges against the fund. To confuse you even more, some companies give you the choice of paying an entry fee at the start or going in for no fee and having it deducted over the next few years.

Exit Fees

These are not common with unit trusts (except for some mortgage trusts) but are becoming increasingly popular in life insurance products such as "nil entry fee" insurance bonds and deferred annuities. These products still pay a brokerage[1] to the agent which is recouped by making internal charges in the fund earnings. The balance is recovered in whole or part from exit fees if the investor quits the fund before the prescribed time, which normally varies from three to five years.

Internal Fees

There are also fees charged within the fund which are often overlooked by investors as they tend to get buried in the small print. The following are some managers' fees from a variety of leading trusts selected at random.

Cash management trust: .75% per annum of the fund value

---

1 Usually around 3%.

Equity Trust A :	1.75% p.a. of the fund value plus an incentive fee of 25% of all returns over 20% p.a.
Equity Trust B :	1.5% p.a. of the fund value
Balanced Trust :	1.85% p.a. of the fund value
Insurance Bond A :	.728% p.a. of the fund value
Insurance Bond B :	.1.32% p.a. of the fund value

Unit trusts have fees to be paid to the trustee in addition to the manager's fees because the assets of investors in unit trusts have to be held by a recognised trustee company. These range from .077% p.a. to .125% p.a. Insurance company funds are not required to have a trustee so their products have no trustee fees.

As you can see the fees are substantial. However, don't be put off by that. Think of the old saying "Don't ask what it costs — ask what it's worth". When you invest in a managed fund, such as a unit trust, all the work is done for you. There are no repair bills to find, no rates to pay, no land tax returns to fill in, no long conferences with your stock broker, no credit checks to carry out, and no advertising or interviewing of tenants. The fund manager will even pay the money straight into your bank account for you.

Don't ask "Are the fees too high?" Ask "Am I getting value for the fees?".

The prices that you see quoted in the newspapers are the prices that the manager will pay you for your units, **under normal conditions**[2], within the time stated in the prospectus. Once you have sent in the request to redeem some or all of your money most funds will have a cheque to you within 14 days.

The Unit Price

This is another area which confuses almost everybody even though it is quite logical. Let's go through it now and get to understand it.

We'll start an imaginary fund to illustrate the principles involved. Assume that Dennis and Cheryl had $100 000 each to start their own fund. To keep track of their money they issued 200 000 units at a face value of $1.00 each. They started off by putting the money into a bank. The bank balance would be

---

2 If any institution suffers panic withdrawals and a "run" develops, a freeze may be placed on redemptions. This happened with Estate Mortgage.

$200 000 and the units remain at that value while the only asset of the fund is the $200 000 cash at bank.

They invest the lot into shares just before the stock market booms. Within eight months their shares are worth $300 000. Now their 200 000 units are worth $1.50 each. They invite their friend Peter to join them and he puts up $75 000 for which they issue 50 000 units at $1.50 each. The $75 000 is banked which increases the trust assets to $375 000. This is represented by 250 000 units at $1.50 each making a total value of $375 000 being $75 000 cash and $300 000 of shares.

The stock market falls and the shares drop to $225 000. Total assets are now $300 000 (shares $225 000 plus the $75 000 cash in the bank) and the 250 000 issued units are now worth $1.20. At this stage Dennis needs to withdraw $60 000 so he redeems 50 000 of his units at $1.20 each.

The fund assets are now:

Cash at bank	$ 15 000
Shares at market value	$225 000
TOTAL	$240 000

which are represented by 200 000 units at $1.20 each apportioned:

Dennis	50,000 units
Cheryl	100,000 units
Peter	50,000 units
TOTAL UNITS	200,000

Notice how everybody's share is still in balance and how simply and fairly the system works.

The unit prices for all the leading funds are quoted in most newspapers each Monday or Wednesday. There are two figures. The higher one (which includes the entry fee) is the one that new investors pay, the lower figure is the redemption value which is paid to investors withdrawing money. Notice that most fund managers have a range of funds so make sure you look at the one in which your money is invested. The first time you look up the figures you may find it confusing, but your adviser will guide you.

When Are Values Calculated?

The prospectus will state the basis of valuation. Equity trusts and bond trusts usually re-value at the close of business each day as the value of these funds can be easily and precisely determined. The valuation is done at the **close** of business each day to prevent unit holders who live in the major cities getting an advantage if the market falls suddenly. Some investors who lived in Sydney tried to

Manager/Fund	Exit Price $	Entry Price $	1 Yr Retn % pa	3 Yr Retn % pa	Manager/Fund
Advance Fund Management Ltd					DA Gateway Growth I
ADF Cap Fd	1.1929		3.05	3.24	DA No.2 Cap G'teed
ADF Cap Stab	2.5227	2.5353	-0.12	5.51	DA NO.2 Div Stable
ADF Cash	1.4127	1.4127	3.54	3.31	DA No.2 Managed
ADF Gth	1.4512		2.35	7.46	FIP Cap Gtd Ser 1
ADF Gth	2.9754	2.9992	5.01	10.37	FIP Div Stb Ser 1
AP RP Aust Sh	1.1707	1.2195	8.19		FIP G-way Aggressive
AP RP Aust Sh NEF	1.1597	1.1597	7.69		FIP Gateway Balanced
AP RP Cap Stbl	1.7656	1.8392	0.12	6.11	FIP Gateway Conserv.
AP RP Cap Stbl NEF	1.7178	1.7178	-0.38	5.58	FIP Gateway Growth
AP RP Mgd	2.0160	2.1000	3.55	8.82	FIP Mgd Ser 1
AP RP Mgd NEF	1.9646	1.9646	3.03	8.28	FIP No.2 Cap G'teed
AP RP Money Mkt	1.3585	1.3585	3.90	3.81	FIP No.2 Div Stable
Imp Fd	1.1364	1.1962	5.09	11.11	FIP No.2 Mngd Fund:
MultiFd Aust Bd	0.9923	1.0445	-5.96	3.75	Inv Bd Gway Aggress
MultiFd Aust Sh	1.4844	1.5625	2.93	9.59	Inv Bd Gway Aust Sh
MultiFd Fut Gth	1.1427	1.2028	0.99	7.17	Inv Bd Gway Balance
MultiFd Inc and Gth	1.2119	1.2757	1.98	7.71	Inv Bd Gway Conserv
MultiFd Inc Extra	1.0846	1.1417	-1.94	5.79	Inv Bd Gway Growth
MultiFd Int Shmkt	1.0221	1.0759	3.43	16.78	Inv Bnd Cap Gtd Ser
MultiFd Mthly Inc	0.9939	0.9939	3.15	3.85	Inv Bnd Div Stb Ser1
MultiFd Prop Sec	0.3876	0.4080	-6.62	4.60	Inv Bnd Mgd Ser 1
MultiFd Worldwide Sh	1.4461	1.5222	1.42	15.48	Inv Bnd No.2 Manag
PS RP Aust Sh	1.1750	1.2240	7.57		Inv Bond No.2 Cap C
PS RP Aust Sh NEF	1.1631	1.1631	7.05		Inv Bond No.2 Div S
PS RP Cap Stbl	1.6956	1.7663	1.18	5.60	Life DA Div Stb Ser1
PS RP Cap Stbl NEF	1.6550	1.6550	0.70	5.14	Life DA Mgd Ser 1
PS RP Int Sh	1.1233	1.1701	5.27		MaxiSafe DA
PS RP Int Sh NEF	1.1123	1.1123	4.77		Per Sup Cap Gtd Ser
PS RP Mgd	1.9226	2.0027	3.26	7.73	Per Sup No.2 Cap G
PS RP Mgd NEF	1.8719	1.8719	2.76	7.25	Per Sup No.2 Div Stl
PS RP Money Mkt	1.3496	1.3496	3.14	3.37	Per Sup No.2 Manag
PS RP Prop Sec	0.9834	1.0244	-5.46		Pers Sup D.Stb Ser 1
PS RP Prop Sec NEF	0.9737	0.9737	-5.92		Pers Sup Mgd Ser 1
Sup Plus Dep	1.3783	1.3783	2.86	3.54	PSB Gateway Aggr
Sup Plus Mgd	1.9417	1.9417	3.69	8.15	PSB Gateway Balance
***Advisor Asset Management**					PSB Gateway Consen
Ret Inc Balanced Pen	1.9208	1.9208	3.25	11.07	PSB Gateway Growth
Ret Inc Conserv Pen	1.6541	1.6541	1.62	7.50	RO DA Cap Gtd
Ret Inc Growth Pen	1.6173	1.6173	7.13	14.07	***ANZ Managed Inves**
Super Balanced	1.8939	1.8939	4.15	10.66	ADF Growth
Super Conservative	1.6461	1.6461	1.79	7.20	ADF Inc Accum

withdraw their funds DURING the day of the 1987 crash by going direct to the fund managers' offices.

How Safe Are Unit Trusts?

In this chapter we are discussing their advantages and limitations, but don't be concerned if it takes you a while to grasp it. Few investors seem to comprehend them completely and it is common to hear questions like "Is a trust a safe thing to invest in?". This question shows a total lack of understanding, for anybody who appreciated the unit trust concept would ask "What type of risk is involved with this particular trust?"

A unit trust is not some complex device but is merely a legal structure that enables investors with relatively small investment funds to participate in the kind of investment that may be beyond the capacity of them as individuals. The main elements for any investor to think about are the skill and reputation of the trust manager together with the area in which the trust assets will be invested.

Because trusts normally keep a cash reserve to meet redemptions, it has become customary to treat investments in them as fairly liquid and unit holders have become used to being able to cash in all or part of their investment within two or three weeks. This flexibility of being able to withdraw part of the investment at short notice is one of the outstanding features of unit trusts.

However, as we have seen with Estate Mortgage, this ready cashability cannot be guaranteed if the trust is investing in assets that are not capable of fast realisation. In July 1990, several unlisted property trusts were forced to place a freeze on redemptions following the investor panic that arose after the Estate Mortgage collapse and the public airing of the problems of OST and Pyramid Building Society.

This freeze was to prevent a minority of nervous investors withdrawing funds from the trusts thus creating a liquidity crisis which could have the eventual result of forcing the trusts to sell prime property at "fire sale" prices. Obviously this would be to the detriment of all unit holders in the trust.

This should not be a cause for alarm but I make the comment so investors will be aware that unit trusts are merely providing an avenue that enables some investors to do the same thing that others are doing, by themselves, without the use of the trust structure. The investor who invests directly in assets such as mortgages, debentures, Government Bonds or property has no guarantee that these investments may be quickly cashed at face value and thus is no better off than the unit holder. Once this fact is understood the mystique surrounding trusts should vanish.

Remember that a trust has no magical power to gild an investment such as shares, mortgages or property with qualities that direct investment in the same areas does not possess. Therefore investors in all managed funds should study the underlying assets before becoming involved with them. This is of particular importance in a depressed market.

Think about two top flight property or equity trusts. One may be fully invested while the other is holding at least 40% of its assets in cash. The one with the cash is beautifully placed to snap up any bargains that come on the market and will fall much less than the fully invested fund if the market crashes. On the other hand the fully invested fund will benefit most from a sudden market upsurge.

It's Your Decision

Only you can decide whether you prefer direct investment, managed funds or a combination of both. After reading this book, and having completed the quiz in the next chapter, you should be better placed to make an educated decision.

Many people fear loss of control with managed funds and are also put off by the fact that some managed funds have got into difficulties. However, once you analyse why some investors lost money in managed funds you should be able to assess the risks of any proposed managed fund investment provided you use a competent adviser with good research facilities.

The main risks in managed funds are:

(1) Loss of value when the share market falls. This will happen whether you invest in managed funds or on your own. If you can't handle that, stay out of the share market.

(2) Loss of capital because a "lender" type fund (mortgage trust or debenture) has lent to bad credit risks. This risk is handled by spreading your money between different funds and choosing only the ones that have been approved by the research source of your adviser.

(3) Loss of capital because the managed fund was a highly speculative one such as a film scheme or an agricultural scheme. Be aware that you should not invest in these areas with money you cannot afford to lose.

(4) Loss of capital because a property trust in which you invested incurred losses because it was involved in a risky project such as a large development. A safeguard is knowing what projects the trust is involved in.

(5) Loss of capital, because of our dollar rising in value, when you invest in a trust with international exposure such as an international equity trust or a resource trust. This risk is ever present with direct or indirect investment in these areas. In any event one of the main purposes for investing in the international area is to give yourself a hedge against our dollar falling.

19

Test Yourself

Should You Be In Managed Funds?

Experience is the name everybody gives to their mistakes.

OSCAR WILDE

In the investment world the debate goes on continually — do you get better returns by having your own property and shares, or should you be in managed funds such as property trusts and equity trusts? There is no correct answer, as so much depends on the ability and temperament of the investor. I have no doubt that direct investment will provide the best returns for about 5% of the population, but these are capable and experienced operators who devote heaps of time and energy into research and management.

The majority of investors have neither the time, nor the talent, to achieve consistently high returns through direct investment and will do better in managed funds.

The following quiz, although a little light-hearted, will help you decide which course of action is most suited for you.

QUESTION A: You go to the mail box and pick up a large envelope from a company in which you own shares. It is marked "This envelope contains important documents". Inside are various documents and a glossy booklet marked "Prospectus".

Do you:

(1) Break into a cold sweat, wonder what it all means, and ask your neighbour or bank manager to help you understand it.

(2) Phone your stockbroker to discuss the proposal and ask for guidance.

(3) Read the proposal, analyse the information and make your own decision.

QUESTION B: It's a fine Saturday morning. Would you rather:

(1) Spend the day driving around looking for undervalued property to buy.

(2) Get up early and play golf or tennis.

(3) Lie in bed as late as possible.

QUESTION C: When the paper arrives do you turn first to:

(1) The general news.

(2) The sports section.

(3) The property and finance pages.

QUESTION D: The hot water system at home fails.

Do you:

(1) Look up the yellow pages and call a company whose advertisement looks good.

(2) Obtain three quotes and then bargain with the lowest bidder.

(3) Fix it yourself.

QUESTION E: Your spouse or partner suggests you sell your present home and move into an old house in which you can spend the weekends and evenings renovating.

Is your reaction:

(1) Divorce has got to be better than this idea.

(2) How soon do we start?

(3) The idea doesn't thrill me but I'm prepared to make the sacrifice if there is the chance of a good profit.

QUESTION F: You arrive at your rental house to collect the arrears of rent and find a tearful tenant holding a week-old baby. She tells you her de facto husband has just left her for somebody else and she has no money and no chance of getting any for at least two months.

Do you:

(1) Take her and the baby home to your place and give them free board.

(2) Tell her you will let her off paying any rent for two months.

(3) Feel sorry for her but tell her if the arrears are not brought up to date within a week you will take eviction proceedings.

QUESTION G: A prime vacant block is put up for auction in your suburb.

Do you:

(1) Have a good idea of what price it should sell for.

(2) Feel it might be a good buy because you have read in the papers there is a boom going on at present.

(3) Ignore it.

QUESTION H: Is the secret of real estate wealth:

(1) Buying any property available and holding on to it.

(2) Buying well located property and taking steps to increase its value.

(3) Marrying somebody wealthy.

QUESTION I: You hold a portfolio of good shares and hear on the radio at noon that the Australian stock market has crashed by 30% that morning.

Do you:

(1) Ring your stock broker and tell him to sell everything.

(2) Go to see your stock broker immediately and discuss buying more shares.

(3) Take little notice of the news as you are a long term holder.

QUESTION J: You are buying an investment property and borrowing most of the purchase price. The bank manager tells you that there is fixed interest money available but urges you to take a variable rate as "we hear that rates are trending downwards".

Do you:

(1) Shop around other institutions to see what they can offer.

(2) Take the variable rate.

(3) Take the fixed rate for an initial two year term.

QUESTION K: You meet a friend in the street who tells you that he has just been speaking to a friend of a geologist from a well known mining company. The geologist has said the company is about to announce an oil strike. Do you:

(1) Sell your house and use the entire proceeds to buy shares in the company.

(2) Buy a couple of thousand dollars worth.

(3) Ignore the information.

QUESTION L: A young couple apply to rent your investment house. They tell you they have had trouble finding a place to rent because of a bad credit rating which was not their fault. They appear to be decent types.

Do you:

(1) Investigate their credit record thoroughly and then make an informed decision.

(2) Take them on face value and give them a six months lease.

(3) Have no idea how to check their credit record.

QUESTION M: How many hours a week are you prepared to devote to doing your own investing.

(1) At least 12.

(2) About three.

(3) Less than two.

ANSWERS: Don't forget to tick your score for each question and find the total at the end.

A.

1. 0 — You can't do it on your own
2. 1 — You know enough to seek proper guidance
3. 2 — It sounds as if you are at home in the stock market

B.

1. 2 — You like to do it yourself
2. 1 — Golf is much more fun than looking at property
3 0 — You don't want to do it on your own

C.

1 1 — You have a broad enquiring mind
2 0 — Why waste time on making money
3 2 — You have a special field of interest

D.

1 0 — There are better things to do than fiddle with repairs
2 2 — You've got the makings of a good property owner
3 2 — You enjoy DIY

E.

1 0 — Why spend your life doing something you hate
2 2 — What a well matched pair
3 1 — At least you will have a go

F.

1 0 — You are a nice person in the wrong business
2 0 — Who pays your mortgage for those two months?
3 2 — You are an experienced landlord.

G.

1 2 — And so you should if you want to be in the property business
2 0 — Stay away from it — you've missed out on the boom
3 0 — Good for you — you are honest about your fields of experience and interest

H.

1 0 — This is a fallacy
2 2 — This is the secret of wealth
3 0 — This is also the secret of wealth even if it may not be the way to happiness. Obviously you prefer somebody else to make your money for you.

I.

1 0 — You should not be in the stockmarket
2 2 — A good rational approach
3 2 — You are obviously "old money" or a skilled investor

J.

1 2 — You know the rules of the game

2 0 — You have to be joking!

3 1 — You are learning

K.

1 0 — You are not safe to let out in the street

2 1 — You like a bit of a gamble

3 2 — You have heard it all before

L

1 2 — That's the best way to go

2 0 — You may be headed for big problems

3 0 — You are certainly headed for big problems

M.

1 2 — You will need it

2 1 — You will be pushing

3 0 — What makes you think it's so easy?

Results

18 to 26 points. You should do well on your own — you probably are now.

12 to 18 points. You should probably stick with managed investments but you should be able to manage an investment house or a few shares of your own.

Less than 12 points. Don't even try to do it on your own. Stick with managed funds.

20

The Dollar Cost Averaging Process

Wealth is the product of man's capacity to think.

AYN RAND

The technique of dollar cost averaging has been used for a long time, but I have found most investors don't know much about it, and never think to use it. It's worth studying because it is a great strategy for those who are unsure which way the market is heading — and that's all of us! It was initially used in share trading, but works just as well with equity trusts or market-linked insurance bonds, as they can be bought in small parcels.

Remember that very few people know the right time to enter and leave a market. Certainly there are plenty of predictions made, and many boast about the time they picked it perfectly, but you never hear about all the other times they got it wrong. The dollar cost averaging process is simple, it works, and it enables an investor to do well in a rising or falling market.

It is a procedure that consists of investing a fixed sum, on a regular basis, into the same product. If you do this you will always be buying units at an average **cost** which is lower than their average **price** over the investment period.

Assume you put $2 000 a year for five years into a market-linked investment such as an equity trust or a market-linked insurance bond. Further assume that during that period the market fell by 80% before recovering to its original starting point. At the end of the five years your position would be:

	Year 1	Year 2	Year 3	Year 4	Year 5
INVESTMENT	$2 000	2 000	2 000	2 000	2 000
UNIT PRICE PAID	$10	$4	$2	$6	$10
UNITS BOUGHT	200	500	1 000	333	200

Notice your total outlay is $10 000 and after five years you own 2 233 units at $10 each with a total value of $22 333. Thus your investment has appreciated by 123.3% (that's a whopping 28.1% a year compound) at a time when the market has been in a slump. All the price did was fall from $10 to $2 and recover to $10 again.

Look first at your average **cost** over the period. You bought a total of 2 233 units for a total outlay of $10 000 so the average cost of your 2 233 units is $4.40 a unit. (2 233 x $4.48 = $10 000).

The average **price** per unit over the same period is the total investment divided by the number of years. i.e. $32/5 = $6.40. The average **cost** per unit is always lower than the average **price** no matter whether the market is rising or falling provided the investment is consistent.

Why does this method work? Because if you keep up your regular investment you get larger numbers of units as the price falls. Thus you acquire your biggest parcel at the bottom of the market so when the market eventually rises you will make your first profit on the largest number of units.

The Noel Whittaker Wealth Creator on CD-ROM contains an interactive module on dollar cost averaging. It allows you to enter a monthly investment amount, and then choose a monthly starting and finishing date between 1 January 1980 and 31 December 1997. The program will then tell you the value of your investment at the finishing month if the performance of your investment matched the All Ordinaries Accumulation Index. For example, if you invested $250 a month from April 1984 to November 1996, you would have accumulated $87 033 for a total investment of $38 000. This is a compound return of 11.68% per annum.

Reducing Your Average Cost

Another method is to buy more units at a lower price to reduce your average cost. Suppose you bought 10 000 units at $1.20 and the price fell to 25 cents. Another investment of $12 000 would give

First Payment	APR	1984
Final Payment	NOV	1996
Investment amount per month		$250
Calculate	Press 'Calculate' to see the results.	
Total Investment		$38 000
Total value of portfolio		$87 033
Average Price over term		$5.13
Average Cost over term		$4.31
Compound gain per year		11.68%

you a further 48 000 units for a total of 58 000 units for a total cost of $24 000. Average cost would be 41 cents a unit. You have now made a profit when the price recovers to 41 cents instead of waiting till it hits $1.20. If the price fell further you could buy more at an even lower price and reduce your average still further.

Here is something you must **note carefully**. This technique will work **only** if prices eventually recover. We therefore recommend it for top quality units/shares or those that are linked to the index for, based on history, you can be sure it will recover to a spot greater than its previous best.

Summing Up

This process is a superb strategy if you are certain the price will eventually recover as you are buying the largest volume at the lowest price. Do NOT use it for speculative investments because all you are doing is pouring good money after bad if their price never comes back.

It works well as part of a savings plan if you are using the techniques of the "Guaranteed Secret of Wealth" I described in *Making Money Made Simple*.

21

Understanding Risk

If you pay peanuts you get monkeys.

SIR JAMES GOLDSMITH

In this chapter we'll discuss risk so that you will have a better appreciation of what the word means, and how it applies to investment. Clients often ask, with a slightly scared look, "Is this investment risky?" They usually mean "Will I get my money back" as if it's like having a bet on a race. This is the wrong way to approach risk, but you should appreciate the word "risk" in our industry has several meanings. Some of them are:

(1) You might lose all your money.

(2) You might lose part of your money.

(3) You might have achieved better returns had you invested elsewhere.

(4) You might find the value of your investments fluctuate.

(5) The Government might change the laws.

Let's look at them now but, before we do, bear in mind that **every** investment has a risk. **Your** job is to understand the risk that goes with each investment, and decide if you can handle it.

Beware of those who tell you what you **should** have done based on an examination of past performance; anybody can make sound decisions **after** the event. The investment world is not as simple as that, for it is forever changing. It was easier to make money in the 1980's than it was in the 1970's, and the 1990's turned out to be a period of both challenge and opportunity.

In Australia the first decade of the new millennium will be a challenging and exciting one because:

- The imputation system introduced in 1987 has had the effect of creating a floor under the prices of quality shares that pay franked dividends.

- The massive amounts of money being transferred to savings by the compulsory superannuation schemes are generating billions of dollars that are going to be invested, instead of being spent on consumer items. The logical home for a large part of these funds is the stock market.
- The "baby boomers" who were born between 1946 and 1964 will be looking to retire with far more money than their parents could have imagined.
- The capital gains tax introduced in late 1985 is now affecting a greater number of investments. By removing the anomalies of the tax it replaced[1], capital gains tax has permitted many investors to make profits that are **guaranteed** free of tax. Investors are now free to switch between investments knowing precisely the amount of their capital gains tax liability (if any).
- International investment will increase because of deregulation, and because investors will become educated about the possibilities of diversification offered by international funds.

The result of all these changes is a new "game" with different rules and one in which all the players are likely to make some wrong moves. By understanding risk you can help to ensure that any damage from a wrong move is minimised.

Two Basic Investment Areas

Funds invested fall into two categories:

(1) "Lending" money to an institution such as a bank, building society or mortgage trust who in turn lends it to borrowers at a higher rate of interest. There is no capital growth. The danger here is **credit risk.**

(2) "Investing" money in areas like property, gold or shares where one of the aims is for the value to increase. The dangers here are **market risk** and **opportunity risk**.

Credit Risk

Credit risk is the chance that the institution to whom you lend money will be unable to pay it back. This may be caused by dishonesty, bad management or because one or more of their

1 The tax that applies to assets purchased prior to September 19, 1985 is discussed in detail in *Making Money Made Simple*.

borrowers have defaulted and the underlying value of the security is insufficient to discharge the debt. Leading examples of losses because of credit risk are Cambridge Credit and Estate Mortgage. Cambridge Credit had its money tied up in unsaleable vacant land and Estate Mortgage had too many non-performing loans.

The cure for credit risk is to use substantial corporations that have been recommended, in writing, by your investment adviser and to spread your money between different companies so that if one does get into trouble it doesn't take all your money with it. I am amazed how often our television stations feature people who have lost their life savings by investing the **whole lot** with one institution.

By asking your adviser to put all recommendations in writing you put yourself into a position to take legal action if you lose money in a "capital guaranteed" investment, or if a "safe" mortgage trust goes broke.

Lending bodies make their profit by borrowing money from one group of people and lending it out to others. Naturally they want to borrow it as cheaply as possible, and lend it out at the highest rate the market will bear. The rates being offered to borrowers increase as the standing of the lending body decreases. Therefore the better the reputation and credit rating of the lending institution, the less they have to offer to depositors.

Consequently the lower rated institutions have to charge more and their borrowers are more likely to be those who are forced to pay a higher rate as they have trouble borrowing from the higher ranked organisations. This is why the chance of your losing your money increases as the rate of return rises.

Market Risk

This relates to a situation where you have bought an asset and its value drops. The asset may be anything from a bar of gold to a share in BHP; the nature of it makes it subject to the ebb and flow of market forces.

You protect yourself against market risk by recognising that any asset that has the potential to rise in value may also fall in value, and then by not putting all your funds into one area. If you do suffer a drop in price you may consider the averaging technique described in the previous chapter but **only** if you believe the asset is almost certain to rise in price.

All investments that include bonds, shares or property have the potential to suffer falls in value yet these areas have historically shown the best returns over the medium to long term. This is what the term "risk versus reward" means. If the best returns were available in prime fixed interest investments, there would be no point in taking a higher risk by going into property and shares.

Written recommendations from an adviser should clearly state that investments that are prone to "market risk" may fall in value as well as rise.

Opportunity Risk

Mark buys $30 000 of shares and Peter buys a block of land for the same price. After two years the shares are still worth $30 000 and the land is worth $45 000. Mark has lost the **opportunity** to achieve two years earnings on his $30 000 and has thus suffered opportunity risk.

It is difficult to eliminate opportunity risk as capital gain cannot be guaranteed; nobody goes into an investment expecting it to do nothing. Thorough research before making the commitment may help to prevent the problem, and on-going monitoring of the performance may help you to say "enough" after a decent period and act to withdraw your funds and look for greener pastures. If you follow my suggestion of writing down the reasons you entered into the investment, it may help you to make a decision to retain or sell.

Inflation

Inflation is a disease that sneaks up on you. Usually you notice it when you stumble across some old papers and stand gaping at the prices of houses or cars 10 years ago. The way to prevent inflation is to invest part of your funds in assets that are likely to show capital growth, and thus enable your money to grow in line with inflation.

Retirees should note that house costs and mortgage payments are built into the official inflation figures, and that their own cost of living might not rise nearly as quickly as the Consumer Price Index. It is thus important for retirees to seek security above all else, and possibly to be overweight in cash type investments at the expense of capital growth.

Legislative Risk

Governments are continually changing the rules and today's perfect financial plan may be obsolete on Budget night. Luckily our Government seems to have learned the lesson about the folly of retrospective legislation, which is why we now have such a range of confusing transitional measures.

About the only way to guard against legislative risk is to stay as flexible as is possible, always seek expert advice about your affairs and make sure your investments are monitored on a regular basis. This applies particularly in the areas of superannuation and roll-over funds which are discussed in depth in *Living Well In Retirement.*

Risk In Lack Of Flexibility

An investment plan needs to stay flexible for the following reasons:

(1) **People's needs and situations change.** A family may give birth to children who will need education in the future, retirement may result in a change of home, while loss of a job or ill-health may wipe out cash reserves.

(2) **The rules are almost certain to change.** In the last 12 years we have witnessed the introduction of capital gains tax, dividend imputation, compulsory superannuation schemes, the abolition and restoration of negative gearing, reasonable benefit limits on roll-over funds and the deregulation of the Australian financial system. How can we believe the changes are over?

(3) **The financial cycles change.** In the 1980's share prices and interest rates fluctuated, while property turned in a mixed performance. To be locked into an investment area is to put yourself in danger of missing out on better opportunities as they occur.

(4) **The best performing funds change.** Investors tend to follow the best performing managers, but it is a sad fact that this year's top performer is often in the bottom quartile next year. In the late 1980's three of the top performing superannuation funds were Scottish Amicable, Capita and Pittsburgh National. Now all three are no more, as they have merged or been taken over.

Risk Of Choosing A Wrong Time Frame

The "capital growth" assets such as quality shares and property should show good consistent performance if held for long enough.

However, investors who invest in these areas for too short a period may suffer a loss if they are forced to redeem at the wrong time.

As a rough guide use:

TIME FRAME	INVESTMENT
1 to 2 years	Cash type investments
2 to 3 years	Capital Guaranteed or Capital Secure
3 to 5 years	Managed investments such as insurance bonds, and income and combined units of property trusts.
5 years and upwards	Growth investments such as shares and property, equity trusts and growth units of split trusts

Certainly there is no guarantee that a market will recover in any given time frame, but investors who buy quality assets and hold them for the long term have a high probabilty of achieving satisfactory results.

Risk Or Volatility

The term risk can also mean volatility which is the degree that the price of a share moves around. There is a term "beta factor" used in investment circles which indicates the degree that a given share's prices move against the index. The index, by definition, has a beta factor of 1.0 so if a share has a beta factor of 2.0 we know that it is twice as volatile as the market. Analysts use a model called the Sharpe Index that is able to measure risk relative to return for any portfolio of investments.

In theory the higher risk (more volatile) portfolios should show higher returns than low risk portfolios, but look at the following "risk/reward" table which shows that a low risk manager can be a high performer, or a high risk manager can be a poor performer.

The left hand vertical column measures return and the bottom horizontal column records volatility. Fund Manager C is the worst performer because he has achieved the worst return while taking the most risk. Contrast C's performance with that of Fund

Manager A who has managed to pull off the jackpot — the highest return coupled with lowest risk!

Depending on market timing a low risk manager may also achieve better cash results than a high risk manager. Compare a conservative fund which earned 20% in the first year and minus 4% in the second, with an aggressive one that earned 100% in the first year and minus 50% in the second. On first glance you may think the second one would do best, but if you invested $1 000 with each at the beginning of the first year you would now have $1 152 in the first fund and $1 000 in the second.

This is **not** a recommendation that you avoid high risk (volatile) investments but rather an effort to show you that a high risk investment need not outperform a low risk one.

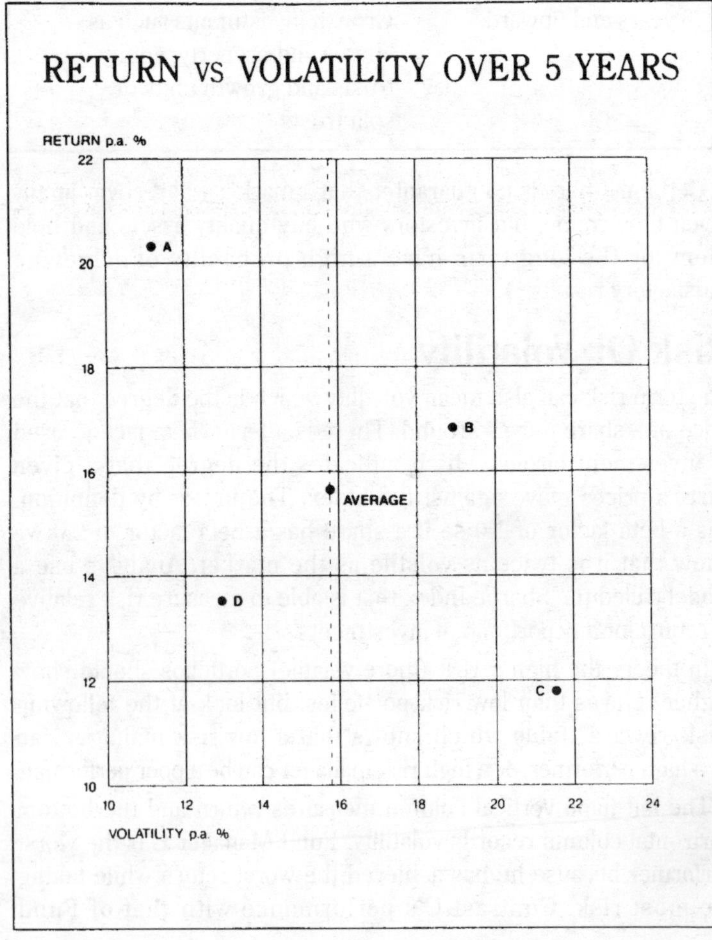

Risk Of Non-Diversification

Reams have been written about the need to diversify and not have all your eggs in the one basket, but many investors end up with no diversification because all they have is a lot of similar baskets. Examples are people whose whole investment portfolio consists of suburban rental houses, or who are entirely invested in industrial shares, or who have cash type deposits with at least four different banks and building societies. It is also common to see investment advisers spread a client's money over four equity trusts who have precisely the same approach to investment. This is **not** diversification.

The table shows the annual returns for the main asset classes for the 17 years ended 30 June 1999. Notice how the best performing areas have changed over the period as the economy moves through its cycles. This shows the virtue of diversification, for nobody can consistently pick the right time to enter and leave the market. By spreading your money

MARKET RETURNS Period ending: June 99

	Aust Shares	Aust Fixed Interest	Int'l Shares	Int'l Fixed Interest	Aust Listed Property	Cash
1983	35	21	73	44	24	14
1984	13	18	2	2	35	13
1985	37	13	62	56	12	16
1986	42	17	55	40	24	15
1987	54	13	33	16	41	13
1988	-9	17	-10	14	-3	13
1989	4	6	18	17	-2	16
1990	4	16	2	14	15	18
1991	6	22	-2	15	8	13
1992	13	22	7	15	15	9
1993	10	14	32	14	17	6
1994	18	-1	0	1	10	5
1995	6	12	14	13	8	7
1996	16	9	7	11	4	8
1997	27	16	29	12	29	7
1998	2	11	42	11	10	5
1999	15	3	10	5	4	5
17 yr return	16	13	20	17	14	11

Source: Macquarie Bank

around you have the opportunity for at least some of it to participate in a sector that is performing well.

Capital Guaranteed?

The crash of 1987 led many investors to flee to the security of "capital guaranteed" investments and away from "market linked" ones where values could rise and fall in line with the stock market. The size of the rush to capital guaranteed is indicated by the fact that in 1987 just over two billion dollars went into this area, but for 1989 it was almost seven billion dollars. As a result, the Insurance and Superannuation Commissioner issued stringent guide-lines (Circular 273) to take effect from June 30, 1989 to ensure the solvency of life offices issuing capital guarantees.

Previously there was a broad requirement that assets must exceed liabilities, but the new provisions put such a strain on reserves that many life offices closed their capital guaranteed funds to the entry of new money. In lieu they started "capital stable" or "capital secure" funds where the money was invested in areas such as fixed interest securities, the money market, and possibly a few prime shares. Although there was no guarantee from the life office, the nature of the investments meant that the policy holder was much less subject to market risk or credit risk.

Clients regularly say to us "I want everything to be capital guaranteed" and then often find it hard to understand that few investments **can** be capital guaranteed.

There is no guarantee if you buy property or shares, either directly or through property and equity trusts, and the only guarantee carried by government bonds is that you will receive the face value at maturity and the scheduled interest along the way. The main investments left are interest-bearing deposits with highly regarded institutions, or insurance products that carry a guarantee from a major life office.

Certainly the term "capital guarantee" gives investors a warm feeling that they will not lose any of their capital, but the question to ask is "Is the price worth paying?". The irony is that the capital guaranteed funds are backed by the same cash, property and shares that back the market-linked funds so should give a similar return over a long period. The rates declared on the capital guaranteed funds are calculated by deducting a **premium** from the market-linked returns. Thus by their very nature, market-linked funds **must** provide better returns over time than capital stable funds, which in turn should outperform capital guaranteed ones.

What Is A Reasonable Return?

This depends on the type of investment and the amount of risk you wish to take. However, all returns are not the same. Consider the following investments, each providing returns of 10% a year:

	Bank a/c	**Share**	**House**
Growth	Nil	6%	5%
Income	10%	4%	5%
TOTAL RETURN	10%	10%	10%

Now assume that each investment is worth $100 000 and that Taxpayer A earns $70 000 a year, while Taxpayer B earns $9 000 a year. Capital gains tax is calculated as if the assets were sold just over a year after acquisition, although this is unlikely in practice, and buying and selling costs are ignored. I appreciate the rates may be unrealistic at the time you read this but the example has one aim only. That is to show how rates can differ because of the nature of the investment and tax bracket of the investor. It accentuates the different tax treatments of interest income, franked dividends and realised capital growth.

TAXPAYER A

	Bank a/c	**Share**	**House**
Growth	Nil	6 000	5 000
Income	10 000	4 000	5 000
	10 000	10 000	10 000
Income Tax	4 850	780	2 425
Cap Gains Tax	nil	970	1212
Net Return	5 150	8 250	6 363

TAXPAYER B

	Bank a/c	**Share**	**House**
Growth	Nil	6 000	5 000
Income	10 000	4 000	5 000
	10 000	10 000	10 000
Income Tax	1 700	743 Cr	850
Cap Gains Tax	nil	340	425
Net Return	8 300	10 403	8 725

Notice how the imputation credit from the franked dividends reduces the tax on the other income and how shares have provided the best after tax return. This is because the shares are a higher-risk investment. The only one of the three categories above that can **guarantee** the return in advance is the bank account, and then only if you are prepared to contract with the bank to leave your money for a 12-month term. This is why the bank account provides the lowest return for it carries the least risk.

How Much Return?

It is impossible to predict long-term future returns accurately because they depend on the everchanging mix of prevailing interest rates, world economic cycles, the rate of inflation and the level of the currency. However, in Australia it seems that an overall return of around 8% to 12% a year from property and share-based investments is realistic. My premise is based on the fact that our long-term inflation is likely to be around 2% and both shares and property may appreciate at around the inflation rate plus about two to four per cent.

This gives a capital gain of between four and six per cent. Add to this a yield that varies from four per cent to nine per cent for quality property and shares and you have a total return of between 8% and 15%. Usually a low yield is coupled with higher growth, and a higher yield with lower growth, so an overall rate of 8% to 12% is reasonable. As we saw in the example above a large part of this return can be tax free if you arrange your affairs properly.

Higher tax-free returns with a reasonable degree of safety can be achieved through negative gearing; a topic that is covered in detail later. You will notice when you read those sections that the effectiveness of negative gearing depends on the investor's marginal tax rate, the interest rate on funds borrowed, the net yield from the asset and the amount of capital growth. If these four elements are favourable tax-free returns of between 15% and 22% a year are realistic. Note, once again, that the higher returns come with a higher degree of risk.

Conclusion

I hope by now you realise why few investments can be described as "capital guaranteed" and why investors pay a high price for investing in capital guaranteed areas. It is impossible to eliminate risk, but by taking the trouble to understand the underlying characteristics of investments you can choose a risk that is appropriate for your own situation.

Now we change course and move on to the fascinating subject of saving tax.

22

Ways To Cut Your Tax

The race is not always to the swift, nor the battle to the strong, but that's the way to bet.

DAMON RUNYON

People's reaction to paying tax is hard to understand. Wage and salary earners seldom complain about having tax deducted from their income but everybody, including wage and salary earners, screams loudly if they have to write out a cheque to pay tax.

So let's agree that nobody likes paying tax. Now instead of wasting time complaining about it we can look for some legal solutions to save it. Believe me there **are** solutions, for we have found that most tax problems are caused by bad budgeting, wrong structuring or inappropriate investments. These can usually be readily rectified.

In this chapter we will discuss ways to minimise tax legally, but first heed a warning. Make sure you talk to your financial adviser and your accountant **before** you try to put some of the more sophisticated ones into practice.

Weapon One – Practise Deferral

It is better to pay tax at some time in the future than **now** for three reasons:

1. You are using future or devalued dollars when you eventually pay it. These are worth less than today's dollars.
2. You have the use of the money which should have been paid to the Tax Office.
3. When the tax is due to be paid you can sometimes arrange your finances so you are in a lower tax bracket that year. Thus you pay tax at a lower rate.

Interest-Bearing Acounts

An easy way to defer tax is to invest your money in a term deposit, or similar account, with the interest payable after June 30. This transfers the interest income from the current year to the following year, and reduces tax for the current year. This works well for people who are retiring in that next year, as their taxable incomes may be drastically reduced.

Another factor to consider is that our marginal tax rates are trending downwards, so you may strike it lucky and find that tax rates are lower in the year to which you defer the income.

Roll Over Funds

These investments are covered in detail in *Living Well in Retirement,* but note that by rolling over a lump sum you defer all lump sum tax till any withdrawals are made. When money is withdrawn the only lump sum tax payable is that on the amount withdrawn. Tax on money left in rollover funds may be deferred till age 65, when the investment must be withdrawn, and tax paid, or converted to an eligible annuity or an allocated pension.

No lump sum tax is payable if the lump sum is converted to an annuity or allocated pension or if the holder dies before reaching age 65.

Better still, the sum that may be received tax free (the first $105 843 for people aged 55 or over) is being increased each year by Average Weekly Earnings. This figure is expected to be four per cent a year. When you leave the money in the rollover fund you postpone the lump sum tax to a time when the tax will be lower and the tax-free portion greater. This is particularly important for people approaching 55, because the tax on the first $105 843 of the post 1983 component will be nil if cashed in after 55, but taxed at 20% flat plus Medicare levy if cashed before the 55th birthday.

Assets Subject To Capital Gains Tax

You must appreciate the importance of timing when cashing in assets subject to capital gains tax.

Capital gains tax is not triggered until an asset is sold, so tax can be deferred indefinitely if there is no sale. If a sale happens, the amount of capital gains tax depends on the length of time the asset has been held, when it was acquired, and the income of the owner in **the year of sale**. The rules changed on 21 September 1999 and there are now three separate classes of assets for CGT purposes.

1. Acquired before 19 September 1985 – free of CGT.

2. Assets acquired before 21 September 1999 – provided you have owned the asset for at least a year, you have the option of paying CGT on the whole gain less an allowance for inflation, or CGT on 50% of the gain but with no allowance for inflation.

   EXAMPLE: *An asset is bought for $120 000 on May 1, 1990 and sold in March 2000 for $164 000 after all costs. The inflation-adjusted cost is $144 000. Therefore the owner has the option of paying CGT on $24 000 (being 100% of the difference between the inflation-adjusted cost and the selling price) or CGT on $22 000 (being 50% of the difference between $164 000 and $120 000).*

3. Assets acquired after 21 September 1999 – provided you have owned the asset for at least a year, you pay CGT on 50% of the gain, with no allowance for inflation.

Note that no concession is allowed unless the asset has been owned for a year.

EXAMPLE: *An asset was bought for $100 000 on July 1, 2000 and sold on June 28, 2001 for $120 000. CGT is payable on the whole gain of $20 000 as less than a year has taken place since purchase. If the sale was deferred till July 1 CGT would be payable on only $10 000 as the taxpayer would be entitled to the 50% concession.*

If the capital gain is fairly small, you can save CGT by trying to effect the disposal of the asset to a year when your income is lower.

EXAMPLE: *You retire on June 30, 2000 and your taxable income for that year was $75 000. To pay for the replacement of your car you wish to sell some shares, which will trigger a capital gain of $30 000. If you cashed them in while you were still working CGT would be $7 050. By waiting till after retirement, when your income is $25 000, you move the capital gain into the 30% tax bracket and pay CGT of only $4 500.*

Weapon Two: Tax Effective Investments

Tax can be saved by using investments that have an in-built tax advantage. The main ones are:

(1) Investments where the tax is paid by the fund itself, at a lower rate than that paid by the investor.

(2) Listed property trusts whereby part of the income may be tax free or tax deferred.

(1) Tax Paid Investments

The main ones are insurance bonds, friendly society bonds and superannuation/rollover funds. These have been covered in detail in *Making Money Made Simple* but it won't hurt to go over them again briefly. In all these investments the fund pays the tax — for insurance bonds and friendly society bonds it should be between 20% and 30%, and for superannuation/rollover funds it is between nil and 15%.

Be aware of the way tax differs when you withdraw monies from these funds. The accruing bonuses on insurance bonds and friendly society bonds are tax free if the bonds are kept for 10 years, whereas funds held in superannuation or rollover funds may have a lump sum tax on exit.

Tax-paid funds offer investors with high taxable incomes the opportunity to place money in areas where the tax being paid by the fund is less than their own marginal rate. Obviously the attractiveness declines as the investors' marginal tax rate falls.

(2) Property Securities Trusts

Income from property often has a tax-free component because of depreciation and building allowances. If you invest in a property securities trust that invests in a range of listed property trusts up to 30% of the income may be tax free. To see the effectiveness of this let's compare a bank deposit yielding 5% per annum with a property securities trust, which at time of writing had returned 9% per annum growth and 6.6% per annum income for the last two years.

For this example, to be conservative, I have used income of 5% per annum (of which 30% is tax free) and growth of 2% per annum.

EXAMPLE: *Let's assume that $100 000 is invested in each investment and the investor has a marginal tax rate of 47%.*

Bank deposit:	Income	5 000 (at 5%)
	less tax	2 350
	Net return	2 650 (or 2.65%)

Property securities trust

Income	5 000 (at 5%)
less tax on taxable portion	1 645 (47% of $3 500)
Net income	3 355
plus after tax capital gain	1530*
Total after tax return	4 885 (4.88%)

* CGT will be $470 if the units are kept for at least 12 months. This is calculated at 47% of 50% of the gross capital gain of $2 000.

Weapon Three: Income Splitting

Income splitting saves tax when the parties involved are in different tax brackets. It involves rearranging the investments so that the income comes to the individual in the lowest tax bracket.

EXAMPLE: *Harry earns $70 000 a year and his wife Carmel earns $10 000 a year. They have $125 000 in term deposits returning $10 000 a year. If this money is in Harry's name tax will be $4 700, and in joint names $3 200. However, if the money was all invested in Carmen's name the total tax would be just $1 700, giving a saving of $3 000 over investing it in his name.*

Weapon Four: Dividend Imputation

Franked dividends carrying imputation credits enable lower income earners to cut their tax down.

EXAMPLE: *Maree has a taxable income of $12 000 on which tax payable is $1 320. Her mother left $100 000 to her which she invests in equity trusts or Australian shares paying franked dividends. If the dividends total $5 000 they may carry imputation credits of $2 142. Maree's tax position is as follows:*

Normal taxable income	$12 000
Dividend income	5 000
add Imputation Credits	2 142
Taxable Income	19 142
Tax thereon	2 234
less imputation credits	2 142
Net tax payable	22

Notice how the dividend is not just tax free. The tax on her other income has **ALMOST** been eliminated by the franked dividends from the shares or equity trust.

Weapon Five: Superannuation

The increased tax deductibility allowed to superannuation contributions in the August 1989 budget makes this avenue one of the best for saving tax. People who are not members of an employer-sponsored fund may claim $3 000 plus 75% of the balance of contributions. From July 1, 1994 there have been limits on the amounts that can be contributed as a tax deduction but they are generous. For example, at date of writing the maximum tax deductible contributions were

under 35	$11 912
between 35 and 50	$33 087
over 50	$82 054

EXAMPLE: Mark is 52, earns $65 000 a year in his own business, and has minimal superannuation. He contributes $23 000 to superannuation in one payment by way of a single premium superannuation bond. He claims $18 000 (calculated $3 000 plus 75% of $20 000) as a tax deduction, which increases his tax refund by $8 460. Thus the true cost of the investment is $14 540.

The Government will immediately take $2 700 (15% of the $18 000 tax deduction) as an entry tax, leaving Mark with a net investment of $20 300, which cost him $14 540. While this money remains in the superannuation fund its earnings will be taxed at no more than 15% – far lower than his 47% marginal rate. My book Superannuation Made Simple *is devoted to this topic, while* Living Well In Retirement *goes into all the complex angles.*

Weapon Six: Negative Gearing

Much has been discussed about negative gearing elsewhere in this book. Accordingly it is mentioned here only briefly as a reminder.

Despite its risks negative gearing is a superb tax-saving technique for high income earners with substantial assets who wish to build up wealth in a hurry. Just remember it will speed up what is going to happen to you — wealth or poverty.

Weapon Seven: Tax-Driven Investments

Around June every year the tax-driven investments raise their heads again. They are usually investments in films or agriculture and come accompanied by optimistic estimates of the profits to accrue to investors at some time in the future. A thread runs through all of them – the lure that all, or part, of the investment is tax deductible.

They are seized upon by high income earners with tax problems who usually have to borrow the money to invest in them, often at high rates of interest. Doubtless they do save tax and some, like *Crocodile Dundee*, turn in a handsome profit for their investors. Unfortunately there are few *Crocodile Dundees* and most fall far short of the projections. The end result is a debt that is just as large as the tax saved, with nothing much to show for it. The fact that the interest is tax deductible is cold consolation.

Read The Case Of The Man Who Tried To Save Tax in Chapter 37 **before** entering into any tax-driven investments. At least you can't say you weren't warned if you end up worse off than before.

Weapon Eight: Loading The Purchase Price

This technique is legal and may save you a lot of capital gains tax. As you know capital gains tax is calculated on the base cost of the asset, so it follows that the higher the base cost the less the taxable profit will be when you sell.

How do you increase the base cost? Just look for opportunities. The examples that follow will stimulate your thinking.

EXAMPLE ONE: *The Wilsons wanted to buy Mrs Jones' house so they could demolish it and erect a block of units. She was a pensioner and had decided to go into a retirement village. The listed price was $185 000 but she was prepared to sell at $170 000. The Wilsons offered her the $185 000 she was asking providing she gave them a year to settle the purchase. They paid the rates for that year. She was thus able to live in the house secure in the knowledge that she would receive the $185 000 in a year. This suited her, because she was in no hurry to move.*

Her alternative was to sell for $170 000 cash, find a place to rent for six months, and invest the sales proceeds till she found *the unit to buy. The interest on the $170 000 would probably cost her most of her pension. It also suited the Wilsons for they had secured the house with minimal outlay of capital and they could now prepare plans and tender documents. They had also increased the base cost from $170 000 to $185 000.*

EXAMPLE TWO: *You are going to buy some shares that pay franked dividends. The shares are currently selling at $6.20 which includes a fully franked dividend of 20 cents. Next week the shares will be quoted "ex dividend", which means the price should drop to $6.00 as that dividend is not payable to investors who buy then. Should you buy now at $6.20 or wait next week till the price is $6.00?*

Wise investors will buy now because the base for capital gains tax purposes will be $6.20 instead of $6.00. Those who buy at $6.00 will have more profit for capital gains tax purposes when they sell as their base cost is lower. The imputation credit that accompanies the franked dividend will eliminate all or most of the tax on it. You win in two ways, a tax-free dividend plus a higher cost base.

Weapon Nine: Capital Drawdown Schemes

Capital drawdown schemes work on the principle that you spend capital instead of income. This sounds a bit frightening, but if all goes well the capital growth on the unspent capital should be more than the amount you draw out. In other words, your capital is increasing faster than you are spending it.

EXAMPLE: *A couple retire with $300 000 and require an annual income of $20 000. They can both earn $5 400 a year without paying tax which accounts for $10 800 of income. This leaves $9 200 to be spent out of capital. Assume $100 000 is placed in income-producing areas where it earns 8% per annum and the couple draw $1 670 a month ($20 000 a year) from it. It should be fully expended in seven years.*

By that time the remaining $200 000 would have doubled in value if 10% growth can be obtained. Now the couple can start to spend some of that.

In practice we would use a combination of split trusts and imputation trusts as well as the strategy above to make the most of the couple's money. In any event they should never have to pay tax again.

Weapon Ten: Paying It Now

This section applies to people in business for themselves. While it won't reduce your overall tax bill it will free you forever from the worries about large unexpected tax bills. I urge you to adopt a system whereby you pay yourself a weekly or monthly wage, and deduct income tax from it by group deduction. You may need to talk to your accountant about forming a company or family trust to do this. The outcome is that you are paying your tax as you go – just like all the wage and salary earners who work for somebody else.

I have heard all the arguments about having the use of the money for a longer period. They are great in theory. The reality is that most people cannot budget to pay their tax when they have kept control of their money. It is no different to your suggesting it would be a good idea if you paid your groceries and petrol once a year. Most could not do it.

If you give yourself a group taxed salary, and keep good accounting records, you come to the end of the financial year with all your personal tax paid. All that needs to be done before June 30 is to work out the profit left after your salary has been paid and liaise with your accountant about ways to reduce tax on the balance or to pay yourself a tax-paid bonus. If you do this properly you arrive at June 30 with no further tax to pay and no provisional tax to worry about.

Weapon Eleven: Paying Off Your House Mortgage

I have frequently stressed the importance of paying off the loan on your own home as quickly as possible. Unfortunately there are still some ill-informed commentators and well-meaning givers of advice saying this is the wrong thing to do. The reasons they give are:

(1) The interest rate may be around 7% and it's silly to pay off a loan carrying such a low rate of interest.

or

(2) If you leave your housing loan high, you will pay it back in the future in the deflated dollars of that time and thus the real repayments are lower than if you made them today.

While the second statement has some truth about it, the reality is that the interest on your housing loan is not tax deductible and is being made from your **after tax** earnings.

Therefore investing money by making extra payments on your home mortgage is equivalent to earning the rate of that mortgage **tax free** in some other investment. For example, if your housing loan is only (!) 7%, any payments made to reduce that mortgage are equivalent to your investing the money to earn 7% after tax in a capital guaranteed fund with no entry or no exit fees. A tax payer on the top marginal tax rate would have to earn nearly 14% in an interest-bearing account to get the same return.

I believe the case is proven beyond doubt, don't you?

Weapon Twelve: Salary Sacrifice For Superannuation

One of the most effective ways of contributing to superannuation is by taking a portion of a salary as employer-sponsored superannuation. For example, a person aged 40 may be offered a salary package of $78 000. It is often possible to negotiate with the employer to have the salary package split as follows:

Salary	$55 000
Contribution to Super	$23 000
TOTAL PACKAGE	$78 000

The employee is still getting $78 000 overall but has reduced his marginal tax rate to the second-highest level instead of the highest. The contributions to superannuation attract an entry tax of only 15% whereas if taken as salary they would be hit with 47% tax (plus Medicare Levy) and the earnings on those funds are taxed at a maximum of 15% a year, whereas they would be taxed at 47% if invested by the tax-payer.

Be aware that money placed in superannuation is tied up until you retire after age 55.

Weapon Thirteen: Using Your Own House To Avoid Tax

In Australia there is no capital gains tax on your own residence provided it is in the name or names of the tax-payer/s personally. If it is in the name of a family company or a family trust, any profits on sale are liable for capital gains tax. As houses in good locations have shown consistent appreciation in price, people who are handy around the home, or who have a flair for decoration, have the opportunity to make large tax-free profits.

Remember the **BAM** formula which is the secret of real estate profits. Buy well, Add value and Manage intensively. The "Manage Intensively" may not apply to your own home (apart from managing your money of course) but the Buy Well and the Add Value certainly do.

You must understand that the technique involves **improving** the property. If you simply buy a property and wait for it to rise in value in line with the other houses around, you are not making any real progress. The big profits are made by those people who can find a neglected property, or a property with potential, buy it, then live in it and do it up at the same time. Those who have a natural bent for this can accumulate a fortune over their lifetime by moving from house to house. It will take a lot of effort, but when you sell you should be paid for that effort in tax-free dollars.

Don't do it too often or you'll become classified as a trader in houses by the Tax Office and all your profits will be taxed at your full marginal rate without the benefit of indexation. The way to minimise the chance of being classified as a trader is to buy successive houses in the name of one party and then the other.

Weapon Fourteen: Strategic Use Of Losses

When you read Chapter 24 you will understand the way losses on assets are viewed by the Tax Office, and how capital losses may be offset against capital gains. Suppose you are having a year of high income, and have just sold an asset that will result in a large profit that will be subject to capital gains tax.

Perhaps at the same time you may have some shares that were bought at a high price, and are now well below their market value. Talk to your accountant about selling the shares in the same tax year as the one in which the capital profit is going to be assessed. This will generate a capital loss, which can be offset against your capital profit, which will reduce your capital gains tax. At some future stage you could buy some the shares back if you thought they had potential.

The fact that capital losses are not indexed makes this such a good strategy. The capital losses will lose their real value over time because of inflation – therefore it is good sense to use them as fast as possible.

Be aware that capital gains tax is calculated using your taxable income for the year of the sale of the asset. It could be that your taxable income could be drastically reduced in the year of sale by using some of the other methods outlined in this chapter. Talk to your accountant and financial adviser.

Many Australians leave the country to work overseas and retain negative-geared properties here. For the period that they are classed as non-resident tax payers the negative-gearing losses accumulate, and can then be used to reduce tax substantially when they return and start to earn here again.

> **EXAMPLE:** *Mike had two investment houses that were making a net loss of $20 000 a year, after all costs including interest were accounted for. He worked overseas for four years and then returned to an $80 000 a year job. The accumulated losses of $80 000 eliminated the tax on the entire first year's income.*

Weapon Fifteen: Employing The Family

If you have a family business one of the best ways to split income is to employ family members. Now don't try to milk this one too hard by doing such things as having a six-year-old writing up the cash book. The Tax Office takes a rather cynical view of family members on the pay-roll and claims for wages will receive close scrutiny. However, there are many businesses where family members can do meaningful work and be paid a reasonable wage for it. Duties may include typing, packing goods, operating machinery such as petrol pumps, answering the telephone, gardening, filing, mail outs and cleaning.

It is important you are familiar with the chapter on children's tax in *Making Money Made Simple* as unmarried children under 18 pay a high tax on "unearned" income once it becomes more than $8 a week. No such restrictions apply to earned income, so a child can earn $6 000 a year from personal exertion and pay no tax at all. It is important that money from earned income be kept separate to money from unearned income, and the best way to do this is to keep separate bank accounts.

Weapon Sixteen: Prepayment Of Expenses

In this country only a select few such as primary producers and authors are allowed to flatten out their tax by averaging their income. This saves them the problem of paying tax on a high taxable income in one year and then having no cash to cope with a following lean year.

A good way for business people to flatten out their tax is to reduce their income by large prepayment of expenses.

EXAMPLE: *It is early June and Mr High Income Earner is thinking about his $300 000 loan on his block of flats. The present interest rate is 8% and the repayments are a whopping $4 000 a month, which adds up to over $48 000 a year. The interest component is $24 000 a year and the balance of the payments are coming from his after-tax income.*

The loan is re-financed on an interest-only basis and the annual interest of $24 000 is paid before June 30 so he can claim the whole lot as a tax deduction in the current year. This reduces his tax bill by almost $12 000 which can be put away to help provide for next year's interest repayment.

Check out the benefits:

(1) The money he has to find each year for his loan repayments is slashed from $48 000 to $24 000. That's a great safety buffer in turbulent times but also may be useful to get the

family over a tough period with such temporary but pressing items as school fees.

(2) He has the security of knowing the next 12 months' payments are taken care of.

(3) He has locked in the interest rate for the next three years so won't be troubled if rising interest rates overseas force ours up.

A similar prepayment can be arranged by those who are purchasing business equipment around May and June. Lease payments are traditionally made in advance, so by arranging for the lease to be made by annual instalments, instead of monthly ones, the lessor gets an immediate tax deduction of the first year's instalment.

Weapon Seventeen: Using A Smart Strategy

Legal tax strategies can be most effective. I am proud of a scheme I thought up to help a man who came to our office for advice on the best way to fund for the education of his children's education in about 12 years' time.

A discussion revealed that he had a high taxable income, a prosperous business and had just paid $50 000 for a new truck. After he explained to me his fear that somehow there may not be enough money to pay for the future school fees, and I had convinced him that leasing was a better way for him to go than paying cash for the truck, we decided on a course of action.

I arranged for him to see a leading finance company who "bought" the truck from him for the price he had paid for it and then leased it back to him at $1 450 a month for four years with a 40% residual at the end. We invested the $50 000 just freed up in a range of top flight growth investments that will more than pay for the school fees in the future.

His leasing payments are tax deductible so he has effectively obtained a tax deduction for the school fees, as well as having the security of knowing his concerns about education are taken care of.

Weapon Eighteen: Including Life Cover In Superannuation

Any items you pay from your after-tax dollars have a much higher cost than those paid from pre-tax dollars. By including your life insurance premium in your superannuation scheme you effectively get a tax deduction for it if you are also claiming the superannuation as a tax deduction or if it is being paid through a salary sacrifice scheme.

Bear in mind your life cover cannot be more than the amount of superannuation allowed under the reasonable benefit limits.

Weapon Nineteen: Starting Off Right

This is not so much a weapon, as a warning, but it may pay for itself in tax saved or because it saves you incurring penalties from the Tax Office.

Buying a business or a property can be an exciting activity, but many prospective buyers are in such a hurry to take possession that they fall into the trap of signing the purchase contract without making sure a detailed breakdown of the sale price is included. They then expect their accountant to unscramble the mess at the end of the financial year.

Experience has taught us that, once the transaction has been settled, the vendors may not be as co-operative as when the negotiations were being carried on. The truth is that it may be to their advantage to ignore your efforts to contact them.

The sale contract for the purchase of a business, or an income-producing property, should list the depreciable assets and the original cost of any buildings constructed after 1982. If applicable, details should also be included of such intangible assets as patents, licences and goodwill.

There may be substantial tax savings if this is done properly, and the buyer may be seriously disadvantaged for tax purposes if it is overlooked. Australia has now moved to a system of self-assessment for tax purposes and the Tax Office is carrying out more audits. It is commonplace for their staff to find tax-payers who are not able to produce the correct documentation following the acquisition of a business or an income-producing property. The result is they may miss out on tax-deductible claims. The seriousness of this is shown by the fact that the Tax Office have advised that where no value was attributed to depreciable assets on a contract of sale, no depreciation may be allowed on any assets acquired.

If people are buying a business it is customary for the stock and work in progress to be clearly spelt out in the purchase agreement, and you should note that the Tax Office requires these figures to be at market value. However, many overlook the necessity to be able to ascertain the cost of the buildings and goodwill (for capital gains tax purposes), plant and equipment (for depreciation purposes), and the original cost of a building (for calculation of the Building Allowance).

The vendor is likely to try to maximise the "selling price" of one asset against another. For example, if the business was acquired by the vendor prior to the start of capital gains tax, any amount received for goodwill is free of capital gains tax. Therefore if the price allocated to goodwill is made as high as possible at the expense of the price of the depreciated assets, the vendor gets the best of both worlds. There is no tax to pay on the high goodwill figure as it is non-taxable, and there is no tax to pay on the excess of the sale price over the book value of the depreciable assets as these assets are valued at low figures.

If the vendor makes this apportionment, it is too late for the buyer to object once the sale is completed. The purchaser is in a position of strength only prior to the completion of the contract of sale, and negotiations after settlement of the sale are difficult at best.

It is also necessary to keep records where an existing business makes improvements to property or builds new buildings on land acquired before (or after) the introduction of capital gains tax. In these circumstances it must maintain sufficient records to calculate whether a capital gain or loss has been made on disposal. Failure to do so may mean penalties or additional tax.

Let me repeat a piece of priceless wisdom. Keep good records and consult your accountant, solicitor and financial adviser before you sign any contract – it may save you a lot of money.

In Summary

I hope this chapter has stimulated your thinking and you now understand there are many legal and effective ways to reduce your tax. They do require thought and planning, so maybe your next step should be to make appointments to see both your accountant and your financial adviser. Discuss this chapter with them and decide what is appropriate for your situation.

23

Buying Assets In The Right Name

I think age is a very high price to pay for maturity.

TOM STOPPARD

It doesn't matter whether you are buying shares or an investment property, building up a cash reserve in the bank, or are trying to start a fund for your children, one of the most important decisions you must make is "In whose name will it be held?"

When deciding, you must look at three factors. Unfortunately it may be a bit like stuffing a carpet snake in a suitcase — you might get one part of it right but fail in another. You must consider:

a) Where the asset is best placed to minimise income tax now and capital gains tax **later.**
b) Who you want to be in **control.**
c) What will be the outcome if the owner of the investment **dies** or if the parties **separate?**

First it's important that you understand the difference between assets held as joint tenants, and assets held as tenants in common.

JOINT TENANTS: If a couple hold assets as joint tenants, and one dies, the entire asset automatically passes to the other holder irrespective of the terms of any will.

This is the usual way that husband and wife hold the family home. Obviously you should not hold an asset as joint tenants unless you wish the other holder to have your share if you die first.

TENANTS IN COMMON: A tenancy in common is quite different. Upon death of one of the owners the survivor/s continue with the present holding, and the deceased's share passes to the beneficiaries in terms of the deceased's will. This is the usual way that brothers and sisters or friends hold property. In this modern age where divorce and re-marriage is commonplace we find more and more couples are holding all their property as tenants in common, to allow their own children to have their share.

EXAMPLE: *David and Shirley have both been married before. He has two children from the previous marriage and she has four. They do not intend to have any more children but hold assets as tenants in common. This enables David's children to have half the proceeds when he dies and Shirley's children to have half the proceeds when she dies. The position would be different if the assets were held as joint tenants and David died. David's half would pass directly to Shirley and how much she then gave to David's children would be at her discretion.*

Certain financial commentators have suggested it is not practical to hold money in joint accounts because of delays in withdrawing the money if one party dies. However, our company's research has shown there are no delays if a joint account holder dies. Provided the account is held as joint tenants the money automatically belongs to the survivor, who may operate on the account immediately. Naturally the banks will require evidence of death where the account requires both parties to sign the cheques or withdrawal forms, in case there is no death and one party is "leaving town".

Most share registries and fund managers will transfer the share or unit holding to the joint owner on production of a death certificate, which in normal circumstances will issue less than two weeks after death.

Split Your Income

To minimise tax, split your income if possible. It is commonplace to interview clients where large sums of money are held in joint accounts, yet one party is a big income earner and one is a low income earner. Provided there is trust between the parties, a transfer of funds to the lower income spouse may reduce tax significantly by bringing the interest into a lower tax bracket.

Franked Dividends

It is best if shares paying franked dividends are bought in the name of the lowest earning **tax-payer** as the imputation credits that go with franked dividends can reduce tax on income from other sources.

If the investor is in the top tax bracket the dividends enjoy a low tax rate, so if the choice is between non-taxpayer and a top marginal rate tax-payer, you would normally choose the one who pays no tax. However, watch the way the investment affects the spouse rebate, for if you are expecting a large dividend it may be better to invest in the name of the highest income earner and keep the whole spouse rebate. Your accountant or financial adviser can do the sums for you.

Negative Gearing

When using negative gearing it is generally best to have the asset held in the name of the highest earner. The Federal Government effectively subsidises tax deductible expenditure (including interest) at the tax-payer's highest marginal rate, so the higher earning negative gearers get the biggest tax breaks.

Watch the Catch 22 here, because capital gains tax on sale hits hardest on higher earners. However, it is not levied until sale, and even then you pay CGT on only 50% of the gain. This is why many high income earners try to defer cashing in assets till after retirement when their marginal tax rate is lower.

Clearly, if large short-term gains are expected it may be better to forgo maximising the tax deductions of negative gearing in the name of the highest earner and opt for the one with the lowest expected taxable income in the year of sale. Do your sums **before** you sign the contract.

The Family Home

The family home is our best tax-free investment but is only free from capital gains tax if bought in the personal names of the occupiers. If you buy it in the name of a company or a trust you are liable for capital gains tax on sale.

If you are selling the family home and buying another on a regular basis, it is better to use the name of one partner and rotate the names on each transaction. This cuts down the transaction frequency and lessens the possibility of your being classified as a trader by the Tax Office, which would cause the loss of the tax exemption.

Children's Tax

Great care should be taken where money is held in children's names or in the name of one or both parents as trustee for the children. Unmarried children under 18 pay tax of up to 66% on "unearned" income above $416 a year so you may find yourself paying harsh penalty tax if the interest goes above $8 a week.

The Taxation Commissioner will use his power to assess interest directly to the parent named as trustee if he believes the money is, in reality, owned by the parents and is only being placed in a trustee account to cut tax. The result can be heavy penalties if the trustee is a high earner. Check your trustee bank accounts and change the trustee to the lowest earner if you believe the Tax Office could regard the money as your own. One of the main tests is control – if parents use the money as their own, the interest will almost certainly be regarded as assessable to them. A whole chapter is devoted to children's tax in *Making Money Made Simple.*

Buying In A Company Name

Investors should be wary of buying assets in the name of a company. The family home will not be free from capital gains tax if bought in the name of a company, but one of the other implications is just as serious. When you buy assets in the name of a company you pay full CGT, albeit at the company tax rate – you do not get the 50% concession that is available to individuals.

Insurance Bonds

It has been customary to place insurance bonds in the name of a low income spouse, so that little or no tax will be payable if they are cashed in before 10 years have elapsed. However, the 34% tax rebate that applies for early encashment means that they may be better placed in the name of the higher income earner.

Consider the following alternatives:

Mr Smith earns $35 000 a year and his wife has no income. They have dependent children so Mr Smith receives the full spouse rebate. Consider what happens if they purchase an insurance bond for $10 000 and cash it in seven years later for $19 000. The $9 000 profit will have to be shown as taxable income and the holder will claim a 34% rebate from tax payable.

The tax rebate of $3 060 (34% of $9 000) will eliminate any tax payable by Mrs Smith, but Mr Smith will lose his spouse rebate for the year.

If bought in his name the extra tax payable will be $2 745, but when the rebate of $3,060 is deducted he will have $315 of surplus credits with which to reduce his other tax. He will also keep his spouse rebate.

Summing Up

The above ideas assume total trust between the parties where there is a suggestion of putting assets in different names. If there is no trust you may be happier investing in your own name and suffering the consequences of higher tax and possible delays on death.

I have written before about the importance of ensuring assets are placed in the right name, but new twists are constantly cropping up. Be aware the right time to seek advice about structuring is before the deed is done. It may be very difficult to change things about once a contract is signed, and harder still after the buying transaction has been completed.

24

Taxation — Treatment Of Losses

Income tax has made more liars out of the American people than golf has.

WILL ROGERS

If you become a serious investor you are going to make the odd loss along the way, so it's surprising we find most clients are totally confused about the treatment of losses in their tax return. It's not too difficult if you first understand there are **two types** of losses – revenue losses and capital losses.

Revenue Losses

A revenue loss occurs when your current year's tax deductions are more than your taxable income. The losses thus incurred can be carried forward to future years and used to reduce taxable income, and thus income tax, in future years. They cannot be used to reduce capital profits.

EXAMPLE: *Margaret earned $23 000 salary but the little restaurant she owned as a "hobby" lost $30 000 for the year. Her taxable income is reduced to nil and she has $7 000 of revenue losses left over that she can offset against future income. If she sold the restaurant these losses of $7 000 could be offset against her future salary to reduce her taxable income.*

Capital Gains

These happen when you make a profit on the sale of an asset that is subject to capital gains tax. The capital profit is added to your taxable income, but note carefully that if you have held the asset for more than a year you are entitled to a 50% concession. As capital gains are treated like ordinary income they can be offset by revenue losses, but cannot be carried forward to future years.

In the example above, if Margaret had made a $14 000 capital profit from shares she had held for over a year, she would have to declare a $7 000 capital profit after allowing for the 50% concession. This would have been eliminated by being offset against her revenue losses of $7 000.

Capital Losses

These happen when you make a loss on the sale of an asset where you would have been liable for capital gains tax if you had made a profit. They can offset against capital profits in the same year as the loss happened or can be carried forward to future years and used to reduce future capital profits.

In the next example we'll follow the fortunes of Bill and Mary Investor and you will see how it all comes together.

> **EXAMPLE:** *Bill Investor was a doctor earning $75 000 a year. His wife Mary earned a salary of $45 000 a year. Bill loved to play the stockmarket and was continually buying and selling shares. He was so active in this area that he was classified as a trader by the Tax Office.*

Understand that all profits and losses made by a trader are **revenue** gains or losses. **Capital** gains and losses are made on assets that people buy with the intention of holding for the medium to long term.

In June 2000 Bill bought 10 000 Mining A Go Go shares for $1 each on a tip from a friend he bumped into at the races. They had slumped to 50 cents by August 1990 so Bill sold them. This entitled him to a revenue loss of $5 000, which could be offset against his salary for the financial year ending June 30, 1991. He got luckier with the 4 000 shares in Jerry Building Ltd that he bought in late 1989 for $2. They had jumped to $5 each by July 1990 so Bill sold half to lock in some profits.

In August Mary was overwhelmed to find she had been left $400 000 in the will of a recently deceased aunt. She went straight to her bank manager who told her she could make a fortune in negative gearing and advised her to buy an industrial building as the yields were much higher than those obtainable from a rental house.

During the regular Sunday tennis game Bill told his medical mates about the bank manager's suggestion. They were all enthusiastic about the idea so Bill and Mary started the exciting task of buying a property.

There was no shortage of property for sale and, after spending a day looking around, they settled on an industrial shed for $900 000. It was tenanted by a local building company, which was paying $90 000 a year rent.

The bank manager told them he believed that interest rates were on the way down and advised them to borrow $600 000 at a variable interest rate, which was 16% at the time the loan was taken out. The purchase looked great. The interest bill was $96 000 a year, but when the rents of $90,000 were taken into account there was only a small annual cash shortfall.

The bliss was shortlived. A few months later the Government decided that inflation was getting out of hand and raised interest rates to curb consumer spending. As a result the builder tenant struck cash problems, started getting behind in his rent and eventually went into liquidation. At the same time interest rates went up to 20%.

Now Bill and Mary faced a vacant building that was bringing in no rent, coupled with a debt of $600 000 that was costing $120 000 to service. All their efforts to find a tenant were in vain and the building sat vacant for months. They tried to sell it, but the reaction from the agents was "We can't sell it until you find a tenant — nobody wants to buy a vacant industrial building". Their frustrated response was "If we had a tenant we wouldn't have to sell it!".

The months went on and their cash reserves were almost gone because of the massive interest bills. Finally, in desperation, they accepted a cash offer of $550 000 from a wealthy investor who had made a fortune picking up properties at rock bottom prices from naive investors such as Bill and Mary who had over committed themselves. They had to borrow $50 000 to make up the shortfall between their debt and the sale price.

This is how their tax returns looked for the year ended June 30 2001.

	BILL	MARY
TAXABLE INCOME		
Salary	75 000	45 000
Profit from share trading	6 000	
2,000 @ $3		

Net rents building (50% each)	4 000	4 000
TOTAL INCOME	85 000	49 000
TAX DEDUCTIONS		
Loss from share trading	5 000	
10,000 @ .50		
Interest Building (50% each)	60 000	60 000
TOTAL DEDUCTIONS	65 000	60 000
NET TAXABLE INCOME	20 000	NIL
REVENUE LOSS CARRIED FORWARD	NIL	11 000

Notice how Bill's trading profits and losses are included when calculating his income for the year, and how Mary's $11 000 can be carried forward to reduce her taxable income from salary and similar sources in the following tax year.

The $300 000 loss on sale of the building is a capital loss and can only be offset against capital profits. To create these capital profits Bill and Mary will both need to generate non-trading profits from the purchase and sale of more assets such as property. Somehow I doubt they are going to try, which means the losses are likely to be wasted.

This example does more than illustrate the way losses work. The experience of Bill and Mary is typical of ones we strike almost every day.

Summing Up

Capital profits can be offset against revenue losses.

Capital losses can only be offset against capital gains.

You can't claim a tax deduction for interest on a loan used to buy an asset if you no longer own it.

Capital gains tax is payable on capital profits in the year they are incurred. These capital profits can be offset against capital losses of the current year or of previous years.

25

Partnerships, Companies, And Trusts

There is no victory at bargain basement prices.

DWIGHT D. EISENHOWER

If you are in a high tax bracket one of the best ways to save tax is by income splitting. That means diverting part of your income so the tax paid on it is paid by a person or an entity in a lower tax bracket. It's unlikely you will want to achieve this by rushing around giving your money away to everybody you meet, but there **are** legal and efficient methods to do it if you follow the rules.

In Chapter 22 you learnt about saving tax through vehicles such as superannuation funds and insurance and friendly society bonds where a tax of between 15% and 30% is paid by the fund itself. Now we'll move on and consider partnerships, companies and unit trusts. Before we start let's remind ourselves of the tax rates.

Under our progressive tax system the **rate** of tax for private individuals increases with income. Since 1st July 2000 personal tax rates are:

Taxable Income	Marginal Rate
$0 – $6 000	Nil
$6 001 – $20 000	Nil + 17% on the balance above $6 000
$20 001 – $50 000	$2 380 + 30% on the balance above $20 000
$50 001 – $60 000	$11 380 + 42% on the balance above $50 000
$60 001 and over	$15 580 + 47% on the balance above $60 000

In addition a Medicare levy of 1.5% is added to the tax payable, but for simplicity I have ignored it in this chapter.

At the outset you will have to understand that partnerships and unit trusts **do not pay tax** themselves. They are a device that **diverts** income to people who pay the tax or companies that pay the tax.

In contrast a company is a taxpayer in its own right and is liable for tax in the same way as you might be. However, company tax is only 30% and there is no Medicare levy. Now you are probably thinking "What a great idea, I'll form a company and enjoy a much lower tax rate".

It's not as simple as that. Companies pay tax at 30% from the **first** dollar earnt whereas, for a person, the first $6 000 is tax free, the next $14 000 is at 17% and so on up the scale. For example, company tax on an income of $50 000 is $15 000. Personal tax on the same income is just over $11 000. It is not until you reach an income of $72 000 a year that the total company tax payable becomes lower than the overall personal tax. Nevertheless, as you shall soon read, companies are still important devices for tax saving.

The next point to understand is that the Tax Office is not happy about taxpayers trying to divert income by artificial means. I'll use an extreme example to illustrate the point. Suppose Luigi is a famous tenor whose entire income comes from the concert performances he gives. He could not reduce his tax by the simple method of setting up a company or a trust because the Tax Office would take the view it was Luigi, not the trust or the company, that earnt the income. Therefore he is the one who should pay the tax on it.

Now we'll consider partnerships, companies and trusts separately and show you how it all comes together.

Partnerships

A partnership consists of two or more people in business together. It is not a separate entity and therefore does not pay tax. Its use in tax planning is to allow income splitting.

The most common use of a partnership is in small business. Suppose Bill is a plumber and, with his wife Beryl, operates a partnership known as Acme Plumbing. Notice this is a different situation to that of Luigi the tenor for both partners contribute. Bill spends his time in the field while Beryl answers the phone, arranges the jobs, does the books and handles all the accounting.

If Bill earnt $80 000 a year, and was working as a sole trader, his tax bill would be almost $25 000. By operating as a partnership half the income is split to Beryl and taxable income reduces to $40 000 each. Total tax is then about $17 000, resulting in a saving of $8 000 a year.

The main benefit of operating as a partnership is simplicity. There are few establishment or ongoing costs and most people find the concept easy to understand. However, they have some major drawbacks:

(1) They do not provide a means for diverting income to children unless those children work in the business. This is why discretionary trusts (discussed later) are growing in popularity.

(2) Members of a partnership suffer the same tax liabilities as individual taxpayers.

EXAMPLE: *Harry and Sally went into partnership on July 1. The partnership made a net profit of $200 000 for the year ended June 30. Thus each partner earnt $100 000 each from the partnership. As no group tax has been deducted they will each have a tax bill of nearly $70 000 in the next year. This is because they are paying two years' tax at once.*

(3) Partners are individually liable for all the debts of the partnership. This is one of the biggest dangers of partnerships as the following example illustrates:

EXAMPLE: *Linda, Don and Fred went into partnership in a landscaping business. Their main activities were providing landscaping for builders. One of their major clients went into liquidation leaving them unable to pay $60 000 of debts to their own suppliers. They were forced to close their business down and Fred was the one who had to make good all the partnership debts. The others had no money.*

You will find similar examples in Chapters 36 and 38 and I make no apology for labouring the point. Knowing about the dangers of partnerships may save you a lot of money one day.

Companies

Companies evolved to solve the problem of the members of a partnership being personally liable for all the partnership debts. Business people formed "limited" companies in which the liabilities of the shareholders were limited to the amount of uncalled capital on their shares. Provided your shares were paid up you had no further liability.

This is why the word "limited" must always be placed after a company's name. This is a warning to those who deal with that company that the liability is limited and the creditors do not have recourse to the private assets of the shareholders. Business practices are continually evolving and it is usual now for major creditors to sneak behind the shield of limited liability by seeking personal guarantees from the directors of a company. Nevertheless the use of a limited company does provide some protection against losing all your assets, particularly if the company is sued for negligence.

Unlike a partnership a company **is** a separate legal entity and can sue and be sued in its own right. It also pays tax at company rates as mentioned above.

The main benefits of a company are:

(1) Some protection against liability.

(2) The ability to employ the owners of the business and thus have the benefit of group taxed wages and full tax deductibility of superannuation provided it is paid by the company. Let's think about Harry and Sally again.

EXAMPLE: *If they had operated as a company instead of a partnership their figures for the year ended June 30 may have been:*

Profit	*$200 000*
Less Salaries ($70 000 to each)	*140 000*
Superannuation ($10 000 each)	*20 000*
Profit earnt by company	*40 000*
Tax thereon (@30%)	*$12 000*

Look where Harry and Sally are on June 30. They have no further personal tax to pay because they received a group taxed salary from their company who is their employer. Furthermore, they have salted $10 000 each away in superannuation where it is safe from creditors if the business gets into trouble. Instead of struggling to pay a joint $140 000 tax bill next April there is only $12 000 company tax to be paid.

Naturally there are disadvantages:

(1) The amount of wages that can be paid to a family member as an employee of the company has to be reasonable for the work done. If Sally was working solely as a typist for the company it could not pay her a $70 000 a year salary.

(2) It is bad practice to hold assets in a company name unless they are trading assets. The reasons are detailed in Chapter 23.

(3) Apart from wages to the owners, profits must eventually be distributed as dividends. This may cause further tax to be paid depending on the tax bracket of the shareholder.

It may also may provide opportunities for tax saving.

EXAMPLE: *Robert and Tess have a consulting business they operate through their family company. As Robert does most of the work it is reasonable to pay Tess only $10 000 a year from the company as wages. On my advice they issued Robert "A" class shares and Tess "B" Class shares when the company was set up. This is a typical year's figures.*

Profit		*$100 000*
Less Salaries		
Robert	*$50 000*	
Tess	*$10 000*	*60 000*
Superannuation		
Robert	*$10 000*	
Tess	*$5 000*	*15 000*
Profit earnt by company		*25 000*
Tax thereon (@30%)		*$ 7 500*
Company profit paid to Tess as dividend		*$17 500*
Tess's taxable income is:		
Salary		*$10 000*
Dividend		*17 500*
Imputation Credit for company tax		*7 500*
Total taxable income		*$35 000*
Tax on income		*6 880*
Less imputatation credit		*7 500*
Tax refundable		*620*

Notice how the franked dividend has reduced most of the tax on Tess's $10 000 salary. It was possible to do it this way only because they had different classes of shares. If they both held the same number of shares of the same class the dividend would have been paid to them equally. Then Robert would have had more tax to pay.

We'll now discuss discretionary trusts and unit trusts, which I believe are the best business structures if your affairs warrant them.

Trusts

A trust is a separate legal entity but it does not pay tax. Instead it acts as a conduit or funnel and sends the income down to its beneficiaries who pay the tax. Thus it has characteristics of both a company and a partnership. However, a trust can employ its beneficiaries provided the wages are reasonable for the work done and deduct group tax from their salaries.

There are two main types of trusts:

(1) Discretionary Trusts

(2) Unit Trusts

We'll now discuss each one.

Discretionary Trusts

A discretionary family trust is another income-splitting device, but it has greater flexibility than a partnership. This is because the trustees have absolute discretion to pay the income where it will be most tax effective.

We'll look at the company owned by Harry and Sally, but this time we'll assume it's run through a discretionary trust. Notice how the income can be split:

Profit	*$200 000*
Less Salaries ($60 000 to each)	*120 000*
Superannuation ($10 000 each)	*20 000*
Profit available for distribution to beneficiaries.	*60 000*

They have two children; Tom, their 18-year-old son, who is at university, and Tina, their 16-year-old daughter, who is at high school. As well as the two children the trust beneficiaries include Harry's mother and a family company. Getting complicated isn't it?

After discussion with their accountant Harry and Sally decided the $40 000 profit should be distributed as follows:

	Distribution	**Tax payable**
Tom aged 18	*$20 000*	*$2 380*
Tina aged 16	*416*	*nil*
Harry's mother	*20 000*	*2 380*
Family company	*19 584*	*5 875*
Total	*$60 000*	*$10 635*

If Harry and Sally had been trading as a partnership the tax on that extra $60 000 would have been $28 200 because it is all liable to 47%, the top marginal rate. By the use of a trust it drops to 18%.

You may wish to re-read the chapter on Children's Tax in *Making Money Made Simple* now. As you can see, Tom is treated as an adult because he is 18, but Tina is allowed to earn no more than $416 of "unearned income" tax free before moving to the 66% bracket. The trust distribution is termed "unearned income" because she has not physically worked for it. If she did work in the business, which is probable, that earned income is treated separately and comes out of the business as wages, not as a profit distribution. Thus she may earn a further $6 000 as wages tax free.

A special benefit of a family trust is that the beneficiaries do not have to work for their distributions of income. Contrast this with the case of Luigi the tenor who would be very happy if he could find a way to bring his business under the umbrella of a family trust.

I hope you realise by now that all actions have disadvantages as well as advantages. Harry and Sally have enjoyed substantial tax savings by diverting part of their income to Tom, Tina and Harry's mother. However, to enjoy the tax savings they will have to pay the money to the beneficiaries. After all, it is the beneficiaries' money. In practice it usually goes to them and is immediately lent back to the trust where it appears as a loan by them to the trust. For example, in the accounting records of the trust Tom is shown as being owed $20 000 by the trust.

The trust may owe Tom over $80 000 after four years if the income splitting continues while he is at university. If a family dispute then occurs there is always the danger that Tom will demand repayment to him of the $80 000 owed by the trust.

You should understand by now that all income splitting involves giving money to other people. Thus there is always a risk it could create serious problems in the event of arguments and divorce.

This is why it should never be done without a full awareness of the possible risks, and without taking expert advice.

Unit Trusts

Unit trusts are also income-splitting devices but lack the flexibility of the discretionary family trust. They are used when the beneficiaries of the trust wish to protect each one's interest.

Let's suppose that Harry decided to buy into an industrial shed with three of his friends, Tony, Ron and Mick. They may have different amounts of money to contribute and in any event want to safeguard the asset for their families. If the building cost $200 000 the contributions may be:

Harry $80 000 Tony $60 000 Ron $40 000 Mick $20 000

They may then set up a unit trust that contained 20 x $10 000 units and issue them in proportion to the funds contributed. Consequently Harry would have an 8/20 share. The main point to realise is that there is **no discretion** here at all. If the net income of the building is $20 000, Harry is entitled to 8/20 of it or $8 000. This may not suit Harry if he is already in the top tax bracket for he will lose 47% of the $8 000 in tax.

It would have been a better strategy for Harry to buy the eight units in the trust in the name of his discretionary family trust. Certainly the unit trust would still have to distribute the $8 000 of income, but this time the beneficiary is the discretionary family trust which can pass the income down to its own beneficiaries as it wishes.

Units trusts are also the vehicle for many managed funds because they best serve the interests of the individual investors. They were discussed in detail in Chapter 18.

Conclusion

By now you should have an elementary knowledge of business structuring, but if you are still confused work through each example slowly till it all comes together. Remember that using trusts and companies for income splitting is a complex matter and all this chapter can do is provide some very basic principles to stimulate your thinking. If you feel your affairs can be improved discuss the position with your accountant and, if need be, with a lawyer who specialises in tax matters.

26

Leasing, Hire Purchase Or Bill Of Sale?

Experience shows there is a natural tendency for plans to go wrong.

SIR LEO PLIATZKY

"Should we pay cash or lease it?" is a most asked question. To answer it you must realise that leasing is a strategy for those who can claim the payments as a tax deduction. It is rarely suitable for items, such as cars, that are bought solely for private use.

Once a person in business understands the rationale for leasing, as well as the way a lease works, a decision about whether to lease should not be a difficult one.

You now know that interest incurred in borrowing for business purposes is tax deductible so if you borrow to buy plant, machinery, equipment or motor vehicles to be used in the business you can deduct the interest from your taxable income. However, there is another tax deductible item called "depreciation".

Depreciation

It is hard to explain without going on for pages and pages, but the term "depreciation" is a measure of how much the item wears out each year. It thus bears a close relation to the useful life of the item, and is used in accounting to try to apportion the cost of wearing out over this useful life.

The amount of tax deductible depreciation allowed for income producing items is set out in the Tax Act, and you are allowed to choose one of two methods to calculate it. One is called the "straight line" method and the other is called the "diminishing value" method. Each is an attempt to apportion the cost of the item over its working life, but the former assumes the amount of depreciation is the same each year, and the latter assumes that a greater portion of value is lost when the item is newer. Notice the second rate is 50% higher than the first.

Example

A business bought a new car for $20 000. The "straight line" rate allowable by the Tax Office is 15% a year and the "diminishing value" rate is 22.5%.

Year One	Straight Line		Dim. Value	
Purchase Price	$20 000		$20 000	
Depreciation (first year)	3 000	(@ 15%)	4 500	(@ 22.5%)
Written Down Value	$17 000		$15 500	
Year Two				
Opening Value	$17 000		$15 500	
Depreciation (second year)	3 000		3 488	
Written Down Value	$14 000		$12 012	
Year Three				
Opening Value	$14 000		$12 012	
Depreciation (third year)	3 000		2 703	
Written Down Value	$11 000		$ 9 309	

The "written down value" is the value of the vehicle in the books of the company at the end of the financial year, after depreciation has been taken into account. In each of the examples above the book value reduces each financial year, but notice how the straight line method produces a lower depreciation deduction than the diminishing value method in the early years, but a greater deduction in the later years.

If the car was sold for $10 000 at the end of the three year period there would be a tax deductible **loss** of $1 000 in the first case.

This is because the true value of the car is less than the value shown in the books of the business. There is a taxable **profit** of $691 in the second case, as the depreciation has been over claimed and the car is worth more than the books indicate.

As you can see "depreciation" is an attempt to spread the costs of the item over its useful life. Obviously it is impossible to know what the final sale price of the equipment will be until the time comes to sell it, so this is the way the Tax Department adjusts for the fact that the deductions for depreciation may have been too heavy, or too light. The loss on sale may be claimed in recognition that the depreciation provision was too low, and the tax-payer did not claim enough depreciation as a tax deduction. Conversely a profit is taxable, because there was too much depreciation claimed.

Apart from running costs, the main tax deductible items that relate to items such as plant and machinery are depreciation (the wear and tear factor), and interest on the borrowings used for the acquisition (the funding cost).

Leasing

When you lease equipment you are **not** the owner of it; the owner is the finance company who buys the equipment and accordingly claims the depreciation. You pay a regular payment to the finance company to "lease" it from them. This is usually a monthly payment, but there can be other periods negotiated such as yearly or six-monthly. The finance company calculates the amount of the leasing payment based on the depreciation rate allowed by the Tax Office, as well as the cost of the funds to buy the equipment.

You don't pay a deposit when you arrange a lease, so you are effectively "borrowing" the whole purchase price. At the end of the lease period a debt remains which, in theory, should be the value of the item. This debt is called the "residual value" and the lessee will usually make an offer to the finance company to buy the item for that figure.

You should note that this right cannot be written into the leasing contract. If it did, the Tax Department would claim the transaction was a terms sale, treat the leasing payments as part payments of the purchase price, and deny a tax deduction for them. To complicate matters even more, and it may seem a contradiction, all leases include a clause that makes the lessee liable to the finance company for any **shortfall** between the residual value and the eventual disposal price. Thus there is an obligation on you to make good a shortfall, but no obligation on the finance company to reward you with a surplus.

Without doubt items such as computers lose value rapidly, and a small residual value is close to their true worth. In contrast some luxury cars **rise** in value instead of falling, and the residual value may be way below the market value. I know of cases where a finance company has seized a car that was worth much more than the residual value to make up for losses on other accounts they had with the same borrower.

This is why it is important to deal with a reputable leasing company. Certainly it is customary for the lessee to make an offer to purchase the goods for the residual value, and for the leasing company to accept that offer. However, this cannot be written into the lease contract, so the lessee is at the mercy of the leasing company and can only hope it does "the right thing" if a surplus over the residual value is the outcome at the end of the lease.

A lease works in some ways like a personal loan — one part of the payment consists of interest, while the other reduces the amount borrowed (similar to a principal reduction). I know the purists will dispute this and say the lessee is merely leasing the item. This is of course strictly correct but the concept as I have explained it will help you understand it better. A wise finance company executive once said to me "Really you don't lease the vehicle — you lease the money".

Lease Or Buy?

A private person has little to gain by leasing when there is no tax advantage, but I generally recommend that a business lease equipment instead of buying it. Here are the reasons:

(a) **YOU PRESERVE YOUR CAPITAL:** It takes a lot of work to save a sum like $50 000 from your after tax dollars. Once this money is used to buy equipment it is gone forever. It is comforting to have liquidity available for such purposes as buying more stock to sell, or for expansion. By leasing you preserve this valuable cash.

(b) **YOU SPREAD THE COST OVER THE LIFE OF THE ITEM:** When you lease you pay for the item each month as you use it, but if you pay cash you are using after tax profits from times gone by. Hence there is no connection between the cost of the asset and when you pay for it. Leasing also keeps you on your toes because the business has to find that leasing payment every month. Remember The Guaranteed Secret of Wealth in *Making Money Made Simple*.

(c) **IT IS EASIER TO BUDGET:** Most of us find it easier to find a monthly payment than to make regular savings of after tax dollars. Even if we do save that money, there is always some large item such as a tax bill that seems to crop up to take it.

(d) **EASIER REPLACEMENT OF THE ASSET:** If you lease something you have only to find the monthly repayment. When the time comes to replace that item all you have to do is pay an increased monthly repayment. This is not as hard as trying to save a lump sum.

(e) **INCREASED ABILITY TO BORROW:** For some reason it seems to be easier to borrow money for leasing than for straight working capital. Although I am not suggesting that you get your business heavily into debt, it is comforting to have the increased borrowing capability that leasing provides.

Hire Purchase Or Bill Of Sale

Many people are offered finance by hire purchase, bill of sale or personal loan. They usually wonder which one to accept, or whether leasing is better.

Hire Purchase

The main difference in leasing and hire purchase is that the HP buyer has an absolute right to purchase the goods at the end of the hire period. Accordingly the monthly hire instalments are treated as payments of the purchase price, and are not tax deductible. The full price of the asset is recorded into the books of the business and depreciation is claimed each year in the tax return. The yearly interest is also claimed as a tax deduction, although the amount reduces each year as the balance owing drops.

Most hire purchase contracts require a deposit of 10% of the purchase price, so the hirer has to find some funds at the start.

Bill Of Sale And Personal Loan Finance

Many personal loans may be secured by Bills of Sale.

A Bill of Sale is a "chattel[1] mortgage" which gives the lender similar rights to one who lends on a mortgage over real estate.

---

1 A chattel is any property other then freehold land.

However, as the "mortgage" is over chattels, such lending does not have the same security value as loans secured by prime real estate. Items such as cars or furniture can be stolen and wrecked, and most machines have a limited life. Hence most lenders regard Bill of Sale security as having "scare" value only. It is common for a Bill of Sale agreement to provide for a "balloon[2]" payment at the end of the term which brings it even closer to a lease agreement in concept.

The main difference between Bill of Sale and Hire Purchase is that with the former the borrower has title to the item from the start. With the latter, the title does not pass until the Hirer exercises the option to purchase from the finance company who is the owner. The treatment in the books of the business is identical.

EXAMPLE: A business buys a vehicle for $25 000 using a Bill of Sale with payments of $723.52 a month over four years when it will be paid off. There is nothing owing at the end of the four years. The tax deduction allowable will be:

	Year 1	Year 2	Year 3	Year 4
Depreciation	$3 750	$3 750	$3 750	$3 750
Interest	$4 137	$3 248	$2 184	$ 914
Total Tax Deduction	$7 887	$6 998	$5 934	$4 663

The depreciation figure is constant as we have used the 15% straight line method, but the overall tax deduction reduces in line with the reducing interest component. Thus, even though the monthly payment is unchanged, the tax deductibility falls each year. Consequently the borrowers have to find increasing amounts of money from their after tax income. This differs from leasing where the **whole payment** is tax deductible.

If the "diminishing value" method of depreciation had been used, the tax deductibility would have been even higher at the start and fallen off faster.

	Year 1	Year 2	Year 3	Year 4
Depreciation	$5 625	$4 360	$3 378	$2 619
Interest	$4 137	$3 248	$2 184	$ 914
Total Tax Deduction	$9 762	$7 608	$5 562	$3 533

2 Balloon payments are covered in Chapter 15 of *Making Money Made Simple.*

Some Leasing Traps

Before you take out a lease satisfy yourself as to the method the leasing company uses to calculate the payout figure if you wish to terminate the lease before the end of the contract. It varies between companies and some have harsh early payment penalties.

A car dealer boasted to me once that he liked to arrange all leases on cars he sold through his own finance company. When clients phoned to ask the payout figure, the dealer knew they were considering changing cars and was in the running to make another sale. Sometimes they loaded the payout figure, and then added this penalty on to the trade-in price they were prepared to offer. Obviously no competing dealer could beat them!

Watch out for "cheap" monthly leasing payments based on a high residual value. Obviously the higher the residual value, the lower the payments will be, as there is less principal to pay off, but many lessees have found to their horror that the market value of their vehicle is far lower than the residual value or payout figure. The fact that this shortfall is tax deductible is cold comfort to a person with no money.

Also beware of residual values that are too low. The Tax Office looks carefully at artificially low residuals as being contrary to the spirit of genuine leases, and has the power to disallow all the tax deductions if this happens. Be careful of residual values for motor vehicles of under 40% for a three year lease, and 30% for a four year lease.

If you are buying a luxury car on which you will be claiming depreciation, try to buy after June 30 each year, as the Tax Office has set a limit on the depreciable cost of motor cars and station wagons which rises each year by the Consumer Price Index. This figure was $52 912 for vehicles first used during the year ended June 30, 1996 and $55 134 for the year ended June 30, 1997.

> **EXAMPLE:** *A business buys a car on June 15, 1996 for $60 000. It can claim depreciation only on $52 912. If the purchase was delayed to July 1, 1996 the business could have claimed depreciation on $55 134.*

Leasing Works Of Art

The leasing of paintings and other works of art has become fashionable in these days of high profile corporate offices.

Naturally the art dealers encourage this practice because it is easier for a business to buy a painting at $750 a month (tax deductible) than to write out a cheque for $50 000 from after tax dollars.

Two important questions arise when considering the matter.

The first is whether the lease payments are tax deductible, and the second concerns the treatment of the residual value. There has been significant developments in this field as the Tax Office has jumped in to close loopholes that have been exploited.

The Tax Office does not object to lease payments being claimed as a tax deduction provided the paintings are used exclusively in the business premises of the lessee. However, the problem is that the Tax Office depreciation rate for leasing works of art is just 1% per annum, so even after you have paid for your paintings over a four year lease you will find that the residual may still be 95% of the purchase price. Therefore, the lease is almost the same as an interest only loan. Certainly if the paintings rise in value you have done well but you still have the problem of paying tax on the difference between the residual value and the selling price if you sell them.

I hope by now you understand the concept of leasing, or paying for your business equipment as you use it. Now let's explore one of everybody's favourite subjects – negative gearing.

27

Negative Gearing

Danger, the spur of all great minds.

(GEORGE CHAPMAN: Bussy d'Ambois)

People have hated paying tax since time immemorial, so it follows that any ideas to save tax will be welcomed. Unfortunately, many go to extremes in their rush to cut their tax bill and their tax-saving schemes cost more in the long run than the tax they save.

Negative gearing is one strategy that is always seized on eagerly by higher income earners trying to minimise tax. It sounds wonderful – if you have a tax bill solve it simply by negative gearing. However, negative gearing is **not** a panacea and should be treated as the high risk strategy that it can be.

Most people have not yet grasped this fact and it has become obvious to me from discussions with clients, and from questions from the public, that many of those leaping into negative gearing are doing so without a full understanding of the way it works, and of its risks as well as its benefits. Many accountants have one way of solving a client's tax problem — "You had better go out and buy a property and negative gear it."

In this chapter we'll cover negative gearing in depth for there is no doubt negative gearing is the **best** wealth creation strategy available **if** it is used properly.

"Gearing" means "borrowing", so a person using "gearing" (or "leverage" as it is sometimes called) is going into debt to acquire assets with the hope that the gain from those assets will outweigh the costs of borrowing.

Once you go into debt you have to pay back interest. The higher the debt, and the greater the interest rate, the more interest has to be paid back. As the debt gets larger in relation to the value of the asset, a point is reached where there is more money going out than coming in. You then have a negative cash flow and have to find the shortfall from your other resources i.e. your other income. You are then said to be "negatively geared" as the cash coming in from the asset is not enough to cover that going out.

The big attraction of negative gearing is that the shortfall is generally tax deductible so our friends at the Tax Office help you pay for it. The higher your rate of tax the more they contribute. If a person on $30 000 a year incurs a loss of $5 000 the Tax Office puts in $1 500 — for a person on $70 000 a year the tax saved jumps 25% to almost $2 350.

Note one important and generally overlooked factor. The taxpayers have to find the balance from their own after-tax income so it is **vital** this income be secure. Also, the tax deduction often takes the tax-payer into a lower marginal tax bracket with a consequent lowering of the tax benefit from the negative gearing and other tax-saving investments.

> **EXAMPLE:** *Harry earnt $61 000 a year and also incurred a net loss of $5 000 from his negatively geared rental property. As a higher marginal tax rate cuts in at $60 000 only the first $1 000 of the loss on the rental home is "subsidised" by the Government at 47%. The other $4 000 saves only 42% in tax. Harry is worse off than a tax-payer earning $65 000 a year who could have deducted it all at 47% marginal rate.*

The Break-Even Point

Most investors don't realise there is such a concept as the "break even point", yet it is this that determines the effectiveness of negative gearing. Look at the following example, which illustrates how the break-even point is worked out. For simplicity I have assumed the whole purchase price (plus costs) has been borrowed using property as security in lieu of a deposit:

> **EXAMPLE:** *Mary Jones earns $70 000 a year and buys a rental property for $145 000 (plus costs of $5 000) making a total investment of $150 000. If she puts down no deposit and borrows $150 000 at 7% her interest bill will be $10 500 a year. If we assume the net income from the property is $7 500 (after allowing for rates, vacancies, maintenance, insurance etc) her net shortfall is $3 000 a year.*
>
> *The tax deductibility of this $3 000 deficit reduces Mary's tax bill for the year by $1 455 (47% + 1.5% Medicare levy). When*

this is taken into account Mary is $1 545 a year behind, after the net cost of interest.

Owning the property is thus costing her $1 545 a year, which she must find out of her own pocket. If the property does not increase by that $1 545 a year she is going backwards. Look at it another way – to break even Mary requires a capital gain of 1.03% per annum on the original total cost of $150 000. If she sells the house for $161 000 clear of all selling costs in four years Mary will just get her money back.

I am not saying the property will not increase by more than 1% a year – it may or it may not. Nor am I saying that Mary should avoid the negative gearing strategy. I am warning you to do your homework and do your sums carefully **before** leaping into negative gearing just for the sake of saving tax. You have to calculate the break-even point to see if the numbers stack up.

Notice also the effect on her personal cash flow. Because the tax refund cheque does not arrive until after the end of the financial year, Mary has to have enough funds available to meet all of the $1 545 shortfall in the first year of ownership. If she found herself short of cash because of the large interest bills, she could solve the problem by asking her employer to reduce the amount of PAYG tax taken out of each pay cheque. This would reduce her tax refund because in effect she is receiving, each pay day, a little of the refund caused by the negative gearing.

Take heed. Drive carefully on the road to wealth through negative gearing.

Negative Gearing Into What?

Now let's consider what types of assets we can use the negative gearing technique to buy.

The effectiveness of negative gearing depends on the investor being able to claim the interest as a tax deduction. For this to happen, the asset purchased must produce assessable income. Obviously the family home, as well as gold, stamps, coins, cars and jewels are out, so what is left — income-producing property and shares.

Borrowing to buy investment property is the traditional way to wealth. Gearing into shares has generally been regarded as a bit of a "no no" for everybody but the most aggressive investors. To understand why, you must understand the fundamental differences between investments in property and investments in shares.

Most property has one unique factor — permanence. It is not portable so cannot be spirited away, so unless you strike an earthquake, atomic bomb, or severe erosion, the land element should have everlasting life. Historically, **well located** property has kept pace with inflation so an increase in its value is virtually guaranteed.

Be aware that locations can go out of fashion, causing property values to tumble. Some of the best examples are the gold rush cities that once sported a hundred hotels — most are now ghost towns. In short, the intrinsic value of property depends on the location of the land.

Because shares represent part-ownership of a business the fortunes of the shareholders fluctuate with that of the business. If the business goes well the shares should provide steady growth and an increasing income stream. Unfortunately, businesses can also be run down, suffer from bad management and can go broke. In short, the intrinsic value of shares depends on the company management, which is liable to change.

The other major difference between property and shares is liquidity. It usually takes a large sum of money to buy property and it generally cannot be sold in part. If you own a block of flats and need $10 000 you cannot sell one of the bedrooms. This keeps the turnover of property low in comparison to shares, which can be bought and sold in tiny parcels.

Now consider that every piece of real estate is unique. Consequently the true value can only be known when a willing buyer has been located, contracts have been exchanged and the sale settled. Until that happens the true value is only a guess. The market is the only judge of value for any asset, but the property market may take many months to give a decision.

Each share in a company is like any other share of its type in the same company. Thus you do not have the uniqueness of each piece of property. Our homes may be different but our Telstra shares are identical.

Couple this with the fact that shares can be traded in small parcels and you have an accurate valuation of your shares whenever a stock market is open. Seldom will the share market keep you waiting for an answer.

As a result share prices are more honest than property prices. If chill winds start to blow, the share buffs may decide to take some profits and sell part of their share holdings. Prices may fall substantially, and rapidly, as the market adjusts.

Investors in property suffer chill winds too when interest rates rise, and the threat of a recession scares off buyers and tenants. Unless the property owners are overcommitted, and are forced to dump properties on a bad market, they sit back and wait it out.

They tell themselves the value of their property has "plateaued for a while but will start rising when times change". Why go through the trouble of trying to sell a property in a bad market, incurring thousands of dollars in buying and selling fees, and facing all sorts of capital gains tax headaches when you can simply wait it out. The strategy is fine, but it is an illusion to pretend the property has not dropped in value — if you don't believe me, have the bank auction it for you as "mortgagee in possession".

Another major difference between the two investments is control over the price. You can buy property and raise or lower its value by improving it or neglecting it – you cannot do a thing to change the price of your shares unless you resort to spreading false rumours about the company. This tactic is not recommended as a jail sentence is the likely outcome.

The Investment House

Most small investors use negative gearing only to buy houses. There are two reasons:

(a) Real estate is all they know.

(b) Houses represent the only income-producing real estate in their price range.

However, the leap in house prices of the 1980s coupled with the high interest rates have not been matched by proportionate increases in rents. The house that cost $95 000 a few years ago may now be worth $190 000 — that is an increase in value of over 100%. Yet the rent of that same house may have gone up by less than 50%. Another drawback is that homes age every year and so become progressively less attractive than newer ones.

It is impossible to forecast accurately what the residential gains will be in future as location has a huge effect on price. However, if low inflation continues house prices will not show huge gains. Therefore those investors who rush into the negative gearing of residential houses may be disappointed unless they research the market thoroughly before signing a purchase contract.

Gearing Into Property Trusts

Investors who are happy to use negative-gearing strategies may consider listed property trusts. Yields of between 5% and 10% are available from prime retail, commercial and industrial properties, and the property trust concept enables investors to pool their money with that of other investors and enjoy part-ownership of quality properties in top locations with long leases to substantial tenants. They enable investors to enjoy all the benefits of investment in higher-priced properties without the problem of having to find millions of dollars to do it. Don't forget that listed property trusts have the same volatility as shares and, like an investment house, must be regarded as a long-term investment.

Borrowing For Shares

Has the volatility of the stock market convinced you it is wrong to negative gear into shares? I hope it hasn't, because soon I will explain why I think it may be a very good tactic for some investors in the right climate.

When deciding whether to borrow to buy shares bear in mind the share itself may be effectively leveraged if the company has borrowings. Taking out a loan to buy shares in a company that has large borrowings is a bit like borrowing money for the deposit on a property you are going to buy with negative gearing.

There are two lots of borrowing involved so we are into "double negative gearing". Wonderful stuff if all goes well, but a recipe for disaster if it doesn't. Remember negative gearing is a strategy to speed up whatever is going to happen — prosperity or bankruptcy.

Do Your Homework!

There is only one way to work out if negative gearing is an effective tax-saving strategy - do the sums. Consequently this section will have a lot of figures in it and I suggest you take out a pencil and paper and work through the examples to make sure you understand them. If you find this boring stay away from negative gearing because it is too powerful a tool to be used without careful analysis. By the time you study this chapter and the next you should be able to do all your own buying and borrowing calculations.

The figures to take into account are the investor's taxable income, prevailing interest rates, the income from the asset being purchased and its likely capital growth. Some of these figures can be estimated with accuracy, but others can't. It's important to know the difference; incorrect forecasts have lured many a person who tried negative gearing into bankruptcy.

Commercial lease rentals are usually linked to the CPI so future income from non-residential property is fairly predictable; income from residential property is harder to estimate because landlords usually charge what the market will bear. Dividend income from shares in solid companies should show consistent increases.

The rate of capital gain on both real estate and shares is very hard to forecast, although one could reasonably expect prices of both over the long term to at least keep pace with inflation. The problem is that real estate has its long flat spots and the stock market has its wild ups and downs.

Most intelligent investors know that it is impossible to pick the right time to enter and leave the property and share markets. Therefore the purpose of feasibility studies when considering negative gearing is to enable you to arrange your affairs to maximise your chances of success.

Earlier I gave the example of the $145 000 house purchased with a loan of $145 000 at 7%. Net rents were $7 500 a year and the interest was $10 500, resulting in a shortfall of $3 000 a year.

After allowing for the $1 455 tax refund created by the interest shortfall, and taking into account the loss of interest on the deposit, the investor needed the property to appreciate by $1 545 a year (1.03% on the initial investment) just to reach break-even point.

Let's compare that to two other alternatives – negative gearing into a listed property trust and gearing into a conservative share trust. Once again we'll have to make some assumptions about entry fees and earning rates. To ensure a valid comparison is made with the house let's assume an investment of $145 000 is made once again funded by a loan of $150 000 at 7%.

EXAMPLE ONE: *Gearing into an unlisted trust that invested in a range of listed property trusts. The assets of the listed trusts would be prime commercial, retail and industrial properties tenanted to major companies on long leases.*

Assume buy-in costs of 5%, no exit fees, net income of 6% a year (of which a quarter is tax free). When the 5% entry costs are provided for $145 000 is invested.

CASH POSITION	
Net Income	$ 8 700
Interest	$10 500
Cash deficit	$ 1 800
TAX POSITION	
Cash Deficit	$ 1 800
add Tax-free portion of income	$ 2 175
Tax deduction	$ 3 975
Tax Saved @ 48.5%	$ 1 928
TRUE COST	
Cash Deficit	$ 1 800
less Tax Saved	$ 1 928
True Cost	$ 128

The property trusts have to increase by just $128 a year (a miniscule percentage of the purchase price) for the investor to break even.

This looks a better deal than buying the house, but two other factors should also be noticed. All purchase costs have been paid and there are no exit fees. Selling commission and legal fees would have to be deducted from the sale price of the house if the investor wanted to sell it. In Mary's example we ignored the $4 000 or more she would have to find in selling costs.

EXAMPLE TWO: *Gearing into a conservative share trust whose principal assets are blue chip shares in companies such as Boral, Telstra, National Australia Bank, BHP and Harvey Norman.*

Assume buy-in costs of 5% and no exit fees, net income of 4% a year (mostly from franked dividends), $145 000 is invested when we provide for the 5% entry fee. I will continue to use a taxable income for the investor of $70 000 a year – the highest marginal rate.

CASH POSITION

Net Income	$ 5 800
Interest	$10 500
Cash deficit	$ 4 700

TAX POSITION

Cash Deficit	$ 4 700
less imputation credits	$ 2 485
Tax deduction	$ 2 300
Tax Saved @ 48.5%	1 115

TRUE COST

Cash Deficit	$ 4 700
less value of imp credits	$ 2 485
less Tax Saved	$ 1 115
	$ 1 100

We can see that the true cost of owning this investment is $1 100 in the first year.

Analyse the three cases above. The house is costing $1 545 a year, the property trust $128 and the equity trust $1 100. It is now a matter of deciding which of the above investments is likely to produce the highest capital gain in relation to the net holding cost. This is the area where you must do your own research helped with input from your financial adviser.

Notice the listed property trusts and the equity trust have a flexibility that the house does not. You can reinvest dividends (the importance of which I stressed in *Making Money Made Simple*) and buy and sell in small amounts. You are also freed from the worry of ongoing management.

A Useful Guide

When you are considering buying property for negative gearing try to think in terms of "net yield" instead of "price". For example, if you see a property on the market for $150 000, work out the net rent after costs such as maintenance and rates. A rule of thumb is gross rents less 25%.

If the gross rents are $180 a week you can assume the net rents are $135 a week ($180 – 25% of $180). The annual net rent is $7 020 (52 x $135) so the net yield is 4.68% on a purchase cost of $150 000. If you can get the price down to $140 000 the net yield jumps to 5.01%. Subtract the net yield from the interest rate and then, assuming you are in the 48.5% tax bracket, halve the answer to bring the tax deductibility of the interest into account. The difference is how much the property must appreciate each year for you to break even.

Look at the example above and assume we bought for $150 000 and borrowed at 7%. The net yield is 4.68% and the cost of interest is 7% so the difference is 2.32%. Half of 2.32% is 1.16%, which is how much the property has to appreciate each year for us to break even. Let's verify the accuracy of the figures:

Net rent	$ 7 020
Interest	$10 500
Shortfall	$ 3 480
Less tax saved @ 48.5%	$ 1 688
Actual cost	$ 1 792

The actual cost of $1 792 is 1.19% of $150 000. The difference is caused by my using the actual tax rate of 48.5% in the worked example instead of 50% when I was showing you how to use the "rough method". The approximation is satisfactory when you are inspecting properties and want to do the figures in your head.

Remember it's no more than a useful rule of thumb.

The Three Essential Elements

Successful negative gearing has three essential elements:

(1) A careful selection of the asset to be purchased to try to ensure maximum capital gain – the chapters on shares and property should help you to choose.

(2) A borrowing plan tailored to minimise risk, which is discussed in the next chapter.

(3) A "fail safe" strategy in case things go wrong[1].

The effectiveness of negative gearing depends on there being capital profits to compensate for the cash shortfall caused by the excess of interest over income. It is up to the buyer to choose an asset that is likely to produce strong capital growth, but remember **wherever there is a chance of capital gain there is a chance of capital loss.**

Make no mistake about it — negative gearing has its risks. I have stressed that gearing is a strategy that will speed up whatever is going to happen. **Negative** gearing will make it happen much faster.

If you use a deposit of $10 000 and borrow $90 000 to buy a house for $100 000 you have doubled your money when the house increases by 10%. If by some chance the house falls in value by 10% you have lost your $10 000 deposit so, in theory at least, you have lost all you invested.

I say "in theory" because neither a profit nor a loss can happen until you create it by selling the asset. If the asset drops by 10%, then rises by 20% a year later, you are still doing well provided you have stuck with it.

Negative gearing is usually undertaken to buy property and shares. While you can expect the values of both to rise in the long term, nobody can say what will happen in the short term. Negative gearing should produce good results over the long haul, so anybody going into negative gearing must ensure they can stay in the game if times get tough. The way to do this is to eliminate as many uncertainties as possible. One way to do it is by using appropriate borrowing – the subject of the next chapter.

---

1 See Chapter 36 Building A Safety Net.

28

Borrowing Smart

If you would know the value of borrowing go and try to borrow some; for he that goes a borrowing goes a sorrowing.

BENJAMIN FRANKLIN

"It's hard to go wrong with property if **you** can choose the time to sell it" is almost a truism. Just as the property prices of 20 years ago seem cheap now, the present prices will seem unbelievably cheap in 20 years time. Most people who lose money in property do so because they are forced to sell at the worst time, thus taking a massive jump backwards down the financial ladder, while giving somebody else a "free kick" by allowing them to grab a cheap asset.

The right type of loan is critical to success in real estate because it is generally pressure from a lender that creates forced sales. An elderly couple I know bought a block of flats in the mid 1980s for $170 000 with a loan of $100 000. The bank manager did not mention the bank had fixed interest loans available and they accepted a variable interest rate.

The rate was 13% when they took out the loan and the repayments were just covered by the rents. Within 12 months the interest rate had shot up to 21% and their monthly repayments increased by $667, which was way beyond their capacity to pay. They had to get out of the game as soon as possible, so their only solution was to sell the property urgently.

There was a major problem. Real estate prices had been strong when they bought because of the low interest rates, but when it came to sell, the interest rate hike had knocked the stuffing out of the market. They were forced into a weak market that was dominated by many other sellers who were dumping prime properties because they couldn't pay their interest.

The couple lost a lot of money because of their lack of knowledge. If they had chosen a fixed rate they could have enjoyed a life free from the fear of interest rate rises sabotaging their budget, and would have remained "in the game" to take part in the inevitable boom when it came a few years later.

You may well ask "why go for a fixed-rate mortgage if rates appear stable?". That's a valid question, but we now live in a time of shorter economic cycles and it is foolhardy to suggest that conditions prevailing now will be the same next year. Negative gearing becomes dangerous in a climate of rising interest rates because, as interest rates rise, the break-even analysis looks progressively worse until it reaches a point where buying becomes foolish.

Establish Certainty

Another way to be chased out of the game is to borrow for shares and give the lender security over the shares only. If share prices drop suddenly, the lender will probably insist you sell some of your holding to reduce the debt. It is a similar situation to that which befell our elderly couple with the flats. You are now forced to dump good scrip on a weak market.

Those investors who fell for the lure of low-interest loans in foreign currencies know all about uncertainty. They have added an exciting element into their investment – the fun of fluctuating currencies.

Certainly the interest rate is lower, but remember the interest rate is a measure of the currency risk. If our dollar is weak compared to that of our major trading partners, foreign currency loans are highly risky. Exporters **benefit** from a weak dollar, and importers **suffer** from a weak dollar. Therefore it may be appropriate for exporters to borrow in the dollars of their export receipts, but never for importers to borrow in the currency in which they pay for their goods. If the importers borrow in a foreign currency, and our dollar drops, they suffer higher interest costs and higher purchase costs. That can be a vicious squeeze.

Interest-Only Borrowing

The importance of tailoring your borrowings for maximum effect is crucial to your success with negative gearing. Borrowing is an essential element of negative gearing and often the type of borrowing makes a huge difference to the outcome. I will now explain why "interest only" borrowing is the most effective strategy for negative gearing.

If you borrow on an interest-only basis you pay back only the interest – the principal does not reduce. If you borrow on a principal and interest (P & I) basis the repayments include both the interest, plus an extra sum to reduce the principal. Note carefully that only the interest component is a tax reduction and that this reduces as the principal drops. As a result you progressively lose the tax benefits of negative gearing.

The repayments are $1 509 a month if you borrow $100 000 from a bank at 7% on a P and I basis over a seven-year period. The same loan at 7% on an interest-only basis would require payments of only $583 a month. The person borrowing on a P & I basis has to find an extra $926 a month.

Notice I pointed out that only the interest component of a loan is tax deductible — thus the investors with the P & I loan have to find the extra $926 a month from their **after tax** income.

It is likely that only people earning over $60 000 would engage in a negative gearing plan of this size, so taxpayers in this tax bracket have to earn an extra $1 852 (2 x $926) to pay the after-tax sum of $926 because tax takes almost half their earnings. Thus the P & I borrower has to earn an extra $22 224 a year ($1 852 x 12) to be on the same borrowing footing as the interest-only borrower.

The principal reduces quickly if you use a traditional seven-year trading bank loan and, as a result, the borrower is likely to suffer tax problems in the final years. By the end of the third year the balance owing is around $63 000. Consequently the principal component of the monthly payment has increased to $1 179 and the interest component has gone down to $330.

After three years have passed the P & I borrowers can claim less than $4 000 as a tax deduction, and have to find the other $14 148 a year from after-tax dollars. They now have to earn over $28 000 a year more than the interest-only borrower just to fund the principal component of the repayment. As the loan continues the P & I borrowers have to find an ever-increasing amount of after-tax dollars to make the P & I repayments.

The major benefits of interest-only borrowing are:

(1) A lower monthly payment is required. Accordingly the borrower does not have such a large regular commitment.

(2) Interest-only loans are usually taken out on a fixed interest rate basis. The borrower is protected from interest rate rises.

(3) Those who are happy with the greater interest commitment may choose a bigger mortgage than if they had borrowed P & I.

The larger mortgage enables them to buy a more expensive property, buy on a lower deposit or buy a property with a lower yield. A well-known property axiom is "the lower the yield the higher the chance of capital gain". Buying the better quality property should result in less problems due to vacancies and repairs, as well as giving larger capital growth.

Summing up, the interest-only loan gives access to a better-quality property or enables a buyer to grab a bargain on a smaller deposit.

I'll Never Pay It Off!

The concept of borrowing on an interest-only basis bothers many people – their reaction is "how can you get ahead when you never get to pay anything off". Obviously this is quite a realistic way of looking at it, but the answer is simple. Start a separate fund (sinking fund) to pay off the debt.

For high income earners the best way to do this is by insurance bonds. A person with a low income earning spouse might be better off to use equity and bond trusts in view of their different tax structure, but in this section I shall concentrate on insurance bonds.

The strategy of higher income earners borrowing on an interest-only basis and investing their surplus funds in insurance bonds is justified by the net tax effect. Market-linked insurance bonds should produce between 7% and 9% a year, on a long-term basis, after the insurance company has paid the tax. No extra tax is payable by the tax-payer provided the bonds are held for 10 years, so the rate after taxation may be 8% net.

As interest for negative gearing purposes is tax deductible the Federal Government is effectively subsidising the interest rate. Thus the 7% investment loan is costing about 3.5% after allowing for tax. Doesn't it make sense to borrow at 3.5% effective and invest your surplus funds at 7% net, instead of using them to repay the loan? If tax rates fell, or interest rates rose, the position may change, so you must monitor it continually.

A rule of thumb when using insurance bonds is to invest, every year, 6% of the amount you owe. For example, if you owe $100 000, invest $6 000 a year into insurance bonds to build the sinking fund. You should find in about 10 to 11 years that your fund will have grown to the size of your debt.

If you require income from the property when the value of the bonds reaches the loan balance, the sinking fund can be cashed in to pay off the debt. Then all the income that was being used for interest will now come to you. If income is not required don't pay off the loan. Leave the funds in the sinking fund intact to accumulate still larger amounts tax free.

Now I'll take you through some examples to show you the way it all comes together. You will gain more benefit if you find a pencil and some paper and work through these examples as you read this chapter. Interest rates, the CPI, and prices will change continually so use the figures here as practice. Then find some real-life examples in your own area using up-to-date rates. You will soon be able to do it easily.

Negative Gearing Examples

The three examples refer to the same property. The different results arise from the way it is financed.

Assumptions

Cash available $200 000 Property Cost $400 000

Cost of acquisition/borrowing $16 000 — CPI 2% p.a.

Net Income 5% p.a. — Net Capital Growth 4% p.a.

Rents increase each year with CPI.

Insurance Bonds earn 8% per annum — their entry fee is 4%, no exit fee.

Tax-payer is on 50% marginal rate Interest rate 7% FIXED

Total Income from property over period = $243 374

Case Study One

The buyer puts down $200 000 deposit and borrows $216 000 @ 7% P & I over 10 years. Annual repayments $30 096

The total repayments are $216 000 Principal and $84 950 interest.

Total Income	$ 243 374
Less Interest	$ 84 950
Surplus Income over Interest	$ 158 424
Less Tax on surplus income	$ 79 212
Net surplus after tax	$ 79 212

Summary

Value of Building in 10 years	$ 592 000
Add net surplus from above	79 212
	$ 671 212
Deduct Principal repaid	$ 216 000
Net surplus	$ 455 212

Case Study Two

In this case $216 000 is borrowed on an INTEREST-ONLY basis for 10 years. Annual repayments are $15 120 – a saving of $14 976 a year.

Total Income	$ 243 374
Total Repayments	$ 151 200
Surplus	$ 92 174
Less tax paid	$ 46 087
Surplus after tax	$ 46 087

Summary

Value of Building	$ 592 000
Add Surplus	$ 46 087
	$ 638 087
Less Loan balance	$ 216 000
Net cash surplus	$ 422 087

The reason this example APPEARS to show a worse outcome for the investor than Case Study One is because it ignores the opportunity cost of the $14 976 a year that is available due to the lower repayments on the interest-only loan. If that had been invested in insurance bonds that earnt 8% per annum there would have been an additional tax-free sum of $228 000 after 10 years.

Case Study Three

In this example the whole purchase price plus acquisition costs ($416 000) are borrowed on an INTEREST-ONLY basis over 10 years, and the available cash of $200 000 is invested in Insurance Bonds.

Total Income	$ 243 374
Total Repayments	$ 219 200

Shortfall	$ 47 826
Less tax saved	$ 23 913
Shortfall after tax	$ 23 913

Summary

Value of building	$ 592 000
Value of bonds	$ 426 000
	$ 1 018 000
Less Shortfall	$ 23 913
Less Loan balance	$ 416 000
Net cash surplus	$ 578 087

Notice these three examples use the same investor buying the same property at the same time with the same deposit. Yet the outcome in each case is vastly different because of differing borrowing strategies. Certainly the results depend on the performance of the insurance bonds, but I believe 8% is a conservative figure for market-linked bonds over a 10-year period.

A different result, and possibly an even better one, would be achieved if unit trusts were used instead of insurance bonds. However, the main aim of this chapter, and the one before it, is to open your eyes to the exciting possibilities with negative gearing and creative financing as well as to alert you to the dangers. Your financial adviser and your accountant should be able to assist you with the fine details.

The bonds or unit trusts create an extra safety cushion for you. I believe it is better to owe $150 000 and have $50 000 invested elsewhere, than to owe $100 000 and have nothing in reserve at all.

I recommend people who are involved in negative gearing into property should invest in insurance bonds that are share based. Traditionally the property and share markets rise and fall at different times. By mixing your investments you are achieving a greater spread and thus security.

In Summary

Now you should be aware of the crucial importance of financing your negative gearing for maximum returns, while at all times making sure there is a safety buffer to prevent the unthinkable; having to dump a property on a bad market.

In the next chapter we'll learn about ways to insure your income, for it is the income stream that makes negative gearing work.

29

Income Replacement Insurance

To be alive at all involves some risk.

HAROLD MACMILLAN

Have you bothered to insure your home? What a silly question! Of course you have. Nobody in their right mind would leave an asset worth $100 000, or more, uninsured.

Have you adequate life insurance? The answer is probably "No" but I hope this will change after you have finished this book. We have found the average family needs enough life insurance to provide **at least $400 000** to the estate **after all debts are paid.** This is calculated on the basis that $400 000 wisely invested should provide about 5% a year income and 6% a year growth. This would provide only $20 000 a year which is the bare minimum most households require.

Certainly a higher income could be produced from that $400 000 but there is a price to pay. If more income is taken, at the expense of growth, family living standards will decline every year in line with the falling value of money.

Families relying on dual incomes or those who have young children should take out life insurance on the spouse's life. Only recently I heard about a senior business executive in a stressful position whose wife died suddenly, leaving him with several young children. He had loads of life insurance on himself but none on her. The payments on his big mortgage were bad enough but the enormous costs for child care were just too much; he had a nervous breakdown and lost his job. Yearly renewable term insurance for a woman of 35 should not cost any more than $5 a week for $100 000 of life cover, including Total and Permanent Disability. Surely that's a small sum to pay for peace of mind.

Insuring Your Income

Your life is insured, your house is insured — what about insuring your earning capacity? World-wide statistics show that one person in every three will suffer a long term disability during their lifetime. Many believe that Workers Compensation will protect them if they are disabled because of an accident, but this is an illusion, because many accidents occur outside of working hours and are thus not covered by Workers Compensation. In any event, only 4% of long term disabilities are caused by accident. Sickness causes the other 96%, so it is obvious that people without some form of income replacement cover are at risk.

A young person has the capacity to earn millions of dollars in a working lifetime, yet few bother to insure this priceless income. A person can gain the knowledge, adopt the savings habit, practise goal setting and do all the other necessary things to speed up attaining their goal of financial independence but find their plans shattered because they did not insure the fuel that drives the

whole plan — their income stream. If a corporate body strikes a serious problem you can bet it is caused by lack of cash flow, if a human body has problems they are often caused by loss of blood flow. Similarly lack of cash flow can cause serious personal financial problems.

There are as many types of insurance to protect against disability as there are disabilities. They range from those which provide cover for total and permanent disability (TPD), to ones which pay you an income if you are sick or injured and cannot resume your normal occupation for a few weeks or even a few years. It is uncommon for younger people to become totally and permanently disabled so insurance for TPD is fairly cheap, and is usually included with a life insurance policy at little extra cost. Notice the wording is "totally and permanently" disabled, which means what it says. That definition does NOT cover your being off sick for a year because of a disease such as hepatitis.

The main topic of this chapter is the income replacement policy — the policy which provides money to compensate you for loss of earnings while you are sick or injured. These policies are costly because of the huge potential cost of a claim. Think about a 30 year old who, for a premium of just $48 a month, takes out a policy which pays a benefit of $300 a week indexed for inflation. If he subsequently suffered an injury which stopped him working for 30 years, the total benefits the insurance company may have to pay him could be as high as **$1.36 million.**

The Choices

I will now take you through the essential features of an income replacement policy; as you read be aware these policies are designed for high income earning professional people such as doctors and accountants. They are desirable for everybody, but the high cost puts them out of reach of lower income earners, and many occupations are not regarded as safe enough to cover.

First we'll cover the choices you will have to make when you choose a policy.

WAIT PERIOD: The wait period is similar to the excess on a motor vehicle insurance policy. The longer you are prepared to keep yourself before the claim period starts, the lower will be the premiums. Few policies will allow a wait period under 14 days and we find that most clients opt for a 30, 60 or 90 day period. The appropriate one for you depends on the type of job you have, and the strength of other resources that can be marshalled in need.

BENEFIT PERIOD: You become seriously ill and are unable to work for eight years. For how long will the benefits be paid? It's a critical question and I am surprised how many clients come in with policies that will pay for only one or two years. These would be worth little to a person with a long term illness. You will have the choice of any term up to age 65, which is when most policies cut out, and I strongly suggest you always go for benefit periods to age 65 for both sickness and accident if you can afford it.

LEVEL OR STEPPED PREMIUMS: A level premium means the premiums are unchanged for the term stated in the policy whereas stepped premiums increase each year. If you choose level premiums you are paying a larger sum now to guarantee lower premiums at some future time. My preference is for stepped premiums which allow you to keep the payments more in line with your budget. The other benefit of stepped premiums is that you are not "locked in" to the policy as you would tend to be if you had chosen level premiums. Few would cancel a policy and change insurance companies after they had paid several years of exceptionally high premiums, just for the peace of mind of having no increase in the future.

THE BENEFIT LEVEL: This is the amount the insurance company will pay you while you are disabled. Usually it cannot exceed two-thirds of your present income. This is to stop people increasing their income by being disabled. You are free to choose a benefit amount that is less than two-thirds of your income.

LEVEL OR INDEXED BENEFITS: Do you want the benefits to stay the same for the term of the policy or to rise in line with inflation? Obviously the indexed one is essential if you are to preserve your standard of living.

AIDS INCLUSION OPTION: Many insurance companies now give you the option of excluding illness from AIDS for a reduced premium. The choice is up to you, but remember you can get AIDS from incidents such as being pricked by a newly infected needle lying on the beach.

PREMIUMS: Do you pay monthly, quarterly, six monthly or annually? Choose the one that suits your budget and note the premiums are tax deductible which reduces the effective cost. The bad news is the benefits are regarded as taxable income, as they are meant to take the place of your normal salary.

OCCUPATION: The cost of cover varies with your occupation and there are some job categories that are uninsurable. Your adviser can guide you in this area and will sometimes suggest a particular insurance company that will accept an occupation that another company would refuse.

That's all there is to the basic policy. You pay the insurance company a premium in return for which they promise to pay you an income for as long as you are unable to work. These payments will start at the end of the Wait Period, and will continue till you return to work or reach the end of the benefit period nominated in the policy.

You are likely to find shopping around for a policy difficult because no two companies have identical policies and many salespeople will confuse you by telling you that no product is as good as the one they are selling.

Here are some points to consider when choosing an income replacement policy. Remember, you get what you pay for:

(1) Are the premiums waived if you are off work because of accident or illness?

(2) What happens if your income has dropped prior to your making a claim so the benefit is now more than two-thirds of your present income?

(3) Will there be a payment for a specified injury even if it does not cause temporary total disability? For example, some policies may pay you a year's benefits if you lose the sight of one eye.

(4) Is there death cover included in the policy?

(5) Are your benefits reduced if you receive additional payments such as those from Workers Compensation?

(6) Is there is period of grace, say 30 days, during which the policy stays in force if you are late making a payment. If you are late with your premiums, does the insurer require a new medical examination?

(7) Is the cost of future premiums guaranteed not to change from that stated in the policy document?

(8) What is the definition of "disabled"? For example, how will the insurance company treat a situation where a surgeon earning $150 000 a year injures his hand and ends up working as a lecturer on $45 000 a year.

(9) Will both premiums and benefit payments increase each year in line with inflation?

(10) Will the company guarantee to renew the policy irrespective of any changes in your health, or claim history, provided premiums are paid on time?

(11) Are you covered throughout the World?

(12) If you have a claim for a specific ailment (e.g. a broken bone) does the policy allow you to claim again for a similar occurrence?

(13) Are you covered 24 hours a day?

(14) What specific exclusions are there — e.g. hang gliding, parachuting.

Summing Up

Income replacement insurance is relatively expensive so it is a luxury for many people. However, you MUST look at your overall commitments and say to yourself "What will happen if I cannot work for a year or more because of illness or an accident?" Certainly those of you who are heavily into negative gearing should have income replacement insurance unless you know that the properties you own are readily saleable.

Most income replacement contracts can be written for a cost of between 2% to 3% of the monthly benefit needed. A person earning $50 000 a year is planning to earn $50 000 when they are well and nothing when they are ill. Maybe it is better to reduce the present income to $49 000 so the family can still have $35 000 a year if the breadwinner is unable to work.

30

The Truth About Life Assurance

In the last analysis it is our conceptions of death which decides our answers to all the questions that life puts to us.

DAG HAMMARSKJOLD

Almost everybody who has ever sat across a desk in our office has had the same reaction towards life insurance, or "assurance" as it is often called. They are suspicious about the product, they have a negative attitude towards life assurance companies, they don't trust life assurance salespeople and they either have a little life assurance but "don't understand it" or "wouldn't touch it". Only one type of client is "sold" on the product — a widow who would be destitute without the large life assurance policy her husband had when he died.

The same people who have a negative attitude towards life assurance take pains to insure their home, car and valuables and would suffer a severe anxiety attack if they woke up one morning to discover their renewal notice had gone to the wrong address and they were living in an uninsured house. Why is there such an apparent conflict in behaviour?

The problem with life assurance is that it is such a complex topic that few will put in the time to understand it. Besides, it involves thinking about death which is a subject we would rather ignore and it is often sold by people with insufficient knowledge. To make it worse there are a few life assurance salespeople who profit by convincing people to cancel good life assurance policies and take out fresh ones, or "sell" life assurance by knocking the other companies' products.

The fact is that life assurance can be a worthwhile investment if used properly, so I urge you to take the time to read and re-read this chapter and discuss it with your family. It should soon become clear. I apologise for the lists of figures in this chapter but there is no other format we can use to discuss it adequately.

I shall explain how life assurance works by discussing a typical family and looking at their life assurance needs. Don't worry too much about the cover levels in the following examples. The aim of this chapter is to teach you to understand the differences between types of policies, so concentrate on the principles of each type of assurance discussed. Notice from the outset that buying life assurance is like buying most other things. You tend to get what you pay for. Also be aware that there are an almost infinite number of options, so you have to settle for the one that suits your budget as well as your needs.

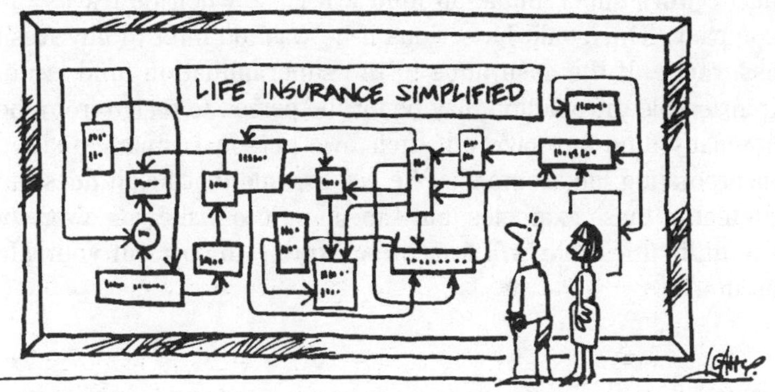

Just before we start, there is a difference between "assurance" and "insurance". Assurance means the certainty of an event happening as is the case with a policy that pays out at age 65 or death. Insurance is for events that may not happen such as when you insure against your house burning down or having your car stolen.

Enter A Young Couple

We will assume that Ralph is aged 30, his wife Donna is 24 and they have just had a baby son named Bruce. Their debts total $65 000 and they have decided they need life assurance on both lives. They are also concerned about building up funds for their son's education.

Our first job is to discover the extent of life assurance cover in Ralph's superannuation fund because almost every superannuation fund has some life cover and it is pointless to over insure. In this case Ralph has only a small cover through his superannuation fund and they decide another $300 000 is an appropriate sum for which to insure Ralph's life.

As we proceed through the chapter we will keep coming to "forks in the road" where we have to decide to go in one direction or another. In the end the decision of which road to take is governed by our budget. We are now at the first one. Even if Ralph's life cover in his superannuation was perfect **today** what is the position if he suffers ill-health and has to resign from his job.

The outcome will depend on the terms of the assurance policy. He may be able to continue his life assurance with the superannuation fund's assurer. Maybe the life assurance included in the work superannuation fund will lapse when he leaves the company. This could be serious if he was too unfit to buy fresh assurance. If the assurance in the superannuation fund is not transferable the solution may be for the person to resign from the company fund and take out their own personal superannuation incorporating life assurance. We will assume that Ralph does not do that in these examples, but I mention it to make you aware of the difficulties that will arise when trying to sort out your life assurance.

Term Assurance

The first option to consider is yearly renewable term assurance which works like car insurance. You pay a sum annually for the assurance and get nothing back unless you have a claim. Each year Ralph will get older, and a year closer to death. Therefore the cost of his life assurance will rise. He has three options:

(1) A level premium with the sum insured decreasing each year

(2) A level sum insured with the premium increasing each year

(3) An increasing premium with the sum insured increasing each year

In this case Ralph opts for (2) so the sum assured stays at $300 000 while the premium increases each year. The figures look like this:

TERM LIFE ASSURANCE ILLUSTRATION

Yearly renewable term cover — aged 30 — non smoker

Policy Year	Age next Birthday	Death Cover	Annual Ins Cost	Total costs paid to date
1	31	300 000	436	436
2	32	300 000	443	879
3	33	300 000	453	1 332
4	34	300 000	462	1 795
5	35	300 000	473	2 269
10	40	300 000	594	4 970
15	45	300 000	792	8 377
20	50	300 000	1 271	13 662
25	55	300 000	2 168	22 402
30	60	300 000	3 847	37 902
35	65	300 000	6 284	63 999

In all the illustrations in this chapter only every fifth year from year five is shown to save space. The figures will increase proportionately in the other years. Notice, in the illustration above, the steep rise in premiums as he gets older.

ADVANTAGES: Ralph has high assurance cover for a low cost when he is young.

DISADVANTAGES: The sum assured stays constant so is falling in real terms as inflation takes it toll. There is never any money coming back out of it, and eventually a time comes when the premiums will be so expensive that Ralph will have to quit the policy losing all he has paid in.

WARNING: There are many types of term assurance available and almost every day I receive "special offers" in the mail. I will remind you continually in this chapter that you get what you pay for and the cheaper policies usually lack many valuable benefits. Your financial adviser or assurance representative will be able to explain the differences to you. If they can't, go to somebody who can.

One of the best additions you can have in a term assurance contract is an option to convert whole or part of the assurance cover to Whole of Life without a medical examination. This is particularly useful if you cannot afford a Whole of Life Policy now because you are paying off your house or car. Once you are free of that monthly repayment in a few years time you will be able to switch, irrespective of what may have happened to your health in the meantime.

EXAMPLE: *A man had a $300 000 term assurance policy which wisely included the option to convert to whole of life. He had a serious heart attack. He knew the benefits of whole of life policies so managed to find the extra payments to convert $100 000 of that policy to a whole of life one. It would have been impossible for him to buy life assurance any other way because of his health.*

If your employer is paying your superannuation contributions, and is claiming a tax deduction for them, it may be cost effective to have your term life insurance included in the superannuation policy. The tax deductibility substantially reduces its real cost.

Whole Of Life Assurance

Now let's examine the Whole of Life Policy. This has been called the Rolls-Royce of policies so expect it to be the most expensive. The contract terms are simple. Ralph will pay the same premium until his 90th birthday or his prior death. On death his estate will receive the sum assured plus policy earnings which are called bonuses. On this policy the premiums are a massive $455.97 a month. That's right, he is paying more a month than he is paying for a whole year's term cover. It is 12 times as expensive **at his present age.**

It may be too expensive for Ralph and I suggest he is better off to take the term assurance and concentrate on getting his house mortgage paid off. But don't overlook the advantages of whole of life for there will be plenty of people reading this book who **can** afford a whole of life policy but are not aware of the benefits.

Look at the figures and notice a column "cash value" which was not in the term assurance illustration. This shows the estimated sum that is available if the policy is terminated and cashed in. It is also the approximate loan value of the policy because the assurance company will always let you borrow against the policy for an amount of up to 90% of its cash value.

ADVANTAGES: The amount of assurance is increasing to keep pace with inflation.

The policy eventually attains a huge cash value which can be accessed at any time by cashing it in or by borrowing against it.

WHOLE OF LIFE ASSURANCE ILLUSTRATION

Death Benefit $300 000. Monthly premium $455.97 — aged 30

Policy Year	Age next Birthday	Death Cover	Annual Ins Cost	Total costs paid to date
1	31	312 600	0	5 472
2	32	325 956	6 626	10 943
3	33	342 813	13 200	16 415
4	34	360 520	19 239	21 887
5	35	380 927	25 843	27 358
10	40	503 278	74 024	54 716
15	45	664 977	148 927	82 075
20	50	885 898	268 743	109 433
25	55	1 185 992	457 080	136 791
30	60	1 559 833	737 305	164 149
35	65	2 043 378	1 144 547	191 507
40	70	2 676 000	1 724 815	218 866

If death duties ever return the proceeds of the policy could be used to pay them so his estate will be left intact for his beneficiaries.

After a few years there will enough cash value in the policy to let it pay for itself if Ralph lost his job and could not afford to pay the premiums. A policy cannot be forfeited by the insurance company while it retains a cash value. If a premium is not paid it is automatically assumed to be taken from the loan value of the policy. The policy can lapse once the unpaid premiums plus interest exceeds the cash value. Consequently a policy on which premiums have been paid for 10 years could continue for many more years with no premiums paid. If he dies the insurance company would pay out the sum assured plus bonuses less unpaid premiums and accrued interest.

As the years go by its cost effectiveness **rises** while that of term assurance **falls.** In this policy Ralph has over $2 million of life assurance at age 65 for his **fixed** premium of $455.97 a month ($5 471 a year). Ralph would need to pay over $40 000 in that year alone for $2 million of term assurance.

It is interesting to observe that most assurance companies do not differentiate between non-smokers and smokers in Whole of

Life contracts but give non-smokers a large discount in term assurance policies. The term assurance rates I have used are for non-smokers so the term assurance premiums would be much higher (particularly at an older age) if Ralph was a smoker.

This policy has a residual value whereas the term policy does not. Compare the two examples and notice that by age 65 Ralph has paid nearly $64 000 for his term cover with **nothing** to show for it. By using a whole of life policy he has paid around $128 000 **more** but has had greatly increased life cover and has a cash value of well over **a million dollars.**

DISADVANTAGES: The policy is expensive. Remember I said you get what you paid for.

Term Combined With Whole Of Life

Don't despair — assurance has plenty of options. Let's see what happens if Ralph takes out $100 000 of Whole of Life assurance and adds a "rider" of term assurance at $200 000 which will last for the first 20 years of the policy.

He will still have his desired cover of $300 000, his premiums will be cheaper, and the Whole of Life Component will grow. However, the premium will be a **level** one so the term assurance component will reduce each year. As there is twice as much term assurance as there is whole of life assurance cover, the term assurance cover will reduce faster than the whole of life portion grows. Notice how the death benefit reduces slowly for the first 10 years then starts to rise again as the effect of compound interest on the whole of life component starts to work its magic.

The cost is $184.98 a month, which may be starting to fit into Ralph and Donna's budget.

I will introduce another phrase before you get too involved in studying the illustration on the next page. That is "paid up value", which **is not the cash value of the policy.** It is the value the assurance company would place on the policy if you decided to pay no more premiums and leave the policy to "sit".

For example in the illustration below you could decide, after three years, to pay no more premiums. The assurance company would then have an obligation to pay your estate $19 821 when you died. Bonuses would make this sum larger but obviously would be much lower than they would be if you kept paying the premiums. If you made the policy "paid up" in the third year and died two years later there would not be an obligation to pay your estate

$36,195 as that is the paid up value for a person who stopped payment in the fifth year. Their estate would receive $276 975 if the policy was current and $36 195 if it had been made "paid up".

You will see this option compares more than favourably with the term cover despite its extra cost. If that cost is still too high Ralph could have had $50 000 whole of life cover with a term rider of $250 000 or any other such option as he decided upon. The advantages and disadvantages are similar to the previous example.

Cashing In Whole Of Life Policies

Often we hear suggestions that those who own Whole of Life policies should surrender them and buy Term Insurance because it is cheaper. That advice ignores the fact that most of those people are paying tax at a higher rate than the Life Office and that the front-end fees have already been paid.

The following example shows that the effective cost of protection under an existing Whole of Life policy is minimal to a high income tax-payer after a few years.

$100 000 WHOLE OF LIFE ASSURANCE ILLUSTRATION

Including term rider of $200 000

Monthly premium $184.98 — aged 30

Policy Year	Age next Birthday	Death Cover	Cash Value	Paid Up Value	Total costs paid
1	31	294 200	0	0	2 220
2	32	288 652	2 208	11 992	4 440
3	33	284 271	4 400	19 821	6 650
4	34	280 173	6 413	27 883	8 879
5	35	276 975	8 614	36 195	11 099
9	39	268 363	19 646	71 783	19 978
10	40	267 759	24 674	81 319	22 198
15	45	271 659	49 642	135 369	33 296
20	50	295 299	89 581	202 419	44 395
25	55	395 330	152 359	287 180	53 866
30	60	519 944	245 768	396 284	63 337
35	65	681 126	381 515	538 286	72 808
40	70	892 200	574 938	725 110	82 279

EXAMPLE ONE: *Consider a male now aged 40 who bought a $100 000 Whole of Life policy with annual premiums of $2 140 six years ago. Let's assume the current cash value of the policy is $12 073, and that interest earned on that sum, if it was cashed in, would be $845 after tax.*

Interest foregone @ 7% net =	*$ 845*
7th premium due	*$2 140*
	$2 985
Less increase in cash value	*$3 070*
True cost	*-$ 85*

The cost of Term Insurance would need to be based on the Sum Insured plus bonuses, minus the cash value of the equivalent Whole of Life policy. Term rates increase each year but at age 40 the rate would be around $3 per thousand for a male smoker and $2 per thousand for a non-smoker.

Apart from its tax effectiveness, the Whole of Life policy has the added advantage of staying in force under automatic non-forfeiture rules if premiums are unpaid. That is one reason Term Insurance lapse rates are higher than those for cash value policies.

The most important point is that few people can afford all the insurance protection they need through whole of life policies, which is why a combination of both is usually the best solution. **Please treat with extreme caution any suggestions that you cash in existing whole of life policies.**

Spouse Assurance

Now that we have Ralph insured we have to consider Donna. The couple are aware that Donna's life needs to be insured because Ralph has a high pressure job and he would need to employ a housekeeper to act as "mother" if Donna was killed. They decide that $50 000 is adequate for this.

They also wish to invest some money for the future of Bruce their child.

Here are their options:

(1) Donna could take out term assurance for $50 000 and invest separately for Bruce. This course of action is quite sound and by now you should know all the good and bad points of it.

(2) Donna could take out a $50 000 whole of life policy and cash it in when Bruce needed the money.

(3) Donna could take out a $50 000 whole of life policy with premiums ceasing when she turned 55, and cash it in when Bruce needed the money.

(4) Donna could take out an endowment policy to mature in 20 years,

(5) Donna could buy term assurance and take out a pure endowment policy to pay $50 000 plus bonuses in 20 years. A pure endowment policy does not incorporate life assurance.

We will now discuss options (2) to (5). By the time we go through all these you should start to have a grasp on the fascinating subject of life assurance.

$50 000 WHOLE OF LIFE ASSURANCE ILLUSTRATION

Monthly premium $61.43 — aged 25

Policy Year	Age next Birthday	Death Cover	Cash Value	Paid Up Value	Total costs paid
1	26	52 100	0	0	737
2	27	54 326	922	5 866	1 474
3	28	57 135	1 804	9 650	2 211
4	29	60 086	2 625	13 606	2 949
5	30	63 487	3 532	17 662	3 686
10	35	83 879	10 155	39 989	7 372
15	40	110 829	20 478	66 704	11 057
20	45	147 649	37 127	99 934	14 743
25	50	197 665	63 804	142 425	18 429
30	55	259 972	104 251	196 787	22 115
35	60	340 563	165 129	267 963	25 801
40	65	446 100	254 036	361 515	29 486
45	70	585 111	381 141	485 346	33 172

OPTION TWO: Take out a $50 000 whole of life policy on Donna's life and cash it in when Bruce needed the money.

The main advantages are the increasing death cover and the high cash values that arise as Donna gets older. If the family find they can cope with the education expenses there should be no need for Donna to cash in the policy. However, it may be worth around $37 000 when Bruce is 20 so will be a useful sum for the family as well as giving life cover along the way.

$50 000 WHOLE OF LIFE ASSURANCE ILLUSTRATION
Monthly premium $76.74 — aged 25
Premiums will cease at age 55

Policy Year	Age next Birthday	Death Cover	Cash Value	Paid Up Value	Total costs paid
1	26	52 100	0	0	921
2	27	54 326	1 084	7 661	1 842
3	28	57 135	2 185	11 685	2 763
4	29	60 086	3 060	15 856	3 684
5	30	63 487	4 034	20 172	4 604
10	35	83 879	11 193	44 349	9 209
15	40	110 829	22 509	73 879	13 813
20	45	147 649	40 705	110 584	18 418
25	50	197 665	69 617	156 885	23 022
30	55	259 972	113 195	216 022	27 626

OPTION THREE: Take out a $50 000 whole of life policy on Donna's life with premiums ceasing when Donna turned 55, and cash it in when Bruce needed the money.

The premiums will now cease. The death cover will continue to grow in line with the other whole of life policy shown in the illustration immediately above because the bonuses are calculated on the sum assured.

I do not favour this option. The premiums are slightly higher than Option Two as Donna is now going to pay a lifetime's premiums in 30 years. This option is shown mainly to further your knowledge of life assurance.

OPTION FOUR: Take out an endowment policy to mature in 20 years.

In this example she has paid in $47 633 to get back $147 649 (3.09 times the money paid) whereas in Option Two she paid in $14 743 after 20 years to get back $37 127 (2.51 times the money paid). But remember you get what you pay for. In Option Two she had much higher life cover and the option to keep it going. The endowment policy is finished when the contracted term expires. With Option Two Donna has paid for the right to have such extra benefits as $259 000 of life assurance at age 55 for just $61.43 a month.

ENDOWMENT POLICY ILLUSTRATION
Monthly premium $198.72 — aged 25
Premiums will cease at age 55

Policy Year	Age next Birthday	Death Cover	Cash Value	Paid Up Value	Total costs paid
1	26	52 100	0	0	2 385
2	27	54 326	3 577	9 326	4 769
3	28	57 135	6 865	14 185	7 154
4	29	60 086	9 669	19 186	9 539
5	30	63 487	12 801	24 337	11 923
10	35	83 879	37 108	52 679	23 846
15	40	110 829	77 708	86 379	35 770
20	45	147 649	147 649		47 693

OPTION FIVE: Buy term assurance and take out a pure endowment policy to pay $50 000 plus bonuses in 20 years.

This policy, being a "pure endowment policy", has no death benefit, which is why the premiums are slightly lower than on the preceding illustration which is an "endowment policy". If the life assured dies before the period of the contract is over the amount payable to the estate is the cash value. A pure endowment policy is often used when the policy holder does not qualify for life cover.

PURE ENDOWMENT POLICY ILLUSTRATION
Monthly premium $191.59 — aged 25

Policy Year	Age next Birthday	Cash Value	Paid Up Value	Total costs paid
1	26	0	0	2 299
2	27	4 506	9 326	4 598
3	28	7 487	14 185	6 897
4	29	10 678	19 186	9 196
5	30	14 099	24 337	11 495
10	35	38 490	52 679	22 991
15	40	77 457	86 379	34 486
20	45	147 649		45 982

This illustration is shown for your information only. I suggest if you decide on endowment assurance you are better off to stay away from "pure endowment" and incorporate the life assurance in an ordinary endowment policy as in Option Four.

Child Assurance

Ralph and Donna have heard about child assurance but don't know much about it. They have heard stories about people who were tricked into buying children's assurance on the pretext that it would pay a large sum on reaching 21. These people are invariably shocked to find they got back not much more than they had paid in.

Children's assurance is controversial because of so many policies being sold that did not contain the features the buyers believed they were getting. I cannot say that this is the fault of the buyers or the salespeople because many people don't understand what they have and there are certainly a few unscrupulous sales people around. Let's hope after you read this you won't need to say "But I thought it was something different".

The following is an illustration for a Whole of Life policy for $50 000 on baby son Bruce. The first feature to note is that there is no death cover until Bruce reaches his 10th birthday. If he dies before age 10 the return to the policy owners (the cash value) is small. Once Bruce is 10 the death cover component comes into force but has been gathering bonuses for those first 10 years so has more than doubled in that time.

By the time Bruce is 21 there is not a huge difference between the cash value and what has been paid in premiums and it is this fact that causes people to say "But I thought there would be enough money there to buy a block of land". That is **not** what the policy was designed to do, so anybody who expected the large sum would have to be disappointed. However, it does have other benefits and if the owners were aware of these other benefits they might not be so keen to cash the policy in.

The first benefit is that the policy will normally nominate several dates at which Bruce could elect to buy more life assurance **without a medical.** In a typical policy these dates might fall on the 18th, 22nd, 26th, 30th, 35th, 40th and 45th birthdays as well as on special occasions such as marriage and birth of a child. The life assurance he could purchase would be in multiples of the initial sum assured.

Now compare the illustration below with the second one in this chapter where we were taken aback to find that it would cost Ralph $455.97 a month at age 30 for $300 000 of whole of live cover. At age 30 Bruce will have nearly $260 000 of life cover for only $38.60 a month. He has bought the Rolls-Royce for the price of the term assurance because he started at a much younger age.

If the parents wished they could add a "rider" that paid the premiums to age 21 if the policy owner (usually one of the parents) died.

These policies are called "Child's Advancement Policies". The question is "Does Bruce need one?". It's a bit like a sun roof on a motor car — nice to have but not essential. My feeling at this stage is **no** because of his parents' tight budget but you now know these policies exist and understand what they are meant to do.

Age next Birthday 1. Monthly premium $38.60.
Sum assured $50 000.

Policy Year	Age next Birthday	Death Cover	Cash Value	Paid Up Value	Total costs paid
1	1	Nil	0	0	463
2	2	Nil	402	5 986	926
3	3	Nil	813	10 045	1 390
4	4	Nil	1 198	14 101	1 853
5	5	Nil	1 624	18 252	2 316
10	10	Nil	4 771	40 809	4 632
15	15	110 829	9 071	66 064	6 948
20	20	147 649	15 711	97 914	9 264
25	25	197 665	26 479	139 075	11 580
30	30	259 972	43 597	192 782	13 896
35	35	340 563	70 938	263 313	16 212
40	40	446 100	114 466	356 455	18 528
45	45	585 111	182 894	480 481	20 810
50	50	767 855	290 284	645 495	22 955
55	55	1 009 261	455 385	865 436	25 100
60	60	1 327 669	702 391	1 158 839	27 245
65	65	1 747 374	1 063 183	1 550 619	29 390
70	70	2 152 920	1 445 614	1 957 020	31 106

Some Points To Know About

Illustrations

The figures used throughout this chapter were supplied by one of the world's largest life assurance companies. They are called "illustrations" as they are nothing more than an expression of what the outcome might be if the company maintained its present bonus rates. The bonus rates declared on assurance policies will depend on the company's earnings which depend on future levels of interest rates as well as the behaviour of the stock market and the property market over many years. No company can accurately forecast these consistently.

There is a relationship between the rate of inflation and earnings from property and shares. If inflation stays high the value of money will fall and bonus rates should rise. If the Government keeps inflation under control interest rates should stay down and naturally bonus rates will drop accordingly.

You will become confused when two assurance salespeople show you illustrations using unlike bonus rates as the end result on the illustration may be vastly different, yet neither company can guarantee the outcome. If this happens you could ask them both for new illustrations using the same bonus rate, but the comparisons could still be meaningless because some companies have a "bonus loading". However, if there is still a large difference in the figures you had better start asking about hidden charges.

Cash Value

Make sure your illustrations show a cash value as well as an illustrative "fund value" or "paid up value". Far too many salespeople sell a policy on the "paid up value" and never get around to mentioning that the cash value is substantially less as well as meaning something entirely different.

Paying The Premiums

You can pay them in various ways but I suggest monthly for most people and annually for those disciplined few who can find a large lump sum regularly. Certainly you pay a little more by paying monthly but after a while it becomes a habit and you don't miss them.

Commitment

Insurance is like any other long-term project — it takes time to start to grow in value. Far too many people start a policy and then let it lapse before it has gained a surrender value or cash it in well before its maturity date. Don't take out a policy unless you intend to keep it up otherwise you will waste your money.

Policy Objectives

By the time most people get around to looking at their policies they have long since forgotten why they were taken out. When you take out a new policy, or change an existing one, ask the salesperson to write down what objective the policy is designed to accomplish. Pin that to the policy when it arrives so your memory will be refreshed next time you look at it.

Savings Plans

You are almost certain to be offered endowment policies or "pure" endowment polices being sold as savings plans. Some of these have high hidden charges and heavy withdrawal penalties if you cash the policy in before it has run its course. Do not sign up for one of these until you have received an illustration showing "cash values" for each year of the policy as well as stating the bonus rate used in the illustration and are satisfied that these are reasonable.

"With Profits"

A with profits policy shares in the profits of the assurance company and accrues bonuses. Do not buy any policy that is not "with profits".

Regular Reviews

People's circumstances are continually changing and the needs for assurance change too. Make sure you sit down with your financial adviser or assurance representative at least once every three years to make sure your current life assurance matches your needs.

Caution

Don't cancel any existing life assurance policies before you understand the full import of what you are doing. In particular be wary of any assurance representative who suggests you replace an existing policy with a fresh one and always refer to the representative who sold you the policy.

Conclusion

By now you should have a better idea about life assurance. Now pull out all your old life assurance policies and read them with your new educated eye. You are almost bound to discover that you need to have an urgent consultation with your financial adviser or assurance representative to make some changes. At least now you will understand what is happening.

Summing Up

1. **Understand that you get what you pay for. If a product appears cheap make sure you know what features you are missing out on.**
2. **Don't cancel a life insurance policy without contacting the person that sold it to you in the first place if possible.**
3. **Don't take out a contract for life insurance unless you intend to stick with it.**
4. **Understand the figures of "future performance" insurance salespeople give you are nothing more than illustrations. There is no guarantee that the results quoted will be achieved. Treat illustrations with extreme caution.**
5. **Don't be taken in by "fund value" or "paid up value". Ensure your illustrations show a surrender value or a cash value. If this cannot be provided go elsewhere.**
6. **When comparing illustrations between one company and another make sure that you are not comparing "apples" to "pears". Always ask for the figures which are the basis of the calculations.**
7. **Attach to all new life insurance policies a short statement of what you expect the policy to do. You'll find this invaluable in future years when you are puzzling why you ever took it out.**
8. **If anybody you know dies do NOT overlook the possible value of insurance policies that appear to be worthless.**

31

Protecting Your Business Interests

There is nothing so stupid as an educated man, if you get him off the thing he was educated to.

WILL ROGERS

Are you taking notice of the quotes that head each chapter? They all have a purpose and the one above typifies most people in business. They are so busy working at what they know that most of them "never get around" to such mundane but vital tasks as making sure they are protected if something unexpected occurs.

First, a warning — if you are in business for yourself this chapter may give you a jolt. Take heart, the first step to solving a problem is to be aware of it.

To explain how it works we'll pretend you are the joint owners of a business with Harry Jones. Even though what follows is made up, the story is typical of what happens in many family businesses. At present you run a profitable business together. You use a company structure and members of both families are shareholders and/or directors of that company.

Business is fine at the moment and everybody is happy and getting on well. What could happen to spoil it? Think about the following:

(1) One of you may decide it's time to retire.

(2) You might have a falling out causing one family to want to leave the business.

(3) One of you might be killed or suffer an incapacitating illness such as a heart attack, cancer or stroke.

You may regard these possibilities as unlikely but consider the following figures:

THE PROBABILITY OF AT LEAST ONE PARTNER DYING OR BECOMING TOTALLY DISABLED BEFORE REACHING AGE 65. (Partners currently aged 35)		
Partners	*Probability of Death*	*Probability of Death or TPD*
2	35 in 100	52 in 100
3	47 in 100	67 in 100
4	57 in 100	77 in 100
5	66 in 100	84 in 100
6	72 in 100	89 in 100

Source: MLC

Do you still think death or disability before 65 is unlikely?

A common thread runs through the above examples; for some reason a major shareholder, and possibly a major contributor to the company's income, is unable or unwilling to continue. Remember this is a profitable valuable business and probably worth over a million dollars. Each family owns a half share of it. Two major questions arise:

(1) What is the half share worth?

(2) Where is your family (we'll assume it's Harry Jones who dies) going to find the money to pay it?

Valuing The Interest In The Business

If a way to value the business is not decided upon while everybody is on good terms and in good health great problems can arise, particularly if somebody is killed. Maybe Harry Jones and you ran the business and your spouses had little to do with it. If that is the case, your families may have little idea of the problems and contingent liabilities that can plague a business — the ones you and Harry fought together for years. The widow's reaction, urged on by an avaricious family, might be "Harry gave his life to that company. His share alone has to be worth nearly a million dollars."

You may feel this is ridiculous but what can you do about it? All the parties involved are faced with a lengthy and expensive court battle if they cannot agree. It is even possible that the only way out is to wind up the company and sell its assets. If this happens much of the value could be lost if a large part of these assets is goodwill that has been built up by the efforts of the owners. You may find years of work has vanished.

The way to solve the problem is to have a method of valuing the business worked out in advance. It may be a formula such as "three years pre tax profits" or it may be a simple number like "$500 000". In any event the simple process of deciding on a method of valuation may save hundreds of thousands of dollars of legal costs and many hours of tension.

Now we have a further complication — preparing the documentation to give effect to the agreed method of valuation. Suppose the parties prepare a simple agreement that states in effect *"I, Harry Jones, agree that my shares are worth $500 000 in the event of my death or retirement from the company and I hereby authorise them to be sold to the XX Family at that figure".* Documents such as these are called "mandatory agreements". Depending on the exact wording of the document it is highly possible this could be construed as a disposal of Harry's shares and be liable for capital gains tax **immediately.** If so, both families could be liable for capital gains tax totalling $500 000 **as soon as the documents were signed.**

The way around that is to prepare put and call option agreements that are just as binding as the agreement mentioned above without the probability of a huge unexpected capital gains bill.

Finding The Money

Now let's assume there was an option agreement in place and the Jones family are prepared to sell you their shares in the business for $500 000. Where does the money come from? There are five main sources:

(1) From cash you have set aside for this possibility. This is most unlikely.

(2) From borrowing. This is expensive and you may not be able to obtain the loan if a large part of your assets are tied up in plant and goodwill.

(3) By bringing in a new partner. A compatible person with the money available may be hard to find. Anyway you want to keep control of the business yourself.
(4) By selling the business. You have no wish to do this and if you did you would be up for heavy capital gains tax on the sale of your shares.
(5) From the proceeds of an insurance policy designed for this purpose. Obviously this is the best course of action.

Fortunately, in this case, the directors had accepted expert advice and had taken out insurance policies on each other that covered death or total and permanent disability. You will now claim on the policy you took out on the life of Harry Jones and you will receive $500 000 tax free. The proceeds are tax free because a tax deduction was never claimed for the premiums.

You use the money from the policy to buy the Jones family shares for $500 000 in terms of the agreement and you now own the company outright. You are doing well but the Smith family have a major problem. They were co-founders of the business and, with the Jones, started it with nothing in 1986. Consequently the cost base of their shares for capital gains tax purposes is the value of their initial capital, $1 000.

Because this base is so tiny, inflation adjustment is of no use, and they have to pay capital gains tax on the profit of $499 000 made when they sold the family shares to you. This could be as high as $240 000. The way to handle this is to ensure the life policies are large enough to pay both the price of the interest in the business **and** the capital gains tax.

There is another insurance policy in existence. Remember Harry Jones and you insured each other. Harry is dead now and you and your family own the whole company. It is now appropriate for your family to request the Jones family to assign the policy on your life back to your family so they can keep it going for their own benefit.

We have just brought more complications into what I am sure has already become a complex matter. If the insurance policy is a whole of life policy your estate will be liable for capital gains tax on the proceeds when you die because the policy was assigned from the original owners.

If it is a yearly renewable term policy, there may be capital gains tax payable by your estate if you die before the next policy anniversary. This depends on whether it was assigned for valuable consideration.

Depending on the terms of the policy the insurance company may allow your family to start a new policy on your life in which case the proceeds will be free of capital gains tax to your estate. If you were in bad health the insurance company may refuse to commence a new policy but you may have the right to keep the old one up. If this happens your estate is liable for capital gains tax when the proceeds of the policy are paid out.

Summing Up

Don't be concerned if you are now feeling confused — this is not an easy subject. However, read through it again slowly and discuss it with your business partners and your family. The topic is far too important to put in the "too hard" basket. If you have any mandatory agreements in place now I suggest you seek urgent advice regarding the immediate capital gain tax implications. It may also be an appropriate time to review all your personal and business insurance policies.

Conclusion

The aim of this chapter is to make you aware of the huge cost of failing to protect your business interests. It is a subject of great complexity and I could devote a whole book to it. If you are in business you should seek out experts in the legal, accounting, financial planning and insurance fields to help you get your affairs in order. It is too late when death or serious illness strikes without warning.

32

An Attitude Of Success

The greatest discovery of my generation is that human beings can alter their lives by altering their attitudes of mind.

WILLIAM JAMES

Congratulations, you have survived 31 chapters of important information that will help take you safely on your trip to financial independence. Let's take a breather for a few pages and think about the power of knowledge to change lives.

The Value Of One Book

In 1989 over 20,000 people attended sales/motivational rallies that were held in all of Australia's capital cities. The rallies were important to me because they featured two men, both world renowned as authors and public speakers, whose books have had a great impact on my life. One of these men was Og Mandino, author of *The Greatest Miracle in the World,* a book that touched me deeply, and the other was Wayne Dyer, whose books such as *Your Erroneous Zones* and *Pulling Your Own Strings* have sold millions of copies and changed tens of thousands of lives.

Unfortunately many Australians see themselves as rugged independent people and the term "motivation" strikes a sour note in the minds of those who object to what they see are "slick Americans" who receive high fees to tell them what they already know. The usual comments are "I don't need motivation" or "I won't let anybody else motivate me".

This is unfortunate, for it is well known that people are a product of their thoughts and the aim of motivational material, in whatever form it comes, is to improve the quality of those thoughts.

James Allen, the essayist from Devon, penned the following words over 100 years ago in his famous book *As a Man Thinketh*:

> *"Man is made or unmade by himself; in the armory of thoughts he forges the weapons by which he destroys himself; he also fashions the tools by which he builds for himself heavenly mansions of love and joy and peace."*

It is well documented that positive thoughts produce positive results, and negative thoughts produce negative results, so it is surely important to understand how our thoughts are influenced. These influences come into our brain from what we hear, what we see, what we read and what we say to ourselves. The main sources are the media in all its forms, those whom we mix with and our own self-talk[1]. The American speaker Charlie "Tremendous" Jones believes where we will be in five years time depends on what we read and who we mix with in that period. Perhaps now is the time for you to ask yourself what you will read and who you will mix with in the next five years.

It is all a bit circular, because negative people are a product of a negative environment, the media tends to focus on stories of death and disaster which are negative, and this sets up a negative environment which creates negative people who enjoy the negative media. Whew!

The speakers at motivational rallies generally teach skills, or share their own experiences in overcoming seemingly impossible odds. Deep down, most of us feel a little inadequate, and it is inspiring to hear about others who have faced and overcome worse problems than we have had to endure.

Og Mandino told the story of the middle aged drunken derelict who was shivering in below zero temperatures in a slum area in some American city. His eye was attracted to a pistol displayed in a pawn shop — it had a price tag of $29.95. Anything had to be better than this hell on earth thought the drunk, so with his last three $10 bills he bought the pistol in the belief that suicide would mean the end of his pain and despair. Something stopped him and he decided to give life one last chance.

The name of that man was Og Mandino.

---

1 Self-talk is what we say to ourselves all day long.

He explained:

"I spent much time in public libraries because they were free — and warm. I read everything from Plato to Peale seeking that one message that would explain to me where I had gone wrong — and what I could do to salvage the remainder of my life.

I finally found my answer in W. Clement Stone's and Napoleon Hill's Success Through A Positive Mental Attitude. *I have employed the simple techniques and methods found in this classic for more than 15 years and they have provided me with riches and happiness far beyond anything I deserve."*

Isn't that incredible! That one motivational book gave him the inspiration to rise from the gutter to become one of the world's most influential writers, a man who can phone a publisher and get a million dollar advance just by quoting the brief outline of the book he is proposing to write.

Fate works in strange ways. I am constantly amazed that a brand new piece of information will come into to my life and be relevant to something that occurs shortly after. Just five days after I heard Og Mandino make that statement in Sydney, I was flying home from Auckland to Brisbane after being a speaker at the Auckland Money Show.

I found myself seated next to a senior vice-president of one of America's largest corporations. His duties included responsibility for the company's operations in the entire Pacific region including Japan, Australia and Korea.

We started chatting and exchanging ideas. After a couple of drinks he confided to me that his world fell to bits on November 5, 1975. His health cracked and he simultaneously lost his job, and his marriage. He, too, was on the point of despair but luckily stumbled across a motivational book. Its title? *Success Through a Positive Mental Attitude.* After reading the book, he pulled things in shape, got back with his wife, regained his health, and went on to become a highly paid executive in a different company.

The retail price of that book is around $15 but I wonder what is the true value of a book that could help a person from the bottom of the heap to the top, not just financially, but also in terms of health and happiness.

An Attitude Of Success

In *Making Money Made Simple* I pointed out that only 8% of people made it financially. The main reason is 92% did not make the decision to succeed. Sure they talked about it, they may have bought books about it, and a few of them may have even gone to motivational rallies. Some of them decided to change, made a start, but the result was the same as the time they started the diet plan or the exercise plan — it petered out.

The reason is few people are prepared to pay the price of success. Their eyes shine when they talk about wealth, they agree it sounds great to have a house paid off, cash in the bank, plenty of superannuation and a sizeable portfolio of investments. Unfortunately that shine dims when the time comes for action and they have to do a budget to allocate their resources, make sacrifices such as cutting out smoking to generate some investment capital, or improve their skills by taking a course so they can generate more income.

The most important thing to remember is to be consistent. Take small steps towards your goal every day, instead of indulging in a burst of activity occasionally. The American time management expert Professor John Lees tells how a publisher paid him an advance of $10,000 to write a book. After several months had gone past and no chapters started to appear the publisher gave John an ultimatum. He had to refund the advance or report to an office in New York that specialised in getting authors into the action mode. As John had no intention of returning the money he decided going to New York was the obvious choice.

Upon his arrival in New York he was given a simple assignment. He had to report to the office every day at seven o'clock in the morning, go to a desk and stay there until he had written 1000 words. That was all there was to it. John found the first day was extremely difficult but he sat there and stuck it out till he had done the 1000 words — the second day was a bit easier, the third day even easier and after two weeks he was writing 2,000 words at a sitting with ease. He finished the book in just six weeks.

Saving money is a bit like that. The hardest thing is starting off, then sticking with it through the hard early stages. Once you have done that it gets easier and easier.

In the next chapter we'll think about ways to help you change direction and start to move towards your dreams.

33

Changing Direction

"Two roads diverged in a wood and I —
I took the one less travelled by,
And that made all the difference."

ROBERT FROST: *The Road Not Taken*

By now your knowledge of finance should be well above average, but knowledge by itself will take you nowhere. Now it's time to put the knowledge into action.

Let's have a moment of truth first. Think for a moment about how you would cope if you were lost in a thick forest with the best quality compass and a detailed map — both would be useless if you didn't know where you were. So your first task is to do something that 90% of the population **never** do. Find out where you are **now.** This knowledge will give you the proper foundation to build on.

In the next few chapters I will encourage you to list your assets and liabilities in detail, set some detailed goals, and rearrange your financial resources if necessary to make them work, better. I know this may be unexciting ground work but once it is over you can move to the next stage and start to use some of the techniques available to speed up your journey to wealth.

Almost everybody "thinks" better on paper, so as a first step buy a loose-leaf binder and some sheets of plain ruled paper. This will become your journal, your log book and your treasure map. Once that is organised we can start work on listing your assets and liabilities.

SECTION ONE

Cash Type Assets

These are a small but important part of your resources. Money in the bank, or even in the pocket, gives out a warm secure feeling. An empty wallet and a heap of money owing on credit cards makes us feel inadequate, frightened and out of control.

The level of money held in readily accessible cash form in such areas as interest bearing accounts depends on the individual, but probably two to three months income is a good guide. It is important to achieve the highest possible return with safety, but be aware that taxation, inflation and the possibility of your not getting your money back are the major dangers. Keeping the balance down to reasonable proportions will solve the tax and inflation problem and investing only with leading institutions, with the benefit of independent advice, should eliminate the chance of you losing your money.

Head up a sheet of paper: **Cash Type Assets.** Now write down all your cash type assets such as savings accounts, cheque accounts, debentures, cash management trusts and mortgage trusts. Pay particular attention to whose name they are held in, the rate of interest being paid, when it is payable, the maturity date if applicable and what charges, if any, are being incurred for keeping the account or for withdrawing the money.

Let's do a general tidy up to start. Along the way you have probably accumulated a few small bank or building society accounts that lie dormant in a drawer. Why not close them and put the money into one bigger account where it will earn higher interest.

There are three ways to lessen the impact of tax on deposits — move the income to a lower income earner, seek out a higher return, or move the money to a tax sheltered area. The first one involves splitting your income. Provided there is trust between you and your spouse, ensure that funds are held for maximum tax advantage. This entails holding the bulk of your available money in the name of the lowest income earner.

Now check out the interest rate you are earning. Our company has noticed that almost all investors who come to us for advice have money invested at below market rates. Every dollar is precious so why accept a low return? I am astonished at the number of people who complain about tax taking half their interest yet they seem content to leave their money in cheque accounts that pay no interest, or in low interest savings accounts.

A before tax rate of 6% gives you possibly 4% after tax whereas a before tax rate of 3% is worth less than 2% after tax – that's 100% more. Can you see why I have stressed that ignorance, or failure to act, are far worse enemies than taxation for most people.

I appreciate that it can be difficult to work out the real interest rate being paid to you as the banks and building societies have so many different products that you can get hopelessly confused. The task is too important to neglect so be prepared to do a little research, obtain and read all their brochures, and take the time to understand it.

Total your money in the cash type section. Is it excessive and causing inflation and tax problems? If you have surplus money here you should consider moving it to more efficient areas. High interest rates are great when the interest is being credited but they lose a lot of their gloss when the tax and provisional bills hit.

SECTION TWO

The Family Home — Your Own Castle

Most of you will own a home or be paying one off. Many more will be trying to get one. Sadly, some are now discovering a home is out of reach because of a misfortune in their life or because they did not buy one before prices rose. The quote that heads up Chapter 17 of *Making Money Made Simple* is an old Scottish Proverb "Home is where you start from" and I urge you to follow it.

Write down the approximate value of your house and land and then find out the amount you owe on your house mortgage, the interest rate being charged and the monthly or fortnightly payment. If possible find out how many years your loan has left to run. The chart in Chapter 14 of *Making Money Made Simple* will guide you, but the best approach is to use my Wealth Creator on CD-ROM. This will print out a schedule of payments for you, calculate how much interest is still to be paid, and let you key in alternative data so you look at the effect of making extra payments.

If you are paying off your house, and also have personal loans, Chapter 2 will show you techniques to knock the housing loan over as fast as possible. If you have lived in the one spot for a few years determine whether you are going to spend your life there or move. People move for many reasons that range from upgrading to their dream home, moving to something smaller because the children have left the nest or moving to a better location.

If moving is likely, start to do the things **now** that make the home saleable. The easiest and cheapest way to add value is by planting trees in the garden and on the nature strip, keeping the lawn in top condition, and by making sure all the maintenance is kept up to date so everything looks good and works.

If you are paying off a block of land, and paying rent, do some arithmetic and work out a 12 month strategy. It is almost always cheaper to pay off the house you are living in than to pay rent and pay off a block of land as well. Investigate trading the land on a home or selling it and buying an established home. The position is a little different if you are still living at home while paying off the land. Hold it by all means if the block is a good one and you intend to build on it, but use every spare cent to get it paid off as fast as possible. The interest is not tax deductible so any money invested in extra repayments is earning the equivalent of the interest rate you are paying after tax.

SECTION THREE

To Cull Or To Keep

You may have a vacant block of land that was bought "as an investment" because "it seemed a good idea at the time". Sadly the reality often fails to match the expectations and there comes a time when you must admit making a mistake. That's not a problem as it's the best way to learn, but better to take action now to cull out the dead wood, than go through more years of vain hopes while paying bills for rates and weed removal.

Apply the acid test. Work out a realistic market price and imagine you have just sold the land and have the money stacked on the table. Ask yourself "If I had that money available now, what would I do with it?" If the answer is not to buy that block of land back, you should sell it.

Don't fall into the old trap of telling yourself you will not sell until you get back what it has cost you. The only measure is what the market will pay, and the market is not in the least interested in how much you may have lost or what you need to achieve your goals.

Similarly you may have shares, unit trusts or insurance bonds that have not fulfilled their promise. What should be done about them?

Let's face facts — nobody can consistently predict the future accurately so don't be too hard on your stock broker or investment adviser for suggesting an investment that has not lived up to expectations. A competent stock broker or adviser can make a recommendation in all good faith and find that the recommended investment doesn't perform.

Some advisers are frightened to recommend investments that have the potential to fall in value, and duck responsibility by recommending nothing but fixed interest products — unfortunately their clients lose purchasing power to inflation and suffer huge tax bills in the meantime. The only way to combat taxation and inflation is to invest in "growth" assets such as property and shares where there is a chance of achieving capital gain.

The dilemma is that wherever there is a chance of capital gain there is a chance of capital loss, so the so-called "growth" investments will not always perform well. Those who seek the growth must also bear the risk. Alas, there is no perfect investment.

Be aware that growth investments need time. The 1987 stock market boom caused many inexperienced investors to be taken in by high short term returns. On October 19, 1987 they learned to their horror that an investment that can rise 40% in one year can drop 40% in a couple of days.

If you have a share-based investment that has fallen in value discuss it with your adviser. If the investment is under-pinned by quality assets you are better off to hold it, or use the averaging technique described in Chapter 20.

Let me stress once more that this process is a superb strategy, if you are certain the price will eventually recover. Do not use it for speculative investments because all you are doing is pouring good money after bad if they never recover. Your adviser should be able to guide you.

SECTION FOUR

Superannuation And Roll Over Funds

Next look at your superannuation and at the same time examine any money held in roll-over funds and list details of what you have. Don't be concerned if you don't know exactly what your superannuation entitlements are, few people do, but it should be only a matter of talking to the Personnel Department or to your financial adviser.

Find out:

- Whether your funds are capital guaranteed, capital stable or market linked.
- How much life insurance and disability insurance is included in the policy.
- Whether your superannuation is a defined benefit scheme or an accumulation one.
- The payout as a multiple of your salary if it is a defined benefit fund.
- The current value if it is an accumulation fund.
- Is it a pension fund, a lump sum fund or a combination of both.
- What you would get if you resigned now.
- What percentage of your salary the employer is contributing if it is an accumulation fund.
- What percentage of your salary you are contributing.
- What is your starting date for superannuation purposes.

Now that you have found out this important information read Chapters 17, 18 and 19 in *Living Well in Retirement*. They will show you what to do next.

SECTION FIVE

Shedding Unproductive Debt

One of our first major goals is to eliminate all unproductive debt, because debt is the killer that prevents 92% of the population from ever reaching financial independence. Take the first step in the war against unproductive debt by listing all your debts on two separate pages. Use the first page where the interest is not tax deductible and the second page where the interest is tax deductible.

For each debt write down the actual payout figure, the monthly repayment, the interest rate being paid, whether the rate is fixed or variable and whether the rate is reducing or variable.

Income

It takes income to drive you along the road to financial independence. This income may come from your own exertion or from your present investments. On another sheet list the expected income from all members of the family for a year and don't forget to deduct the tax that will be payable on it.

If you are a salary earner it is only a matter of looking at your pay packet. If you are self employed it may be easier to use last year's tax return as a guide.

Summary

Congratulations — you have now listed your resources and are aware of strategies to make those resources work hard for you. You have made a solid start on the road to financial independence. However, don't become complacent, for there are many enemies that are waiting to block your progress. You'll learn about them in the next chapter.

34

The Investor's Enemies

Every man is his own chief enemy.

ANACHARSIS (6th century BC)

Almost every day, on radio talk-back programs, during consultations, or in letters, we hear the same message: "I'm afraid the whole topic of money and finance confuses me, it just seems too hard to understand". It's almost as if people felt there was a secret out there waiting to be discovered but they could not get their minds around it. They had read *Making Money Made Simple* and believed things could be different. But the problem remained — how to turn the new found knowledge into reality.

There **is** a formula, it usually works (if you do) and it is not a secret. However, it does take effort as well as the ability to face reality. The formula is: PMA + K + A = R which translates into:

Positive Mental Attitude + Knowledge + Action = Results

Throughout this book I have encouraged you to keep a positive mental attitude, which is essential to success, and I've tried to increase your knowledge in easy steps so you don't get discouraged. Now we'll consider techniques to overcome the enemies you will face.

As you study them remember a great truth American lecturer Brian Tracy spoke about in his audio cassette program *The Psychology of Success.* "The difference between winners and losers in every field is that the losers blame any successes that come their way on good luck and anything bad that happens on somebody else. Thus they forever deprive themselves of an opportunity to learn. In contrast the winners take full credit for their successes and failures." In other words, the winners in all areas take responsibility for their lives.

Take note of those words — make them a part of your thinking as I do, and you will find they will help you make the right decision in many areas. These include dealing with employees, children or in sport. Whenever you find an individual continually blaming somebody else for their troubles you will now realise that the person has the problem[1].

1. The Wrong Attitude

The first enemy many of us have to fight is a bad attitude of mind about ourselves or about prosperity. If we were born to a poor family we may have been encouraged to think that prosperity was not our right because of some accident of birth, which is how I felt for many years. We then convince ourselves that people from our background can never achieve success.

This is a cop-out and a useful way to dodge the discipline you need to be successful. I convinced myself I was too dumb to go to University which got me out of four years of study. I paid the price later with many years of study after work which was much harder. Don't let a modest background stop your dreams. The press is full of stories about people from humble backgrounds who have achieved enormous success by putting in the work to overcome their humble beginnings. Even if you have no wish to make the front cover of *Time* magazine, you can still achieve a prosperous and happy life style if you start doing the right things now.

One evening my family and I were at a combined church/school Christmas picnic. About eight "street kids" arrived at the invitation of one of the committee members who believed these teenagers might benefit from mixing with "average people". All went well until they started to drink too much beer and we refused to give them any more. Their reaction was violent. They turned over the bar, kicked in the side of a car and started tearing street signs out of the ground. Their leader claimed this bad behaviour was the fault of the person who had invited them!

---

1 This knowledge alone will repay the cost of this book many times over.

None of us blamed these young people for what they did — they are a product of the deprivation they have suffered. We did ponder what chance they have of getting anywhere in life with an attitude like that. This degree of violence may be unusual, but the overall attitude is still typical of the way most people look at any obstacles that get in their way.

In my *Road to Wealth Course* I ask the students to chant together "I am a good money manager" to help them overcome the habits of many years of saying "I am hopeless with money" or "Money just slips through my fingers". It sounds strange at first but try it — you will soon get used to it. Start to tune your mind into listening to the way other people talk about themselves and you will start to notice that most of them continually say negative things about themselves. You will then realise this is one of the main reasons they have problems.

I have stressed that only 8% of people achieve success in any field. Look at it another way — 92% of the population are doing wrong things continually. Attitude is one of the major FACTORS that makes the difference.

TEST ONE: *How is your attitude towards prosperity?*

Do you feel a person from your background can never achieve financial independence?

Have you fallen into the trap of continually putting yourself down?

Are you blaming others for your mistakes?

SOLUTION: *Spend $12.95 and read my book* Getting it Together. *Follow this with books such as* The Greatest Miracle *by Og Mandino and* Psycho-Cybernetics *by Maxwell Maltz Then start finding out more about mind control courses such as The Silva Method that use autogenic techniques.*

Then study the biographies or autobiographies of famous people. When you discover that most of them worked hard to overcome enormous problems you will not feel so bad about your own background and abilities.

2. Failure To Set Goals

Yale University surveyed a graduating class in 1953. They asked the students if they had life-time goals and if they had written them down. Guess how many had goals? Only 10%. How many had these goals written down? Only 3%.

They resurveyed the same people 20 years later and found an amazing fact. The 10% with goals had not only achieved more wealth than the other 90% **combined** but were also healthier and happier. They also found out that the group with the written goals had achieved far more than those who had goals but had not written them down.

One of my favourite books is the autobiography of Anthony Trollope, a most prolific novelist, who wrote such works as *The Pallisers* and *The Barchester Chronicles*. He attributes his success to his habit of rising each morning at 5.30 and writing for two hours at a steady rate of 500 words an hour. To make sure he got up in time he paid his groom an extra five pounds a year to wake him without fail.

His method of working was simple. He would decide the number of words his book was to have and divide it by 1000 to find the number of days needed to complete the manuscript. He put this data on a wall chart where it was always in view and each day would mark off his progress. Trollope was proud of the fact that he always delivered a book within a week of the promised deadline. Obviously this technique shows great discipline but it also illustrates the power of specific goal setting.

Elsewhere in this book I have talked about the importance of budgeting. Budgeting is really nothing more than financial goal setting, because in a budget you list the expected income and match it against the expected expenditure and savings.

Goals help provide the energy to keep going when you are tired and to refuse the temptations that seem to keep cropping up. A company executive once said to me: "We wonder at your discipline to produce five newspaper columns a week — it is such an effort for us to produce the company newsletter twice a year." I replied "It's really simple. I can do the columns every week because the editors impose strict deadlines. It's hard for me to put the same energy into writing a new book because there is no deadline pressure." They then realised what was their problem with their newsletter. It came out about every six months, but as there was no firm deadline, nobody made an extra effort to have it out by a set date.

A goal to write a book, prepare a newsletter or save a certain sum of money is of no value unless it has a deadline. One of the essential elements of setting a goal is to write down a date for its attainment.

TEST TWO: *Is failure to set clearly defined goals your major problem?*

SOLUTION: *Re-read Chapter One and start to put those principles into practice.*

3. Ignoring The Tax Laws And Putting Things In The Wrong Name

If you are unhappy about the unfairness of the tax laws you are not alone. Almost every tax-payer feels unhappy about the tax system. Yet tax is not the enemy people feel it is — the enemy is ignorance, which hits our pocket and our money tree much harder than the top marginal tax rate.

The main problems are buying assets in the wrong name[3], holding interest bearing accounts in the wrong name, selling at the wrong time, wrong structuring and failing to use tax-effective investments.

These topics are covered in such detail elsewhere in this book that I will not dwell on them here. Just be aware that few people pay sufficient attention to them.

TEST THREE: *Are you sure your affairs are properly structured for tax and do you seek expert advice BEFORE you buy and sell assets?*

SOLUTION: *If the answer is NO you had better find a good financial adviser or accountant and keep in regular contact with them.*

4. Bad Advice

"Bad advice" is the appropriate enemy to follow "failure to use the tax laws to advantage" because they are so closely related. The problem for you is that bad advice can come in so many forms. These include predatory "advice" from people who are trying to hard sell you a product, wrong advice from professionals who are incompetent, and ill-informed advice from well-meaning relations and friends. No matter what disguise it comes in, it can still cost you heaps.

3 In Chapter 22 of *Making Money Made Simple* I relate the story of a client who incurred a $100,000 tax bill just by buying a house in the wrong name.

Elsewhere in this book I tell the story of the person who ended up in severe financial strife because of advice to borrow to buy speculative investments to save tax. This advice was given purely to enable the person giving it to make a commission on the investment.

Unfortunately many members of the public expect certain people to have an inexhaustible and infallible fund of knowledge because of their position in the community. They then put them on a pedestal and ask their advice about everything. I am referring to accountants, bank managers and to a lesser extent lawyers. Thankfully only a minority are at fault but their inability to say "I'm sorry but that is not my field and therefore I won't comment on it" has cost many of their clients a lot of money. A client of our company went to his accountant to ask about investing in a film. The accountant waved his hands and said "Don't touch it!". Our client took this advice and did not make the investment. The film was *Crocodile Dundee*; it gave its investors huge returns.

Continually we encounter clients who have suffered at the hands of well-meaning bank managers. Bad "advice" that has come to our notice includes:

(a) A recommendation that a 54 year old customer cash in an Eligible Termination Payment to pay off her housing loan.

(b) Advice to pay cash for a business and borrow for a house that was to be the customer's residence.

(c) Advice to take a variable interest rate on an investment loan.

(d) A suggestion that a shy young couple who won $500,000 in the Lotto buy an industrial building for $1 million with the $500,000 shortfall borrowed from the bank.

Bad advice costs more than all the other enemies of the investor combined. Don't let it ruin your financial plan.

TEST FOUR: *From who are you taking your advice? Are you certain they are competent to give it?*

SOLUTION: *If you are not certain check out their qualifications and experience and, if in need, seek a second opinion.*

5. Putting It Off

Let's face it. We are all human beings with human weaknesses and much of our time is spent trying to battle these weaknesses. One of the worse human traits is putting off those important but not urgent tasks that we know should be done. Typical examples are exercise, diet, the assignment, the household budget and the savings and investment plan.

The main obstacle for most of you is not the skill to do the job but the motivation to start it and the persistence to keep at it until it is finished. You have proved your willingness to tackle the tough but rewarding road to financial independence by reading this book. Now you need to develop some techniques to keep you on track.

The way to tackle a job that requires discipline is to get into a set routine and build your life around it. Once you start this pattern it will stay in place until a major change, such as a vacation or ill health in the family, interrupts it.

For example, I find I will go to the gym regularly if I set aside three set times a week for exercise. I can resist the temptation to have a drink after work if I declare Monday to Thursday alcohol free days. I reinforce this by ensuring I use that time for tasks such as writing and exercise that require a clear head. To make sure I get out of bed early I set two alarm clocks, a little one next to the bed and an old-fashioned booming one in a place where I can't reach it from the bed. The second clock is set five minutes after the first one which forces me to jump out of bed to turn it off before it goes off and wakes the district.

You will notice most of the things I use to stay on course are "tricks" but they do work and I could not achieve much without them. You will have to work out your own but I am sharing some of my "tricks" with you to get your mind working.

A financial plan starts with a budget so why not allocate a set time each month (maybe the first Monday night) for a family meeting, a bill paying session and a budget review. At this meeting you can discuss the progress of your financial strategy and monitor the progress of your investments. Once this is in place you can use automatic pay-roll deduction to ensure your savings get priority and do not wither on the vine of "we'll start next week".

TEST FIVE: *Do you have the ability to set a budget and follow a financial plan but are held back by procrastination?*

SOLUTION: *Re-read Chapter 40 of this book and then have a family meeting to discuss ways to put in place routines that will keep you on track.*

6. Looking For The Magic Wand

Man has searched for a formula for miracles since time began. King Arthur's knights searched for the Holy Grail, the chalice used at the Last Supper, in the belief that it had magical healing powers. The alchemists of old spent centuries trying to turn ordinary metals into gold and to find the elixir of youth.

All failed, yet many people in these modern times still believe there is a magic wand waiting to be found or that there is a guru just around the corner with all the answers. Let me save you some time in looking and hoping. There is no magic wand and there is no guru. Furthermore there are no "secrets" because all the techniques for success are well known and well documented.

Certainly there are new strategies (this book is full of them) that are always being developed to cater for the everchanging regulations but that is nothing more than a normal reaction to an evolving world; the **basics** remain the same.

Richard Bach made a fortune when he wrote *Johnathan Livingstone Seagull* but in a further book *Illusions* he tells how he entrusted his money to a "financial adviser" who promised to double it by "investing" in currencies. The adviser was successful for a while and made some large profits on which Bach was liable for a lot of tax. The tide turned, as it always does. Bach lost the lot and ended up owing a huge sum in back taxes.

When I was writing this I had a phone call from a stranger who claimed to have had "advice from sources close to the Treasurer" that the price of gold was about to jump. He was going to invest "about a million" into gold bullion but wanted me to confirm the accuracy of the information before he invested his money. He seemed stunned when I told him that I had no idea which way the price of gold was going to go. I hope he held off because gold went into a slide for the next few months.

It is well proven that those who try to predict volatile markets are wrong as often as they are right. The key to wealth is, and has always been, to build it slowly and surely.

TEST SIX: *Do you believe there is a guru somewhere who can change your life?*

SOLUTION: *Understand that the road to success for most people is made up of a lot of short steps. If you spend your life waiting to find the guru or win the Lotto you might never get across the starting line.*

7. Not Keeping Up To Date

As we embrace the 21st century change is happening faster and faster. Many people, especially the elderly, find this change threatening and stay in a state of immobility. They are scared to change their investments for fear of losing their money.

Despite the changes the main areas for the bulk of your money are cash, property and shares. However, there are new products being released regularly that invest in these areas. Just a few examples are allocated pension funds, imputation trusts, capital guaranteed futures, trading funds, split trusts, neutral gearing plans, margin lending plans, and negative gearing allied with capital guaranteed bonds.

Many of these new products are useful for saving tax, or for boosting returns, but sadly those people who don't keep up to date miss out on the benefits. We regularly come across older people with $200,000 or more in debentures and who prefer to suffer the ravages of taxation and inflation rather than invest in other areas.

TEST SEVEN: *Are you up to date with the latest investment products? (You would be an exceptional person if you were!)*

SOLUTION: *The good news is you don't have to be — just make sure you have an adviser who is.*

8. Ignoring Inflation

Inflation is called the "creeping killer". There is seldom a sudden attack, or a 20% fall in one day, but just a slow relentless whittling away of capital. The Rule of 72 is an inflation calculator. Divide 72 by the inflation rate and you have the length of time it will take for your money to halve in value.

Assume inflation is 4% a year. 72 divided by 4 gives us an answer of 18. We have just worked out that $100,000 will buy $50,000 worth of goods and services in 18 years and only $25,000 in another 18. In other words 75% of our capital has been lost in 36 years.

When I quote these figures at seminars there is never much of a response so to reinforce the point I do something that guarantees a mighty reaction. I hold up a current copy of *The Australian* newspaper and show today's price. I then hold up a 1970 copy with a price of FIVE CENTS. That is a graphic illustration which I follow by showing a 1980 newspaper where petrol is advertised at 37 cents a litre.

TEST EIGHT: *Are you ignoring inflation and leaving the bulk of your money in the interest bearing area?*

SOLUTION: *Understand that cash should only be a part of your overall portfolio and consider moving funds that you can leave untouched into the property and share area by direct investment, unit trusts or superannuation.*

9. Failure To Insure Your Life And Your Income Adequately

The matter of adequate insurance is of such importance that I have devoted two chapters of this book to it.

I appreciate that insurance is a difficult topic and one that tends to be put aside in the "Too Hard" basket. However, I urge you to make the time to study the insurance chapters and then to make sure you are not under insured.

TEST NINE: *Have you adequate insurance?*

SOLUTION: *Get enough NOW.*

10. Inappropriate Investments

At seminars I often hold up two golf clubs, a driver and a putter, to show that different tools are needed for different objectives. The driver is used from the tee to hit the ball as far as possible and in the hands of a Greg Norman may send a ball over 300 metres. A putter is used on the green and may have to hit the ball just a few centimetres.

The dangerous mix of changing laws, new products and the army of so-called "financial advisers" means that many investors are suffering loss by being in inappropriate investments. Here are some examples:

- People who are a long way from retirement with superannuation in capital guaranteed areas. Capital guaranteed products must show lower long term returns than market linked products so young people in the wrong fund are paying a huge price in the form of a lower end benefit.

- People on low incomes with investments in Friendly Society Bonds and Insurance Bonds. These funds pay tax at up to 39% so it makes no sense to have money here when you can pay less tax by having money in interest bearing accounts or unit trusts.
- Long term investments in mortgage trusts. Mortgage trusts have no capital growth and the interest has no tax advantages. Those with low exit fees may be appropriate for up to 18 months but most investors would fare better in income trusts for longer terms.
- High income earners using short term P and I loans for negative gearing. They are better off to borrow on an interest only basis and start a separate sinking fund as discussed in Chapters 27 and 28.

The investment scene is now a complex and changing one. Those who are serious about becoming financially independent will not waste precious time and resources with inappropriate investments. That is like hitting off the tee with a putter.

TEST TEN: *Are your investments appropriate for your situation?*

Do you regularly review your portfolio to make sure you are always getting the best after tax returns?

SOLUTION: *When you finish this book carry out a full review of where you are and make the necessary changes.*

Conclusion

By now you should know where you stand on the road to financial independence and have some idea of the enemies you will encounter along the way. What you have covered so far is basic matter but you will need to understand it to go any further. In the next chapter we'll get into budgeting — the area where most plans succeed or fail.

35

Starting A Financial Plan

When in the box the money rings
The soul from Purgatory springs.

JOHANN TETZEL 1517.

Isn't it strange that we usually expect a higher standard of behaviour in others than we expect from ourselves. If we are taking a plane trip we know the pilot will take the time to prepare a flight plan, if we have an operation we know the surgeons and their team will have done a lot of preparation before we are wheeled into the operating theatre, if we see a building being started we can see the massive amounts of time and money poured into the foundations.

We also expect the progress of the flight, operation or building will be monitored continually and adjustments made when necessary. In most cases the eventual outcome is success. Why should the preparation for our journey on the road to financial independence be any different?

You are going to earn **millions** of dollars before your working life ends if you are young now. Surely it's worth taking some time to make a plan for all this money, and to spend an hour or two a month to monitor progress.

The journey along the road to financial independence is like any other long trip. Your chances of success are greater if you have a plan. In this plan you will have to think about the four essential elements:

(1) The goal — the destination

(2) The income — the fuel that drives the vehicle

(3) The assets — the vehicle itself

(4) The strategy — the tactics to be used for the journey.

The cornerstone of a financial plan is a budget, for it is the budget that determines how every drop of the precious income fuel will be allocated. Unfortunately 90% of the population never gives a thought to the way the income should be used. Consequently their financial vehicle is like a car with a faulty carburettor that is spraying out great bursts of fuel at random. The natural result is failure.

Before we start the trip let me ask you a question. How much money do you think a person will earn in a lifetime? If they start on $15,000 a year when they finish their studies and receive the normal increases they will probably earn over **six million dollars** from salary and investments before they die.

Think about that — teenagers starting work now are going to earn many millions of dollars in their lifetime and yet less than 10% of them will take the time to sit down and make a plan for it. Could you imagine a business with a turnover of six million dollars not having a budget?

Let me assure you that budgeting is simple, budgeting does not take much time, and budgeting does not take much effort. It is a simple but magical technique that will lift you out of the mire of financial problems and set you firmly on the path to financial independence. It is so important that every well-run company has one. That is why one of the major causes of business failure is inadequate or non-existent budgeting.

Why do so few people take the trouble to prepare a budget?

The typical reaction is "It's only a month till Christmas — I won't start until New Year". New Year comes in a twinkling and you can't start then because you're paying off the debts you ran up over Christmas. Next the new school year starts with all its attendant expenses, then it is the Easter holidays . . . And so the year goes by until it is four weeks from Christmas again. Does that sound like you?

Let me tell you a true story that illustrates the theory behind budgeting. A man drove a Rolls-Royce car into a service station for petrol. The attendant, an accountancy student doing part-time casual work, was interested in how anybody could become wealthy so he asked the driver what was the secret of wealth. Without hesitation the driver pulled a handful of bank notes out of

his wallet and said "Most people spend the notes and bank the silver — I spend the silver and bank the notes".

If you understand that story you will appreciate why budgeting is so powerful. Financial success involves adopting the theory that was espoused in the classic best-seller *The Richest Man In Babylon* : **a part of all you earn is yours to keep.** Just as the wealthy man kept his bank notes, so does a budget force one to allocate part of each week's income for investment.

Now let's look at ways to get going. A budget is no different to writing that "Thank you" note you have been putting off. Once you sit down at the table with a pen and paper the rest is easy. The hardest task is to get you to the table.

Creating The Desire For Change

External events such as having your power cut off or your car repossessed may force this desire on you, but it is much more effective to be pro-active and take appropriate steps **before** things get to the critical stage. It is far easier to repair a fence than round up 1000 cattle after they escape.

A good method to stimulate the desire to change is to use some psychological tricks. Probably the most effective way is to use the same visualisation techniques that are now used by leading sports coaches.

Don't laugh at these techniques. In her superb book *Strategies of the Champions*[1] (Pan Books) Vicki Peterson states "John Bay, the sports psychologist who works with Australia's leading swimmers,

1 The book is about techniques now used to produce champion athletes and draws heavily on material provided by the Australian Institute of Sport.

told me that twenty-one days on a thought diet of visualisation and affirmation had a visible effect on attitude and performance . . . American athletes keep a visualisation file which contains . . . reminders of what it will be like to succeed". Many other books on sport and management stress these meditative or visualisation techniques.

These techniques are not new although they have only recently come into favour. They were demonstrated effectively by Charles Dickens in *Christmas Carol* where Scrooge was given a look at the past, present and future by the three ghosts.

Dickens created the ghosts for Scrooge but you will have to create your own. Sit in a quiet spot, close your eyes and visualise your financial world as it is now. If things are tight for you just now, feel the fear of watching the mail for bills, see your present debt as a pile of rubbish filling up and spilling out of black garbage bags that have dollar signs all over them. Visualise the pile becoming larger as you add to it by thoughtless spending and by reckless borrowing. Watch it grow till it starts to suffocate you. That's what your life will be like if you stay on your present course.

Now create a picture of yourself taking charge of your life and sitting at a table preparing a budget. See the budget as a huge broom that starts to sweep away those black garbage bags and eliminates the debt that surrounds you.

Visualise yourself having savings accounts with healthy balances eagerly awaiting the bills coming in, your filing cabinets bulging with folders full of Title Deeds, Scrip and Unit Trust Certificates and see the black garbage bags replaced with white cloth bags containing bank notes and gold bullion.

If you do this at least once, and preferably twice a day, for the next few weeks your desire to change should be well in place.

Be conscious of the power of human influence. Unless you live alone, a budget will never work if all the family are not part of it. If you are serious about getting ahead financially, start on your budget this week. Call a family meeting and announce that the household is preparing a budget so it can do some financial planning so as to have a happier and more prosperous lifestyle for all its members.

In *Making Money Made Simple* there is a chapter on doing a budget, so why not re-read that now. You will need to compile a list of expenses, so ask everybody to help in finding the information. This will help get them involved.

Take a sheet of paper and write down approximately what you spend every year. Split it into three main categories:

(1) The essential fixed expenses such as rates, home repayments/rent, insurance, school fees and car registration.

(2) The essential variable expenses like electricity, food, repairs and petrol.

(3) The discretionary expenses such as entertainment, holidays, cigarettes and clothes.

Now make a list of the household's net income and make it crystal clear to everybody that a family that spends more than it earns is headed for trouble. Compare the income to the expenditure and discuss the answer.

There are three possible results:

(1) **WAY IN FRONT:** There is a large surplus of income over expenses. If this is the outcome you should have plenty of surplus money in various accounts and no pressure when the bills come in. If there appears to be a large surplus but you are still continually strapped for cash you had better check your figures.

(2) **IN TROUBLE:** There is a large shortfall between income and expenses. This is a serious position and needs urgent attention. You are probably in a tight financial bind and are surviving only by adding to existing loans or taking out more loans. You had better re-read Chapter 39 (We're in Trouble) in *Making Money Made Simple* before going any further.

(3) **JUST GETTING BY:** Income and expenses are fairly close. This is the most common result because almost everybody spends all, or just a touch more, that they earn. You probably experience pressure when an unexpected bill hits the mailbox. Fine tuning is needed to create and maintain a large enough surplus for investment.

Don't panic if you are in Categories Two or Three — the majority of people will **never** make the time to do what you have just done. Congratulate yourself on taking the first step on the road to financial independence.

Handling The Family

If you are in Category 3 **Just Getting By** the family is on the point of over-spending. Make it clear to everybody that there are only two courses of action open to the family — spend less or earn more. A lively, but hopefully, productive discussion is bound to follow as the family canvasses ways to do both. Parents may well need the help of the special section for younger people at the back of this book during this meeting.

Here are the remarks that are likely to come out together with possible responses:

(1) *"How come we are spending more than we are earning?"*

It has happened gradually. The problem is that if our expenses exceed our income we have to make up the shortfall by borrowing, with its slowly mounting interest bill. This reduces our future income and the situation grows steadily worse. This budget will show us exactly where the money is going so we take steps now to get our affairs back on track before it is too late.

(2) *"How do the neighbours have so much when they earn no more than us?"*

All financial advisers know that if you try to judge a person's financial worth on appearances you are likely to be wrong. Sure, our neighbours appear to live well but for all we know a rich aunt might have died and left them a tidy sum[2].

(3) *"How can you expect me to give up . . .".*

Nobody is asking you to give up anything at this stage. Clearly we have a problem to resolve and the purpose of the family meeting is to decide by mutual consent the best way to tackle it. If we can bring more money into the household there will be no need to give anything up. Why don't we look at ways to earn more money as a first step.

* * *

These discussions are most important as they focus on people taking responsibility for their own life. Once anybody has learned how to do that, and starts to think in that way, they are well on the road to success.

Notice the obvious area in which to make spending cuts is the discretionary area. This is why it is so difficult, because the discretionary area includes all the things we enjoy such as holidays, gifts, alcohol, cigarettes, dining out, and clothes. It is natural to think that spending on these is a reward for all our hard work and if we cut down here life is not worth working for.

---

2 If you know the neighbours well enough you might ask them what is their secret. They may tell you that it's because they are good budgeters.

Consequently most people spend on these items first and as a result have nothing left over for insurance or repairs. They have to make up the shortfall by borrowing and so start the financial slide.

It **is** important to let your salary buy you some things for your personal enjoyment so allow a sum in the budget to spend on some treat to reward yourself for sticking to it. It need not be a big treat — the rewards of having a budget will more than compensate for the pain of doing it.

Conclusion

Don't forget the success of your financial independence plan depends on how much you can squeeze out of the budget for savings and investment. The budget is the tool to help you do it. Now I'll show you how to prepare your defences.

36

Building A Safety Net

Distrust and caution are the parents of security.

BENJAMIN FRANKLIN

Life holds no guarantees. You can do all the right things, make the best plans and still a hailstorm may come and wipe out your crop. Certainly there are ways we can protect ourselves from disasters, but they must be done in **advance.** It is too late to think about making your house cyclone proof when the roof is about to be lifted off and blown into the sea.

I have broken this chapter into two sections: "Things you should do" and "Things you should not do". Some of these you will regard as obvious, and some may surprise you. The major question is "Are you doing them?".

Things You Should Do

1. Get Ahead In Your Loan Repayments

One of the first things my wife said to me when we took out our housing loan was "I won't be happy until we are a year ahead in our house repayments". I confess this idea had never occurred to me so I asked why. Her answer was simple, "In case something happens". I agreed with this indisputable logic so we wrote the target on a piece of paper, stuck it on the pantry door where it was continually in view, and started to use every spare dollar to reduce that debt. It took only a few months for us to get a year ahead in our payments, but by that stage had got so excited about the prospect of paying it off early that we kept going and paid off the whole debt in record time.

We were fortunate because at that stage my wife worked and we had no children, and I appreciate that many families do not have the earning capacity to pay off a loan so quickly. However, the methods described in this book for getting well ahead of your mortgage obligations will ensure that there is a safety cushion if "something" does go wrong.

2. Take Out Insurance

Few people buy insurance voluntarily, and unfortunately much insurance that they do buy is wrong for them. I admit I was luke warm about insurance until I encountered my first young widow client — then I was hooked. Death is such a remote possibility until you sit facing a crying 39 year old woman and her three teenage children and try to plan a secure financial future for them with "only" $200 000.

The problem is that paying off the home mortgage will take $50 000 of the insurance proceeds, and the balance of $150 000, although it sounds a lot, is not enough to pay for the funeral, replace the car in a couple of years and put the three children through higher education.

You need to make sure you have your income, your life and your property adequately insured. Please make the time to understand the chapters on insurance in this book.

3. Improve Your Skills

The world is changing at a faster pace. Employment opportunities are rapidly dividing into two categories — highly paid skilled workers who are becoming almost impossible to find, and another tier of workers who do routine jobs and can be easily replaced. Your job security depends on the value of what you do and the difficulty of replacing you. Only by improving your skills can you generate the income and the security that is essential to your sound financial future.

Employees should also cultivate the principle of "doing more than paid for" that Napoleon Hill described in his classic book *Think and Grow Rich.* I vividly remember being at a local convenience store at dusk. The young girl was checking my groceries through the cash register and the radio was playing. Suddenly the time signal for six o'clock beeped. She did not bother to finish ringing up my few remaining groceries but told me she was leaving and called the proprietor over to finish off. What sort of job security does that attitude provide?

In America in 1988 the Sears retail chain offered special training courses to employees who were looking for advancement. They were to be held after work for one night each week. Less than 2% of the staff were prepared to sacrifice that time for the sake of future promotion.

In *Making Money Made Simple* I started off by telling my readers that only 8% of people will make it financially. The reason is simple — the other 92% are not prepared to make the sacrifices that success demands.

4. Watch Your Interest Rate

In 1989, Australia witnessed the heartbreak that happened to ordinary families as their mortgage payments escalated as a result of rising interest rates. Sky-rocketing home prices, combined with these high interest rates, meant that mortgage repayments took an ever increasing share of the family budget.

Many investors who opted for the "glamour" of negative gearing have seen their plans turn sour as rising interest rates played havoc with their cash flow, and falling real estate prices took away their safety net.

The **only** way to protect yourself from rising rates is to opt for a **fixed** interest rate. It doesn't cost any more in establishment fees and you have the security of knowing that you won't be forced to sell your property on a depressed market if rates rise. At time of publication our rates were the lowest in 30 years — what better time to think about moving to a fixed rate. Even if fixing the rates does not seem appropriate when you are reading this watch the trend and be ready to move to a fixed rate if an upsurge in rates appears likely.

5. Do Some Good Turns

This may seem a strange recommendation in a book that is mainly about finance, but there is **nothing** like having some good friends to assist you if times get tough. My father taught me that every good turn you do brings two back to you, and my own experiences have taught me this is true.

What is even more mysterious is that the good turns that come back to you often don't come from the people you have helped. It is just as if there is a bank of favours out there somewhere into which we can all make deposits, in the certain knowledge that there will be favours in the bank when we need to withdraw some.

Sceptics will say this is hogwash so you can make up your own mind. I guarantee it works for my family and for many people I know. We now go out of our way to help others in any way we can, and have invariably found that there is somebody about just at the time we need help.

6. Keep Adequate Records For Tax

Unfortunately most people fail to keep adequate records for tax purposes and consequently leave themselves open to heavy penalties.

Our tax system now works on self assessment so your tax returns may appear to be in order but, in reality, have never been examined by the Tax Office. One day it may be your turn to be chosen for an audit, and your file will receive a detailed examination.

If you can't produce the necessary records to substantiate your expenses you leave yourself open to having several years tax deductions disallowed. Consequently you might have to find a large amount of back tax as well as some non tax deductible penalties. Wouldn't that chop a few branches off your money tree?

7. Have Some Emergency Money Available

You never know when an emergency will arise. Maybe a relative in another city takes ill, or the bargain for which you have been waiting for years suddenly becomes available. No matter what the reason is, it is always comforting to have some ready money available. Many financial advisers recommend having three months salary on hand, which for most people would be close to $7 000. This may seem a lot, and my own view is that a sum as large as that is better used to reduce your housing loan either by paying it off the debt directly or by placing it an "offset" accounts.

Another way to create an emergency fund is to obtain a Bankcard with a large limit, and then lock it away in a safe place. If ever you need cash in a hurry it is only a matter of going to the nearest bank and you have got your money in a few minutes. The beauty of this is that there are no annual charges, no unused limit fees, no valuation fees and you pay interest only for the time you use the money.

Please note that this technique is **only** for the disciplined, and the Bankcard is to be used exclusively for genuine emergencies.

Things Not To Do

You will have developed a good safety net if you have put the above recommendations in place. However, danger can come from other areas so now it's time to look at some things to avoid.

1. Avoid Getting Out Of Your Depth

There is enough about negative gearing in this book to alert you to the dangers, as well as the advantages, of excessive borrowing. One way of creating a safety net when borrowing is to borrow more than you need and lodge the surplus in a secure cash type area such as a cash management trust. I would much rather owe $120 000 and have $20 000 invested than owe $100 000 and have no liquid funds to fall back on.

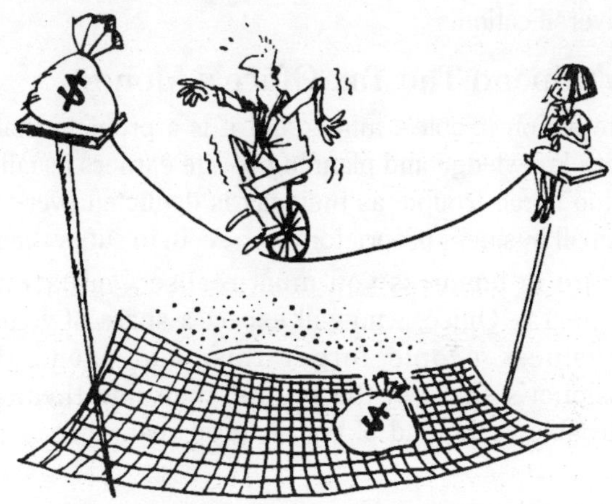

Bridging finance has devastated the finances of many home buyers. They see a property which they "must have" and take out bridging finance at high rates to buy it in the hope they can sell their present one before they have to pay for the new one. Their home takes longer to sell than they imagined, and after a few months they find they are unable to pay the interest on the bridging finance as well as make the repayments on their existing home mortgage. Often the only way out of the crippling bridging finance is to sacrifice their present home at thousands below market value.

2. Don't Put All Your Eggs In The One Basket

This statement has been made so often that you would think nobody would get caught any more. Alas, not so. Every day we encounter clients who have ignored this rule and suffered badly. The worse case I saw was a couple who retired from a prosperous business late in life and put their entire fortune (well over two million dollars) into the shares of a company that at best could be described as "entrepreneurial". The shares are now worthless and the couple are destitute. If they had put just half their money in a different area they would still be wealthy today.

There are many different types of baskets. Putting all your money into the shares of 10 leading companies still means all your eggs are in the share basket; if you have all your money in various Adelaide houses that are being rented out, you have got all your money in the "Adelaide residential" basket.

By now you should have a good idea of the varying investment opportunities open to you — there is no excuse for your not having diversification.

3. Don't Spend The Tax Office's Money

Tax is always on people's minds, but it is a problem that can be solved with knowledge and planning. Wage earners usually do not get into too much trouble as their tax is deducted every pay-day, but it is small business proprietors who seem to suffer the most.

If you are in business you must realise you have another partner, the Tax Office, who will expect a share of your profits. Many business people forget this, and spend the Tax Commissioner's share of the profits, then find themselves in terrible trouble at the end of the financial year when he puts his hand out.

The worse thing you can do is pay your personal expenses from the business account as this only aggravates the problem. All the items become mixed up, and it is impossible to find out quickly if you are spending your own money or that which is rightfully the property of the Tax Office.

There is a simple method that will forever end tax problems for sole traders and people in partnerships. Keep your business account and your personal account strictly separate and never borrow from the business for yourself. Work out at the beginning of the year your average tax rate in consultation with your accountant. As a general guide, your average tax rate at $20 000 per annum is 20%, at $30 000 it is 28% and at $40 000 per annum it is 31%. This is the amount the Tax Office is entitled to.

When you need to draw money from the business to replenish your personal account, ensure that the Tax Commissioner's share is withdrawn at the same time, and placed in a separate account.

EXAMPLE: *Assume you were earning $40 000 per year from your business and decided to draw out $500. When you withdraw that $500 place 25% of it ($125) in the Tax Account and pay yourself the balance of $375. Do not spend or borrow from the money in the Tax Account. Treat that money as if it belonged to a good friend and you were keeping it for him.*

This system ensures that you, just like a wage earner, are paying for your personal needs with money on which tax has been provided for. If the business is profitable any surplus profits are building up in the business. As they have not yet been drawn the money will be available to you to pay tax with if the amount in the Tax Account is insufficient.

This system also ensures that you live within your means. If you find you are having trouble making ends meet in your personal account after putting the tax away it proves that you have been using the Tax Commissioner's share of the profits to live on, so you had better have an urgent meeting with your accountant to find out what is happening.

If you have the kind of business where a large stock is carried, be careful that the Tax Commissioner's share of the money is not being used to fund stock. If this is the case you may have to arrange a working capital loan to finance your increased inventory.

4. Stay Clear Of Guarantees

The Case of the Gullible Guarantor in *Making Money Made Simple* shows the problems that going guarantor can cause you. That story was about a man who went guarantor for a mate and ended up losing his own house. While I have no objection to a parent going guarantor for a child because the child has no credit rating, I caution you to avoid signing guarantees for anybody else.

The only reason a lender asks for a guarantee is because they are not satisfied that the applicant is credit worthy in their own right. If you become guarantor you are assuming a risk that the finance company is not prepared to take. That's quite a gamble.

If you are in business, and are using a limited company, try to avoid signing personal guarantees. Many creditors will insist on personal guarantees in which case you should try to keep the spouse's name off it. It is often better in business to get your accountant to arrange a structure, such as a company, that will shield you from liability. When that is done make sure the family home is in the wife's name and that she does not sign any guarantees. This is not being dishonest; it is merely a recognition of the fact that businesses can go broke and it's much better to come out with at least a roof over your head.

5. Be Wary Of Low Start Loans

Low start loans enable borrowers to make lower than normal repayments in the first few years of a housing loan. Instead of the usual housing loan where the payments remain unchanged[1] for the duration of the loan, the repayments increase each year, but from a lower level than the normal repayments. As a result the first few years payments do not quite cover interest and the loan balance actually rises, instead of slowly reducing as happens with conventional loans.

Low start loans sound attractive when the house market is booming and buying property is all everybody is talking about. I know they have enabled many couples to grab a house at the start of a boom and ride the price up. The excitement can quickly fade for buyers who bought at the peak of the boom. The moment house prices drop, they discover their debt is thousands more than their house is worth.

I am not advising you not to use them — just treat them with caution and use them only as a last resort, and only when you believe a boom is about to get under way.

6. Understand The Dangers Of Partnerships

Partnerships sound like fun. You and a friend go into business, make heaps of money and then both live happily ever after. Unfortunately the reality is usually quite the opposite and you end up deep in debt and on bad terms with each other. Understand that each partner can be solely liable for any debts incurred by the partnership.

CASE STUDY: *Kay and Margaret decided to go into partnership in a dress shop. Kay knew fashion but had no money whereas Margaret had some money but no great sense of fashion. They signed a five year lease on a shop at $2 000 a month and Kay bought $50 000 worth of garments on credit. The credit was easily obtained because of Margaret's credit rating.*

1 Subject of course to the usual interest rate variations.

The shop never became profitable and the losses grew. It was not possible to sell it because it was losing money, so they decided to have a clearance sale and quit the business. They raised only $30 000 at the closing down sale so all the creditors looked to Margaret to make good the shortfall. After all why chase Kay — she had no money.

Conclusion

The aim of this chapter is to increase your awareness of ways to protect yourself from financial disaster. The next chapter continues the theme and explains more of the dangers lurking around each bend of the road to wealth.

37

More Tales From A Counsellor's Casebook

It is commonly seen by experience that excellent memories do often accompany weak judgments.

MONTAIGNE: Essays I.ix

The following case studies are genuine. The names and some irrelevant details have been changed to preserve the confidentiality of the parties involved. They are reproduced here in that hope that you can avoid falling into similar traps.

Case No. 1

The Case Of The Devastating Debt

Mr and Mrs X were conservative people. They had always taken a cautious attitude to investment but had made some reasonable amounts of money by buying run-down houses and re-selling them. They became less cautious when they were approaching 60 and decided to try just one big project that would "set them up" for life. They purchased a large vacant block of land after a real estate agent had produced detailed feasibility studies showing the big profits that could be made by subdividing the land into a number of industrial blocks.

Even though their income was only around $45,000 a year, they persuaded a finance company to lend them the entire $300,000 purchase price of the vacant block.

They signed the purchase contract during a property boom when there was a big demand for vacant industrial blocks in the area. Because they intended to get the project finished quickly, and had little ready cash, they made an arrangement with the finance company to add the first year's interest to the loan. This is called "capitalising the interest" and is a particularly potent form of negative gearing.

Neither they, nor the finance company, were concerned about capitalising the interest as it appeared there was a huge safety margin in the project. Unfortunately development projects seldom go smoothly. Because of the usual delays with the local authority the subdivision took longer than budgeted to be approved, and while these approvals were being negotiated the property boom on which they had staked their fortunes ended suddenly.

Interest rates jumped and they found themselves with a debt of $300,000 and interest accruing at 18% per annum. We know from the rule of 72[1] that the debt would double in just 4 years if allowed to compound at 18% a year.

They now faced a frightening dilemma. The market for subdivided industrial blocks was now almost non-existent and it would be pointless incurring further borrowings to complete the subdivision because there would be no buyers for the finished blocks.

If they did not subdivide the blocks, the debt would double in four years. If they borrowed money to complete the subdivision, there would be a much higher debt and the blocks would not be saleable. Their only solution was to sell the block.

The property boom that was occurring when they bought the land had now ceased. There were no buyers willing to give them what they had paid because that price depended on there being a ready market for the finished blocks. Who is going to buy land for subdivision when there is no market for the finished blocks?

They were so devastated by what had happened that they let the debt build up for over a year by which time it was nearly $400,000. By then the only course open was to take anything they could get for the land, and sell all their other assets to cover the difference between what they got for the land and the debt. In the end they lost most of the wealth they had spent a lifetime building up.

LESSON: Development projects seldom go as well as planned. It can be extremely dangerous to borrow for them unless you have other substantial resources including a strong cash flow.

---

1 See *Making Money Made Simple* Chapter Nine.

Case No. 2

The Case Of The Cheap Home

Bill and Mary were quiet living, honest people who had bought a neat house in a middle-class suburb when they were first married 15 years ago. They worked hard and by 1990 had paid off the loan on their house which had appreciated greatly in value as most houses do if kept for long enough.

They decided it was time to move to a better house and started looking avidly in the daily paper, and at the pictorial magazines, for houses they could buy. It seemed from all the glowing advertisements that their dream home was well within their reach so they telephoned a local real estate agent for an appraisal. The agent put a value on it of $85,000 and they listed it for sale at that price.

Within a day, this agent had found a buyer for their house, who offered $83,000 cash. They accepted this figure and signed an unconditional contract for the sale of their house. They then went off happily to buy their dream home.

Then they discovered the dreadful truth. The only research they had done was to look at advertisements!

When they came to inspect the properties which sounded so beautiful in the newspaper and looked so good in the magazines, they found that they were mostly "advertisers". They certainly wrote up well, but the advertisements omitted to mention "features" such as "situated on a major highway", "in a run-down suburb" or "the exterior hides a house that needs many thousands spent in maintenance". Their dream home was way out of reach.

Looking about gave them more bad news. They discovered the agent had given them an "urgent sale" valuation and they probably could have got $90,000 if they had waited. They had sold too cheaply.

After they got over the shock they looked to buy back into a similar home to the one they had sold. It cost them $90 000 and they also spent another $8,000 in fees for selling and re-buying. What an expensive lesson.

LESSON: Do your research in detail BEFORE you sign a contract to sell your home.

Case No. 3

The Case Of The Fast Finance Approval

Tim and Helen were still aglow from their recent engagement when they went out driving one Sunday afternoon to look at blocks of land for sale. They had always wanted acreage and their attention was drawn to signs along the highway advertising cheap acreage blocks.

They stopped at a small sales office and were soon in the grips of a fast-talking salesman who drove them around the area showing them several blocks. He eventually talked them into buying one for only $15 000. The price seemed a "steal" compared to the others he had shown them.

The salesman prepared the contract in his car, and included in it a clause as follows: *"This contract is conditional upon the purchasers obtaining finance from the vendor's own finance company to complete this purchase"*. In this case the seller of the property was the company that was developing it.

Tim and Helen signed the contract and paid a $500 holding deposit. The agent congratulated them on the purchase and said everything would be fine because finance would be approved straight away.

Naturally they rushed off to tell their families the good news but got a bit of a jolt when a friend stated that he thought blocks in that area had drainage problems. They made further investigations the following week and discovered the friend was right — the block had severe water problems.

They dashed back to complain to the salesman who said "the contract is now unconditional as your finance has been approved so you can't back out. However, if you wish to buy a better block for $40 000, we will cancel the original contract and transfer the deposit to the new contract". This incident happened in 1982. $40 000 for a block was way beyond their means.

They reported the matter to me to be publicised in a column which I was writing at that time in the Brisbane *Courier Mail*. I tried every avenue including the appropriate government departments and the Real Estate Institute but could not obtain a $500 refund for this young couple who had suffered so badly.

The law is biased towards the powerful and it takes people with commercial experience, capital and a lot of courage to take on a large land development company. They were not prepared to do it and in the end they forfeited their deposit of $500.

Five hundred dollars was a lot of money to that young couple in 1982 and I tell their story here in the hope it will save other people of the dangers caused by signing contracts to purchase property before having them vetted by solicitors.

LESSON: Do NOT sign a contract to purchase a property until your solicitor has checked it out.

Case No. 4

The Man Who Tried To Save Tax

A French fable tells of a farmer who was annoyed by a rabbit nibbling his lettuce. The Lord of the Province offered to help and brought most of his soldiers and entourage to assist in the hunt. After several hours of galloping over the property they killed the rabbit but the fences were ruined, the crops were trampled and the entourage ate and drank all the farmer's provisions at the celebration party that followed. There was more damage done in that day than all the rabbits in France could have done in a lifetime.

The moral of the fable came to mind when I was trying to help a friend. He is a high income earner, extremely hard working, and does not have the time nor the inclination to handle his finances. He is also an honest and generous person and like most people of that nature expects honesty in others.

On the advice of an investment adviser he had taken out a series of investments with the sole motive of reducing tax. At the time we spoke their current value was minimal.

The best, or perhaps we had better call it the worst, had yet to come. On the advice of this adviser my friend had borrowed heavily to finance these investments and now owed $360 000 secured by a mortgage against his house. The adviser had extolled the virtues of the tax deductibility of the interest on these investments which were now costing my friend $70 000 a year.

That argument didn't impress me — there is cold comfort in getting a tax deduction for interest paid to finance worthless assets. Despite the alleged virtues of this tax deductibility my friend was still digging into his own pocket at the rate of $36 000 a year.

This incident highlights the severe consequences that can arise as a result of making investment decisions purely on the basis of saving tax.

My friend's tax problems were caused first by bad structuring of his business and were made worse by bad budgeting. The succession of investments that were made solely on the basis of solving the tax problems acted like a Band-Aid placed over a festering sore — they did nothing to correct the cause.

I don't doubt that the tax saved may be close to the amount of the debt — that is not the issue. Because no remedial action was taken, the final outcome is a huge debt with nothing concrete left to show for it.

In this situation there is one clear course of action — change the structure of the business to eliminate the tax problems (this is easily and quickly done) and then apply every spare cent to reducing the debt as a matter of urgency.

LESSON: Don't fix the symptom — treat the cause.

Case No. 5

The Expensive Insurance Policy

This one came from a caller to a talk back program I was hosting.

He had decided to set aside some money for his two children's education, but gave in to pressure, and decided to accept financial advice from an insurance salesman.

After listening to the salesman's patter he signed a document believing he had placed $5 000 in a single premium insurance bond for each child. A year later he discovered to his horror he had signed a contract requiring him to pay $5 000 a year for each child for the next 40 years. In view of the long term contract a large part of the first year's premiums had gone in fees.

Obviously payments of $10 000 a year for the next 40 years were way beyond his capacity. In any event one would hope, in 40 years time, the children would no longer be requiring paid education. Naturally he phoned the insurance company but discovered the salesman had left for greener pastures. This is not surprising — no career-minded insurance representative would act in such an underhand manner.

LESSON: Make sure you know exactly what your insurance policy means.

38

Doing Your Dough!

When a person with money meets a person with experience, the person with the experience ends up with the money and the person with the money ends up with the experience.

Swim with the Sharks: HARVEY MACKAY

You know the two ways to have more money to invest are to spend less or make more; hundreds of thousands of words have been devoted to these topics in books, magazines and newspapers. Yet few have mentioned an even more important matter. How to hang onto to it once you have it.

The information in this chapter is special because it is not taught in regular schools. It comes from a different place — the school of hard knocks. This school has a high price on its lessons; unfortunately many "students" pay this price year after year and still never get the message. You are privileged for you can have the lessons just for the price of this book. Other people, including me, have paid the high price of the research.

Let me start with a word of warning — some of the dangers are hard to spot until it's too late. Worse still, just to make it more difficult for you, occasionally what appears to be a trick is genuine. It can be a grey area so all I can do is give you some pointers and hope you will stay alert so you can enjoy both the money and the experience.

Lesson One

Guard against those who have nothing but ideas of ways for you to invest your money

As you go along the road of life and pick up a little money you will discover, or be discovered by, people with some great ideas but no money to put them into practice. Edmund Burke described them thus: *"Those who have much to hope and nothing to lose will always be dangerous".*

Their ideas will often sound exciting and you might wonder why they have not been snapped up by some other eager investor. Usually the reason is that no other investor has fallen for it.

As a first step find out why this guardian angel offering to change your life has no money. Sure there **may** have been a legitimate catastrophe in the past and this is a genuine attempt to start again so listen closely to the reasons for failure to date. Separate those that show an acceptance of responsibility, and a sense of a lesson learned, from those that blame somebody else.

Exercise extreme caution once you hear stories about how the bank closed them up, how the employees stole all the money, how the shop next door started forcing them out of business, or how the spouse ran off with somebody else and took the money as well. Sure, there will be the odd occasion when it's true — you may strike it once in a lifetime.

> **CASE STUDY:** *Eric was a thrifty type who had saved a fair amount of money and Fred was the entrepreneurial type who had made and lost a lot in the same time. Fred got an idea to buy a half wrecked house, repair it and sell it for a big profit. As he had no money himself he persuaded Eric to go into partnership with him on the basis that Fred, having found the property, would take half the profits as long as Eric put the money up.*
>
> *The project ended up making a loss. This was partly because the house cost far more to fix than Fred had calculated, and also because the property market had gone flat between the time of purchase and the time of completion of the restoration.*
>
> *Now the awful truth dawned on Eric. He had to make good the entire loss as Fred had no money; if the project had succeeded Fred would have taken half. Fred was on a "no lose" basis. There was more bad news for Eric when tax time came around. Despite having made good the whole loss, he could claim only half of it as a tax deduction, Fred was entitled to claim the other half as he was a partner in the venture.*

Lesson Two

Beware of advertisements offering to make you rich

Some magazines are full of those alluring advertisements offering ways to get rich quick and they are **always** couched in terms that sound as if they are foolproof. Often the price is not a lot either — just $29.95 or so sent to a box number.

Just ask yourself one question — if you had such a secret would you be peddling it in the press?

If you want to get rich quick buy a Lotto ticket. At least you have a chance, although the odds might be a million to one.

Lesson Three

Stay Away From Schemes To Beat The Tax Man

There **are** legal ways to minimise or defer tax, and most of them are discussed in detail in other chapters of this book. However, around June 30 every year comes a plethora of schemes to "Slash Your Tax Bill". They are often seized upon by high income earners such as barristers and doctors who devote so much time to their work that they never learn about money.

In many cases they **do** save you tax but there is a massive side effect — they generally replace the tax bill with a debt. After all, the only reason you cannot pay your tax is because there is no money available, so you have to borrow for the tax scheme.

We have found that those who enter into these schemes end up in the same trouble next June 30 and the only way out is to borrow more money to save tax. Now they are like a drug addict, the debt for the tax schemes keeps growing and they cannot get off the merry-go-round.

Lesson Four

Watch Out For Cheap Overseas Loans

Every two or three years a person will crop up who is offering **low interest** loans in **Australian** Dollars. The interest rate is just low enough to be enticing, and not so low as to sound ridiculous. For example, if our current lending rate is 11%, they might offer 6% to 8%.

When you ask questions about why the money is cheap you will be told one or more of the following:

(1) It's from a questionable source. The lenders wish to launder it by leaving it on mortgage in Australia for a few years.

(2) It's from investors who have faith in Australia and believe our dollar will rise substantially against the other currencies.

(3) It's been borrowed overseas at 2% and the lender wants to get 6% here to make a profit.

They may ask you for a fee of around $500 to "get the deal on the road" and another 1% of the amount to be borrowed once an approval letter is issued. It is going to sound so good that you will be straining at the leash to hand your money over. Before you do just ask yourself why, if this money is genuine, institutions such as the Commonwealth Bank are not taking advantage of the cheap money and lending it out at the higher rate?

Trust me — you will save yourself a lot of time, money and excitement if you say **no** at the outset.

Lesson Five

You Have Won . . .

One morning a girl at our office got off the telephone, flung her hands in the air and yelled "I've just won a trip to Hawaii". We all congratulated her but within a few hours the excitement had waned when she found out the fine details. What she had actually won was three nights free accommodation in Hawaii, provided she paid for her own air fare on the airline nominated by the marketing company who had offered the prize.

It wasn't a prize a all. It was a marketing ploy put on by a group selling timeshare.

At least once a month I receive a telegram or a lettergram stating that I have won some prize that ranges from a set of glasses to a holiday. All I have to do to "collect the prize" is to attend a marketing presentation for one and a half hours to learn the benefits of timeshare.

Isn't it a pity this "luck" doesn't extend to the rare occasions I buy a Lottery ticket?

Lesson Six

Don't Tell Anybody

The mystifying feature of a lot of these ploys is that intelligent mature people actually fall for them. One of the best is "I am being allowed to take part in a special investment opportunity that is limited to a small number of select people and have promised not to tell anybody about it".

A client of mine fell for this. Only a year later I found out that it was a pyramid selling scheme where the success of the project depended on finding more and more people to pay the huge initial joining fee.

Another one was the "plane" scheme I encountered in New Zealand. Everybody who joined the scheme had to recruit four others. It worked well for the first people in the game who made tens of thousands of dollars but rapidly ran out of steam as the numbers grew.

Lesson Seven

Beware Of High Returns

I gave a seminar one night for the Mazda group and during dinner afterwards a man approached me and asked me if I had heard of the Keel Corporation. I told him no.

He showed me their card and told me how they were working from one of the most prestige buildings in Brisbane and had been getting huge returns on money invested with them. A friend of his had made 20% in the last month and had persuaded him to invest $20 000 with them.

"Take it out now," I said. His reaction was a shocked look followed by a long argument as to why it was a good investment. I could see it was impossible to convince him so I gave him my card and asked him to ring me in six months with a progress report.

This is the problem with human nature — deep in my heart I knew it couldn't work but yet something urged me to investigate it further "just in case" it was genuine (luckily not till after a six months trial).

It didn't take six months; just six weeks later the inevitable headlines appeared. The investors had lost their money.

If you think of it logically there is no need for a person with a money making scheme that gives genuine high returns to have to offer it to the general public. The scheme itself should keep them rich forever if it worked.

Lesson Eight

Beware Of Anything Dishonest

You are considering buying a business and the seller gives you a "wink wink" and hints at the vast sums of money being skimmed off the till to escape the clutches of the tax man. Naturally these can't be shown in the books so all you have is the seller's word. What he has told you proves he is being dishonest with the Tax Office, so why would he treat you any differently?

The problem with dishonesty is that it is like pregnancy — you either are or you are not. In my experience the truth always comes out eventually and you could be the one left holding the bag.

I have noticed from time to time, in both the real estate and the financial advisory industries, businesses spring up that break all the rules. They entice hordes of customers with misleading advertising, they use shady high pressure selling methods and misrepresent their products. For a while they appear to prosper and attract hordes of clients while the ethical operators wring their hands and wonder how long it can last. Inevitably the shonky operator goes broke leaving those who are left behind with the task of trying to rebuild the good name of the industry. This is a demonstration of the long term effects of dishonesty.

Summing Up

As you travel the road to financial independence you will encounter plenty of "hitch hikers" who want to slow you down. Stay alert and remember two old maxims "anything that sounds too good to be true usually is" and "there is no such thing as a free lunch".

39

How Do We Help Our Children?

The easiest way for your children to learn about money is for you not to have any.

KATHERINE WHITEHORNE

Most of us who are over 50 know the average young person today has the ball at their feet, for never in world history have there been so many opportunities offering. Education is available to all, sexual and racial barriers are being swept away and most industries are suffering a drastic shortage of skilled employees.

Unfortunately so many of our young people don't bother to give the ball much more than a light kick, which is why I devote so much time to showing young people they can have far more than they ever thought possible if they make the best use of what they have.

My book *Getting it Together* was written to give young teenagers a simple guide to success in all areas of their life. However, for the sake of completion, I shall mention a few basic rules in this chapter.

Helping Your Children

"We want to help our children financially so they won't have to struggle like we did" is something I hear so often.

It reminds me of the story about the birds who lived on a lonely island where their food was the fish they caught. Sometimes the fish were plentiful and the catching was easy, at other times the gales blew and fish were scarce. Fortunately the birds had learned their skills over generations and they could always catch enough fish to survive.

Progress came to this peaceful island when a whaling station was built there. Because of all the scraps from the whales and the frenzied activity in the water, the birds had to hunt for fish no longer. From that day on generations of birds lived on easy street and grew fat and lazy. Eventually the whaling station closed and the island reverted to its prior state. What happened to the birds? They had long lost the skill to hunt and quickly became extinct.

As a father of three young children I know that it is one of the most normal and natural feelings to want to help your children — the problem is ensuring what you do is a help and not a hindrance.

It is also an instinctive feeling to want to spare your offspring pain, and that includes the pain of long hours of study, scrimping on a budget and living in a home that may have boxes for chairs for a while. Yet just as steel has to be plunged into cold water to become tough, so do people have to be exposed to hardship to become strong.

A welfare state is bad, but not for the generally publicised reason that the receivers of it are a drain on the public purse. The main drawback with excessive reliance on welfare is that we are creating generations of people who have never had the opportunity to learn to solve their own problems. As the Chinese proverb says "Give a man a fish and you feed him for a day — teach him how to fish and you feed him for a lifetime".

So what can we do to help our children? Remember the two basic tasks of a parent. The first is to instil in them feelings of self worth, the second is to encourage self reliance. Gifts of money do neither. History is full of tales of a grandfather who started from scratch and built a fortune, died and left it to a son who maintained it because of the early input from the grandfather. Many of the third generation children are like the birds near the whaling station. They have never learned to make it, or maintain it, so they squander it. Hence the saying "Shirt-sleeves to shirt-sleeves in three generations".

Giving children the right help is exceedingly difficult and it does **not** take money to do it. Any fool with money can write a cheque, pick up bills for smashed cars or pay for expensive toys. If life was as simple as that, all the wealthy people in the world would have perfect children.

One of the first things parents can do is set a good example. Children seldom listen to what their parents say, but they usually **will** imitate what they do. The family with the radar detector in their car will find it hard to convince their children to have respect for the law just as the family that is heavily into cigarettes, alcohol and all kinds of medications may find it difficult to persuade their offspring that taking drugs is harmful.

I am sure we agree that we want our children to be happy. Despite the difficulty of defining what that means, there is a general agreement that people are happiest when they have self respect, feel in control of their lives and believe they are making a contribution to life in general.

Four Tasks For Parents

Parents who want to help their children, and agree with that definition, should encourage the development of the following qualities. You will notice that none require the outlay of money — just time, skill and effort.

(1) The ability to confront and solve their own problems. In his wonderful book *The Road Less Travelled* Scott Peck points out that life is difficult, but the majority of people waste their life wishing it was different while making little effort to do something about it. The only way we can grow as human beings is to face problems, make mistakes and do our best to learn from them.

I regularly meet wealthy people who complain that they have to keep giving their children handouts. They are almost invariably puzzled when I say "Why do you keep depriving your children of the opportunity to learn to cope for themselves?"

(2) A comprehension of the law of cause and effect. It is human nature to want to take the easy way out, or as the American novelist Ayn Rand described it "to yearn for the unearned". One of the best examples of this is the number of young people who forgo further study and choose instead to enter the workforce early. This gives them an immediate income as well as freedom from the drudgery of further study.

There is a huge price to be paid. They never allow their brains to reach their full potential and so cheat themselves of a huge sum of money in future earnings. If they realise their mistake when they are older, as I did, they have to make it up with years of study after work.

(3) The ability to live within their income, and save 10% of it — this is tied to the law of cause and effect and is a subject I have written about many times before.

(4) An understanding of the importance of honesty. The more I look at life the more I am convinced that nothing succeeds as well as simple honesty. Repeatedly I have seen people in business adopt shady practices and appear to prosper — inevitably the tide turns and they slide back down the ladder. All the people I know who have adopted honesty as a basic moral precept have continued to prosper and be happy. Napoleon Hill summed it up in his classic best-seller *Law of Success. "Every man takes care that his neighbour does not cheat him. But a day comes when he begins to care that he does not cheat his neighbour. Then all goes well. He has changed his market cart into a chariot of the sun."*

Children are one of the greatest joys of life. Should you help them? Of course you must. Just do it in a way that will help them to turn their market cart into a chariot of the sun.

Twelve Rules For The Young

In this section I shall re-produce my *Twelve Rules for the Young* which have been circulated in many newspapers throughout Australia. There has never been a free lunch so you will find that most of the commandments involve making a sacrifice of some sort. The good news for people who are keen to get ahead is that there is very little competition out there.

RULE ONE: Be aware that everything has its price. An American billionaire, whose name I have forgotten, once said: "Success is easy. All you have to do is decide two things — the first is what you want, the second is what you will give up for it".

RULE TWO: Continue living at home as long as you can. Sometimes it may seem irksome living with Mum and Dad but remember about paying the price. Living at home usually means better food and far cheaper living costs. As a result you can save a lot more money and start moving along the road to financial independence more quickly.

RULE THREE: Put off buying a car for as long as possible. Ownership costs of a car are now over $100 a week so you can see what a dint it makes in your budget.

Delaying buying a car is made much easier if you are still living at home as you can usually have a share of the family car if you play your cards right. Our staff regularly see people in their early 20's with $20 000 or $30 000 in the bank. Almost invariably they

Which road will you choose? The easy one that becomes difficult or the difficult one that becomes easier.

are still living at home, dress conservatively and have not yet bought a car.

I was driving through one of Sydney's poorer suburbs once and the person I was with said "In this area the young people have one goal — to turn 18 and rush out and buy a car on hire purchase". It is this attitude which ensures the children will stay as poor as their parents are.

If you must borrow to buy a car, pay it off in the shortest possible time to save interest. $10 000 borrowed from a credit union costs around $73 a week over three years. The same loan over five years through a finance company may well cost $60 a week — just $13 a week less. Total payments to the credit union would be $11 388 and to the finance company $15 600. That small extra outlay of $13 a week for three years will save you over $4 000.

RULE FOUR: Learn to live within your means. We know about the temptation to borrow a small sum by using a credit card. Unfortunately these small sums soon turn to bigger sums and the easy to pay monthly account becomes a monster. Financial independence is guaranteed for anybody who establishes the habit of living within their means at an early age. It has been said that "Birth is easier than resurrection". Similarly it is **easier to stay out of debt than get out of debt.**

RULE FIVE: Try to avoid borrowing for items that drop in value. One of the main differences between the financial winners and the financial losers is that the former borrow at fairly low rates of interest to buy assets such as houses that rise in value. The latter pay horrendous rates of interest to buy consumer items such as furniture, or worse still holidays, that have no permanent value.

RULE SIX: Save at least a tenth of your income. Young people living at home should be able to save far more than a tenth, but I guarantee that anybody who saves just a tenth of their income and does not get into debt for consumer items will seldom have a money worry. Save a tenth of your income for seven years and you should have a year's salary invested. That's a great backstop.

RULE SEVEN: Don't pay off vacant land if you have only a low deposit. It is almost always cheaper to pay off a house in which you live than to pay off land and pay rent as well. If you buy a block of land for $100 000 using $10,000 deposit at 8% over 7 years the repayments are $1403 a month. Add to this rent of $500 a month and you have total monthly outlays of $1 903.

Look what happens if you borrow $164 000 at 7% to buy a house and repay it at $1 903 a month. The whole package is paid off in 10 years which is just three years more than it took to pay off the vacant block.

RULE EIGHT: Homebuyers with single incomes or low incomes should borrow from the local State Housing Authority if possible. This topic has been covered in detail in *Making Money Made Simple.*

RULE NINE: Learn as much as you can about the complex world of finance by reading as much about it as possible. Start a separate fund called your "play money fund" and don't be frightened to dabble in a few shares or in some equity and property trusts. Young people have plenty of time to experiment and to invest in growth investments that are subject to the ups and downs of the real estate market and the share market.

RULE TEN: Acquire the habit of doing more than you are paid for. In many businesses the only time the staff move quickly is at finishing time. The people who see the job as a springboard to better things and put their energy into helping the business prosper cannot fail to succeed.

RULE ELEVEN: Start to learn to exercise discipline. One of the best ways to do this is by taking up a sport, learning a musical instrument, or taking up a fitness program. It has been said that the best fruit is always high up on the tree. It takes discipline to stick with a task until the rewards start to flow.

RULE TWELVE: Remember the greatest investment of all — the development of your own skills. The world is becoming an exciting and complex place and many industries such as computing, accounting, finance, hospitality and science cannot find enough good people to fill the vacancies. Time invested now to develop skills in these areas will pay handsome dividends in the future.

Conclusion

From my discussions with young people it seems the greatest problem they have is lack of faith in themselves. The practice of these 12 rules will help them to create a pattern of successes in life which will provide the confidence needed to progress further.

If you also buy them a copy of *Getting it Together* you will have given them a great start.

40

Now Do Something With It

We are all guilty of crime — the great crime of not living life to the full.

HENRY MILLER

The story of the magic train graphically illustrates the riches anybody can develop if they start early enough. However, we cannot turn back the clock so there is no point wasting time thinking about what might have been. You have now read this book and can congratulate yourself on taking a major step on the road to wealth.

The theme of *Making Money Made Simple* was that we could have far more than we thought possible if we made the best use of what we have now. My main goal in writing that book was to let you know the Road to Financial Independence existed.

The aim of *More Money with Noel Whittaker* is to get you started on that road and to indicate clearly the obstacles along the way, as well as to show you strategies to speed up your journey. However, nothing works unless you do and I offer this quote from Richard L Evans[1],who was a writer and broadcaster in America.

He writes

"Somewhere the story is told of a talented girl who seemed not to be doing enough with the gifts and abilities that she had been given. Under some urgent impulse her mother one day impatiently shook her head and, in substance, said 'I've given you life. Now do something with it'.

---

1 *Thoughts . . . for one hundred days* (Salt Lake City Publishers Press 1970).

We could conceive of the Father of all of us saying about the same 'I've given you life. Now make the most of it'. I've given you time, opportunity, talent, intelligence, the good earth and all it offers – now use it do something with! This brings to mind a line, not often heard or said these days but full of meaning: 'We are not here to play, to dream, or to drift.'

One of the greatest wastes in the world is the waste of time, of talent, of opportunity, of creative effort, and of indifference to learning and indifference to work; the don't care, drop-out, what's the use attitude. There are times for preparation, and times for serious responsible performance, and we had better be finding direction, finding ourselves and moving forward, avoiding indifferent drifting or wasteful delay in using the priceless abilities and opportunities God has given."

There is no doubt that, at the same time as a multitude of labour saving devices make our daily living easier, the pressures of life itself make it harder. The level of technology now needed to run this country is becoming more complex by the day. The continual advances in science, medicine and associated fields require rapidly increasing skills, while the maze of new laws pouring out of governments is taxing the skills of everybody in associated fields.

But there is always the paradox. As the world demands more from its citizens so do the opportunities grow for those who will go out and tackle the problems. In this book, and in *Making Money Made Simple*, you have read priceless information that is known to less than 10% of the population. Despite the fact it is freely available, the majority will **never** take the time to learn it.

You should now understand the way the financial advisory industry has evolved in Australia, know the range of investments available to you and appreciate the importance of eliminating non-productive debt. Neither real estate nor shares should be a mystery to you any more, and you are armed with the knowledge to make money in both the property market and the stock market. Negative gearing is now a tool you can use if it suits your situation, and you appreciate the way properly structured borrowings can maximise its impact.

No longer is insurance a puzzle to you and, at last, you can review your own income replacement insurance and life assurance policies.

Here is a check list to let you see if you are on the right track:

1. Do you now have a budget and does it allow a margin for saving?

2. Have you a system that forces you to make regular investments?
3. Have you made a plan to eliminate all debt for which the interest is not a tax deduction?
4. Have you worked out when you intend to retire and the amount of money you will need to achieve this goal?
5. Is your superannuation adequate for retirement?
6. Do you have adequate life assurance?
7. Are your financial affairs properly structured?
8. Have you a system in place that provides for regular monitoring of any money you may have in roll-over funds?
9. Have you adequate income-replacement insurance?
10. Is there money being invested for the education of your children?

You may be feeling overwhelmed by the amount of material I have given you. This is a natural reaction but today is decision day. **Are you prepared to make the effort to travel the road to financial independence?** Select the chapters that have the most relevance to you and re-read them several times.

If you are aged 40 or over look out for my new book *Living Well in Retirement* which will provide much of the information you will need for a secure and happy retirement. If you are really serious, complete the coupon in the back of this book and send away for my *Do It Yourself Wealth Course*. This contains more books, a one hour audio tape to let you learn as you drive, and an interactive CD-ROM that is a teaching tool as well as an invaluable calculator. Your understanding will grow as you learn and then you put the ideas into practice.

Keep the book handy as a reference guide and consult it **before** you make any investment decisions. It will be an invaluable friend. Remember studying this book has given you a tremendous advantage over the majority of people. Not only do you know that you **can** do it, you also know how to do it. Today you should have realised that the only factor holding you back until now has been lack of knowledge; now that gap has been filled.

The future is up to you. You have but one life – make sure you do something with it!

APPENDIX 1

The Christmas Trap

We are not punished for our sins, but by them.

ARTHUR CAESAR

In November 1989 I wrote the following article which appeared in two of Australia's major newspapers. As we were inundated with telephone calls asking for reprints I am reproducing it here for you all to profit from.

* * *

Today we are exactly four weeks away from Christmas. Have you calculated that this means only four more pay-packets for those who are paid weekly, and two pay-packets for those who are paid fortnightly? "Tis the season to be jolly" booms the carol, but there is little joy in finding out that it will take many more pay packets than the next two or four to cope with the costs of Christmas.

Borrowing to cope seems the only solution but, if we do, the joy of Christmas will probably turn to gloom when the New Year arrives. Suddenly we have to face the consequences of having spent a large part of next year's income before next year arrived.

The traditional family season of Christmas is fast becoming a time when people are demanding more and more. The true significance of Christmas as a time for celebrating the birth of Christ is turning into an orgy of expensive gift giving and over indulgence. It is no coincidence that New Year's Eve finds most people trying desperately to make resolutions to help them solve the problems that were created by an inability to say "no".

Life is like a garden — always under attack from pests and diseases. Unfortunately Christmas brings with it a particularly harmful crop of diseases that attack not only our savings but also our way of life. Sadly, the enemies often come disguised as friends. We have to be on guard as the ads "help" us to beat the last minute rush by telling us "there are only 20 shopping days left to Christmas". Those who are short of money are consoled by such attractive lures as "buy now and don't make your first payment until March".

The worst thing about so much of the Christmas advertising is that it encourages people to give presents, and to go into debt, for the wrong reasons.

"Was it all worth it?"

It is particularly unpleasant when advertisements start with the assumption that all members of the family deserve a bonanza of gifts at Christmas and that somehow the breadwinner has to find the money. Around 1600 the English poet George Herbert said "A gift much expected is paid, not given". The words are just as true 400 years later and it is a sad truth in today's society that the reaction to many gifts is not excitement so much as "what else have you got for me?"

One of the major differences between good money managers and bad money managers is that good money managers borrow at relatively low rates of interest for items which gain value, while bad money managers borrow at very high rates of interest for items which lose value. While the achievers are paying around 10% interest on their rapidly appreciating homes the bad money managers are happily forking out up to 20% interest on such necessities as water beds, videos and expensive presents.

I have never known a family to lose their house due to rising interest rates **if they had no other commitments.** However, it is common for bad money managers to have their homes repossessed, because an increase in home repayments was the last straw that broke a camel's back which was already bent beyond all reasonable limits by repayments on consumer loans.

Success in life, whether it be in the areas of sport, study, business or human relationships, requires discipline and sacrifice. People who get into debt to buy Christmas presents, or for other indulgences, are practising none of these good habits. Worse still they are setting a bad example for their children that may have far reaching consequences.

One of the major tasks of parents is to teach their children to cope with life and take responsibility. How can children learn personal responsibility when they see their parents mortgage next year's income to buy items that turn to rubbish in a few days?

It is a fallacy that expensive presents will make children happy and creative. I remember a Christmas several years ago when our young children received an over-abundance of presents from well meaning family members and friends. Within two hours the expensive toys had been discarded and the children were having a wonderful time on the floor inventing games with the fancy coloured wrapping paper.

Books are great gifts for Christmas and almost every other occasion. A book is enduring, can be personalised by a note in the front cover, and will still be giving pleasure when most other presents have been long forgotten. I am still using the Oxford Concise Dictionary that was given to me 28 years ago by a family friend. He has been dead for many years but the inscription in the front still brings warm memories.

We do not come into the world endowed with wisdom and so our knowledge must be gained by our own experience or through the experiences of others. Unfortunately the lessons of experience can be extremely costly and the course of instruction may take many years to complete. A book enables us to share the experiences of others. The famous American speaker Jim Rohn summed it up when he said "We are all affected by the books we haven't read".

It can be hard to get young people to read but sport will usually catch their interest. Fortunately success factors are universal. The qualities needed to succeed in sport are the same as those needed to succeed in business, in health or in relationships. Basically it involves a knowledge of what to do, coupled with the discipline to do it.

Biographies and autobiographies make good presents for younger people. The young tend to believe successful people have inbuilt talents, are particularly lucky or lead glamourous lives. The actual life stories of most high achievers reveal most have faced, and overcome, quite daunting problems. In contrast, the stories of any of the Hollywood stars reveal a miserable existence plagued with self doubts and propped up by drugs.

Don't be sucked in by offers from companies that will put you into debt now with no repayments for three months. Remember there is no such thing as a free lunch. People who fall for this trap are agreeing to have their interest "capitalised" for three months. That's a fancy word for adding the interest for those first three months onto the loan balance. You are then paying interest on interest!

Bankcard, ever conscious of profitability, may let you off your monthly payment over Christmas. Why not, they are still charging you interest at high rates on the whole balance owing. It's a better Christmas present for them than for you.

If you buy a car in the next four weeks some motor dealers will offer cash back to spend on Christmas. In other words you are adding the Christmas spending onto the car loan. This practice is even worse than borrowing on a credit card, because by doing so, **you are paying for one Christmas over the next four years!**

Don't give up hope if you find yourself with a tight financial situation now. The solution is not to borrow to indulge yourself this Christmas but to make a decision today that next year will be better. Forget about making this Christmas a spending spree. Instead, make it memorable by starting to plan the next one.

Get the family together and put the situation on the line. Explain that, because of bad budgeting, money is short and ask for suggestions for ways to solve the problem. The resulting discussion is likely to have more value than a lot of junk bought on credit cards.

Start by opening a special purpose account and depositing $10 or $20 per week into it so that the money you require is waiting to be spent when next Christmas comes. Do you find it is impossible to bank $10 or $20 per week to provide for next Christmas? If that is so, you must ask yourself how you are possibly going to pay back the $2 000 that you were going to put on a credit card at an interest rate of between 13% and 19%.

Would you like to receive regular bulletins from Noel by e-mail free of charge?

Just simply send an e-mail to Noel at

noelnews@gil.com.au

and ask to be put on the mailing list.

There is no cost, no obligation and you can unsubscribe at any time

The Noel Whittaker Wealth Creator

ON CD–ROM

Design your own future

The interactive tool that will enable you to take charge of your own finance and monitor your progress on a regular basis.

The Wealth Creator *includes:*

- A retirement planner so you can work out when you can retire
- A capital gains tax calculator to aid you in buying and selling decisions
- A loan calculator incorporating a gearing calculator
- A budget planner so you can simply prepare and update your budget
- A net worth statement that lets you keep track of where you are
- An insurance list on which you can record all your possessions

It is also a teaching aid. It includes an animated section that teaches the basics of compound interest, negotiating, business structuring and borrowing.

Don't stop now!

Mail or fax this coupon today for a comprehensive brochure and order form.

☑ **YES Noel, I'm serious about becoming financially idependent and want to improve my knowledge.**

Please forward me an ORDER FORM containing full details of the material you have available to help me.

Name: ______________________________

Address: ______________________________

______________________ Postcode: __________

Tel.: ______________________________

MAIL or FAX this coupon to:

Noel Whittaker
Whittaker Macnaught Pty Ltd
Level 5, Santos House
215 Adelaide Street
Brisbane Q 4000

Tel.: (07) 3221 1022 Fax: (07) 3221 9682
E-mail: noelwhit@gil.com.au

Keep up-to-date with what's happening in the financial world

Visit Noel Whittaker's Web Site

http://www.noelwhittaker.com.au

Index